Stephen Prui

LIVES
TRANSFORMED

LIVES TRANSFORMED

A Revolutionary Method of Dynamic Psychotherapy

David Malan
Patricia Coughlin Della Selva

KARNAC
LONDON   NEW YORK

First published in 2006 by
H. Karnac (Books) Ltd.
6 Pembroke Buildings, London NW10 6RE

British Library Cataloguing in Publication Data

A C.I.P. for this book is available from the British Library

ISBN: 1-85575-378-2

Edited, designed, and produced by Communication Crafts

Printed in Great Britain

www.karnacbooks.com

CONTENTS

ACKNOWLEDGEMENT

We wish to express our heartfelt thanks to Jennie Malan, who—without any formal training in psychotherapy—has come to a profound understanding of the issues involved in intensive short-term dynamic psychotherapy and so, by making blind judgements on the clinical material, has transformed the scientific value of the work presented in this book.

ABOUT THE AUTHORS

David H. Malan, DM, FRCPsych, is a former Consultant Psychiatrist at the Tavistock Clinic in London and is a well-known author. In addition to the practice of psychiatry, psychoanalysis, and dynamic psychotherapy, his background has included research in the physical sciences. He has been particularly involved with the development of short-term psychotherapeutic methods. Many of his publications have been concerned with the long-term outcome of various forms of psychotherapy. His book *Individual Psychotherapy and the Science of Psychodynamics,* a textbook of dynamic psychotherapy, has had a considerable influence on psychotherapists throughout the world. He was one of the first to recognize the significance of the work of Habib Davanloo—hence the present book, which is the fruit of collaboration with one of Davanloo's outstanding ex-trainees.

Patricia Coughlin Della Selva, PhD, is a Clinical Psychologist trained by Habib Davanloo in intensive short-term dynamic therapy (ISTDP). She holds a doctorate in clinical psychology from Syracuse University and is currently Adjunct Professor of Psychiatry at Albany Medical College, Albany, New York. In addition to treating patients in her private practice, she trains other professionals in the theory and technique of ISTDP. Her previous book, *Intensive Short-Term Dynamic*

Psychotherapy: Theory and Technique, sets out the principles of this method with great clarity, and her international teaching is currently making an important contribution to the acceptance of ISTDP throughout the world. Information on the services she provides can be obtained via her website at www.patriciacoughlin.com

PART I

OVERTURE, TECHNIQUE, LITERATURE

CHAPTER 1

Overture

In view of all that has happened since the foundation of psychoanalysis, surely few dynamic psychotherapists would allow themselves to indulge in the following fantasy:

> A method of psychotherapy is developed that is based entirely on psychodynamic principles; it is applicable to a high proportion of nonpsychotic patients; therapeutic effects appear within the first few sessions; and the whole neurosis disappears, so that termination comes smoothly, sometimes within 15 to 40 sessions, or within 70 with some more difficult patients; at termination no trace of the original disturbances can be found; long-term follow-up shows that this position is maintained; moreover, certain adverse phenomena that bedevil traditional dynamic psychotherapy and psychoanalysis—such as regression, intense sexualized or dependent transference, acting out, and difficulties over termination—do not become a problem. Finally, it is possible to train other therapists in the required technique, leading to the hope that the efficiency of therapeutic clinics is greatly increased, and waiting lists are much reduced.

The above passage is adapted from an article that appeared more than 25 years ago, based on observation of the work of Habib Davanloo (see Malan, 1980), and the present book is concerned with evidence that this fantasy has been fulfilled.

The method of therapy was named by Davanloo *intensive short-term dynamic psychotherapy* (ISTDP)—though the duration sometimes goes beyond the usually recognized limit of 40 sessions. The present book is based on the therapy of seven patients treated by Patricia Coughlin Della Selva (PCDS), one of the authors. She was trained by Davanloo but has modified his technique to suit her own personality.

Brevity requires that three of these patients are only briefly summarized in the book, thus dividing the seven patients into four "detailed" (The Man Divided, The Cold-Blooded Businessman, The Good Girl with Ulcerative Colitis, The Woman with Dissociation) and three "summarized" (The Reluctant Fiancée, The Masochistic Artist, The Self-Loathing Headmistress). Nevertheless the latter provide much striking evidence, some of which is presented below and the rest in part III, the General Discussion. In fact little is lost, since all three of these patients have been described elsewhere, as indicated below.

At follow-up (with one possible exception: The Woman with Dissociation, chapter 7), *all* the original disturbances of these patients had not only disappeared, but had been replaced by what we may call "positive mental health". This is the empirical definition of "total resolution".

In order to give a foretaste of the quality of these therapies and their results, we give here vignettes from the three summarized patients.

The Reluctant Fiancée
(age 36, 16 sessions, follow-up 8 years):
The discovery of commitment and true happiness

This severely disturbed woman (described in Coughlin Della Selva, 1996, pp. 96ff., under the name of "The Woman with Headaches") went into fugue-like states and became *literally* paralysed with fear at the very thought of marriage. In addition, she suffered (1) from lifelong depression with strong suicidal impulses; and (2) from headaches, at least once a week, which were so severe that she had been repeatedly hospitalized from the age of 8 years to the present time.

In her background she had been exposed to systematic physical and sexual abuse by her father, from which her invalid mother had never been able to protect her.

The criteria for resolution of her problems, formulated by two judges blind to the events of therapy, included: "Loss of all symptoms" and "To have a warm, satisfying, and committed relation with a man who reciprocates. To be able to accept and give love and tenderness without reserve."

The main issues in therapy were: murderous rage against her father, followed by love; rage against a previous boyfriend; anger and love towards her mother; and grief about what she had missed in childhood.

At 8-year follow-up, she said: "I don't have any of those symptoms any more—it's a distant memory."

In connection with her problem over commitment, she spoke as follows:

"Something amazing happened. Once I walked down the aisle there's been no looking back. It was as if I was crossing a bridge from my old life into a new one. I saw him standing there at the altar, and suddenly a feeling of peace and happiness came over me. Now I am happier than I ever imagined possible. I just love being married. I have the family I always wanted and never had. It's the same for my husband. We had a foundation of tenderness and trust. From that, passion emerged."

The Masochistic Artist
(age 39, separated, 32 sessions, follow-up 4 years):
The discovery of sexual closeness

This patient (described in Coughlin Della Selva, 1996, pp. 161ff) was complaining of depression, anxiety, and guilt, which were precipitated by leaving her abusive husband.

She had never been able to reach an orgasm with a man and could only do so with fantasies, dating from the age of 6 years, of being raped and tortured.

The criteria for true resolution of her problems—formulated as before by two judges blind to the events of therapy—included: "To find a man who respects and loves her, with whom she can form a mutually fulfilling relation"; and "Disappearance of her masochistic sexual fantasies, with the ability to enjoy loving sex."

The main issues in her therapy were anger against her father for sexualizing the relationship with her; anger and grief about her mother's physical abuse and lack of caring; and mourning for her mother's death.

At 4-year follow-up, she had a relationship with a new man who treated her kindly, and the masochistic fantasies had entirely disappeared. She made the following remarks about their sexual relation: "I love his body and he delights in mine. It's an enraptured sense of this other being. I guess what's different from before is that the desire is for him as a person, which is expressed physically and sexually."

The Self-Loathing Headmistress
(age 29, 58 sessions, follow-up 5 years):
The discovery of joy

For this married woman (described in Coughlin Della Selva, 1992), all pleasure in life had been destroyed by a state of self-loathing and self-punishment. She was afraid to have children.

Her mother, who clearly wished she could have got rid of her, seriously and deliberately neglected her. The patient lost the warm relationship with her father at puberty.

Criteria included the following: "Loss of self-hatred and self-punishment, with a major increase in her capacity to enjoy life. We would like to see her enter motherhood with confidence and enjoy her children."

The main themes of therapy were anger with both parents and identification with her mother's hatred of her.

At 5-year follow-up she recounted the following incident:

> She and her 5-year old daughter had been watching a videotaped play in which a young girl was left alone and bereft after the death of her mother. The patient said: "She looked at me as if she would take me in with her eyes and keep me inside her. She said, '*I will love you when you're dead*'. Wow! She's only five! What was I to say? Well, I said—and even though I don't know what it means—'*I'll love you*, even after I'm dead". And she cried and cried. And I just held her, and it was a moment of such profound joy, just beyond the limits of this universe, beyond words."

This unforgettable moment was experienced by a woman who, before therapy, could feel nothing but self-loathing.

* * *

We hope these vignettes speak for themselves.

We write as scientists, and the question may well be asked: What has science to do with concepts such as emotional closeness, happiness, or joy? Our answer is that if the science of psychotherapy cannot deal with these concepts, then it can only be concerned with superficialities and irrelevancies. If we do use them, then all that is needed is that the evidence on which they are based should be published in full.

THE AIMS OF THIS BOOK

The following are some of the principal aims of the work presented here: to describe with examples how these extraordinary therapeutic results can be achieved; to help to instruct the reader in how to do it; to survey the literature confirming the efficacy of dynamic psychotherapy through randomized controlled trials; and to show how each element in the technique is supported by objective evidence, including that from neurobiology.

This is not all. We show how these therapies unmistakably confirm, with detailed evidence from videotaped interviews, many of the concepts and principles of dynamic psychotherapy. In addition, we have tried to introduce as much science into the study of these therapies as the subject can bear—neither too much nor too little. The initial interviews or "trial therapies" conducted by PCDS are routinely so deepgoing that it is possible for judges blind to the events of therapy to make accurate formulations of the patients' problems and their origin, and to lay down the criteria that would indicate that the neuroses had been truly "resolved". These criteria are then matched against the findings at follow-up, which makes potentially highly subjective judgements far more objective.

We have also explored the possibility of *predicting* the main issues that would be dealt with in therapy and that would lead to therapeutic effects, thus trying to convert each therapy into a scientific experiment.

THE RELEVANCE TO THE HISTORY
OF PSYCHOTHERAPY RESEARCH

By now it is generally accepted that there are three primary sources of evidence for the efficacy of psychotherapy: randomized controlled trials (RCTs), studies of process, and studies of individual patients.

RCTs have always been regarded as the "gold standard" of research in psychotherapy, but they have serious limitations. Chief of these is their reliance on *averages,* together with "objective" outcome criteria, which reveal nothing about the *true quality* of the therapeutic results or about the *distribution* of scores for outcome in the experimental and control series—suppose, for instance, that in spite of the averages being essentially equal, the "best" results are clustered together in one of the two samples rather than in the other? Mental health practitioners need data on individuals, not groups, and in particular they are interested in knowing how (and if) improvements occur during a series of therapeutic interventions. Furthermore, practitioners need to know what particular interventions are followed by therapeutic effects. For these purposes, *process research* and *studies of single therapies* (N=1 studies) are required.

For many years there has been a recurrent theme in the literature—insufficiently heeded and with very little influence—consisting of disillusion with RCTs, because of their questionable relevance to clinical practice, and a corresponding advocacy of N=1 studies. This goes back to the 1960s, when it was expressed even by some leading researchers who had devoted their lives to "gold-standard" RCT studies, represented by Carl Rogers, Allen Bergin, and Arnold Lazarus (see Bergin & Strupp, 1972, and a review by Malan, 1973). Interestingly, this situation was exactly repeated in the 1990s. The following is a single illustration chosen from many: Safran and Muran (1994) reiterated Bergin & Strupp's criticisms of RCTs and wrote: "There is an important need for more intensive analysis of single cases in order to yield clinically useful information."

Now, in the 2000s, this view is gradually coming into its own. It is represented by the U.S. National Institute of Mental Health (NIMH), which has "re-written nearly all its funding announcements to reflect the change in priority from large scale clinical trials in controlled settings, to research designed to study large numbers of diverse patients in real-world settings . . ." (Foxhall, 2000).

More recent spokesmen for this trend are Ingram and Mulick (2005), who write in a letter to the Editor of the *APA Monitor on Psychology* that, in addition to RCTs, at least two other methodologies "deserve to be included as part of the pillar of empirical validation". One is qualitative research involving the study of small groups of patients, and the other consists of "single-case design methods in clinical practice, through which an appropriate treatment is empirically validated for a unique client, not for groups of patients who share a diagnostic label". This is both encouraging and discouraging. It is *encouraging* that such a view is being expressed; yet it is *discouraging* that, instead of just being universally accepted and acted on, it still *has* to be expressed. We—quite independently—have seen this need, and the present book is a response to it. We are also responding to what Lazarus advocated in his interview with Bergin and Strupp (1972)—namely, the study of "patient–therapist pairs in all their complexity".

An important theme running through these studies is that sometimes it is possible to demonstrate the effectiveness of a method of psychotherapy beyond all reasonable doubt, without the use of a control series. This applies in the following circumstances:

• The patients have suffered from crippling symptoms and other severe disturbances (e.g. self-destructive behaviour patterns, grossly unsatisfactory human relations) for many years, often since child-hood.

- In some patients, years of previous therapy, both dynamic and non-dynamic, have failed to produce improvement.

- Patients are taken into ISTDP and begin to show major improvements within the first few weeks, and at termination they show complete recovery. No relapse occurs during a follow-up period of many years, even when the patient is subjected to severe stress (e.g. see The Good Girl with Ulcerative Colitis, chapter 6).

- Careful records, taken from videotapes, show that improvements began *immediately after* certain types of event in therapy, particularly the de-repression of buried feelings of grief and anger about people in the patient's early life.

- These feelings are experienced with such intensity as to leave no doubt of their significance.

- The connection between the patient's disturbances, on the one hand, and the buried feelings, on the other, can be clearly inferred.

Under these circumstances, even the most determined sceptic would find it hard to maintain that the improvements were due to "spontaneous remission", which just happened to occur during a period when, by coincidence, the patient was being treated with dynamic psychotherapy.

All these conditions were fulfilled by the seven therapies with which this book is concerned.

THE IMPORTANCE OF STUDYING OUTCOME

Finally, it is worth saying that one of the main emphases throughout this book is on the extremely detailed and psychodynamically based examination of *outcome*—that Cinderella of psychotherapeutic variables, so inadequately studied in the literature.

CHAPTER 2

Introduction to the theory and technique of Davanloo's ISTDP

THEORETICAL UNDERPINNINGS

The techniques used throughout this book were developed by Davanloo (1980, 1990, 2000) and evolved from his understanding of the psychoanalytic theory of neurosis (Fenichel, 1945). In particular, Davanloo based his strategic interventions on Freud's second theory of anxiety (Freud, 1926d [1925]. This theory suggests that anxiety is a *signal* to the ego, warning of danger or trauma; "danger" here is any feeling, impulse, or action that could threaten the primary bond with caretakers. In other words, any feeling, impulse, or action that results in separation from a loved one, or the loss of his or her love, is experienced as threatening, evokes anxiety, and is consequently avoided, giving rise to intrapsychic conflict between expressive and repressive forces within the psyche.

The two triangles

The Triangle of Conflict

This dynamic conceptualization of conflict can be depicted in operational terms by the Triangle of Conflict (see Figure 2.1, left). At the bottom of the triangle are the core emotions. When the expression of these emotions results in negative interpersonal consequences, they

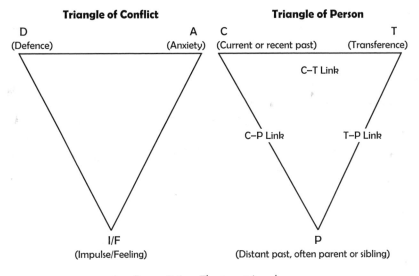

FIGURE 2.1.   The two triangles

become associated with the aversive states of anxiety, guilt, and shame and are avoided via the use of defences (for more detail, see Coughlin Della Selva, 1996, pp. 6–7). The Triangle of Person (Figure 2.1, right) was added to the Triangle of Conflict (by Malan, 1976) in order to depict the interpersonal nature of human experience and emotional expression. What begins as an interpersonal interaction becomes internalized in the form of an intrapsychic conflict over time. In other words, if a child is consistently punished for the expression of anger, he will begin to get anxious when angry and will learn ways to avoid its expression. Let's say that passivity and withdrawal become the child's strategies of choice for avoiding the experience and expression of anger (and its feared consequences). Eventually, he may retreat to this position so automatically that even he is unaware of feeling angry inside. The defences come to *replace* the feeling itself and can result in character pathology (e.g., passive aggressive or avoidant personality disorders), affecting all future relationships.

The Triangle of Person

The Triangle of Person (Figure 2.1, right) depicts the way in which conflicts involving core emotions get over-generalized, affecting patients' interactions with others in their current life, including the therapist.

The use of the two triangles aids the therapist in organizing the patient's material and serves as a guide to intervention. For example, if the patient arrives to his therapy session with anxiety, it is a signal to the therapist that some threatening emotion is being experienced, in all likelihood towards the therapist. This theoretical understanding guides therapeutic interventions, as the overarching goal in this therapy involves the direct experience of the patient's complex mixed feelings towards others. In the hypothetical example given here, the therapist would work to facilitate the direct experience, and clear expression, of feelings towards the therapist (T in Figure 2.1). Those feelings would then be tied to current conflicts in contemporary relationships (C), as well as being linked to unresolved feelings from the past (P). Research has demonstrated the therapeutic utility of making these T–C–P links (Malan, 1963, 1976b; Winston et al., 1991).

Any feeling or impulse that has caused rupture or trauma to the attachment bond can become suffused with anxiety and be avoided via defensive processes. Davanloo (1990) has stated that "only the capacity to develop warm emotional ties to caretakers is innate". When this innate capacity is frustrated or thwarted, it creates internal pain and generates reactive anger towards the depriving other (see Figure 2.2).

Feeling and defence

Figure 2.2 represents the layering of feeling and defence that can develop when emotions get contaminated with anxiety and become chronically inhibited:

1. At the core we find the *love and attachment strivings* that are innate in our species.

2. When the desire to attach is frustrated, this causes *pain and grief*, which gives rise to

3. *retaliatory anger* towards the depriving other.

4. This anger is suffused with *guilt*, and it also leads to *anxiety*, because it threatens the very attachment bond towards which the individual is striving.

5. Finally, if these innate drives towards connection and attachment are neglected or disrupted often enough, the individual begins to create *distance*, both from his or her own affects and from other people. This barrier against intimacy and closeness—with one's own inner world and with others—is depicted by the outer layer, described by Davanloo as "defences against emotional closeness". These defences are almost always characterological and pervasive. Reich (1933) referred to them as "character armour", while

1 Love & attachment

2 Pain & grief

3 Anger

4 Guilt

5 Defences against emotional closeness

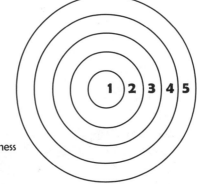

FIGURE 2.2.   Genetic system within the unconscious

Winnicott (1960) used the term "false self". Davanloo has taught us that we must break through and disrupt this barrier against intimacy and closeness in the transference if we are to have any hope of gaining access to all the disavowed feelings lying underneath.

Clearly this is all a matter of degree. Some rupture and misattunement between a child and his caretakers is unavoidable. When the rupture is relatively minor and repair efforts are made, there is no trauma. When the rupture is significant in intensity or duration, or is not repaired, this experience tends to generate reactive anger, and even sadism, towards the cherished family members who provoked it. In addition, the ensuing *guilt* generated by aggressive impulses towards a loved one may itself prove difficult, if not intolerable, for the child to bear, and this may also be repressed.

Self-directed aggression

Since humans are dependent for so long, their survival depends upon secure attachments to adult care-takers. The child will attempt to preserve the bond with parental figures at great cost (Bowlby, 1969, 1973, 1980). In order to protect the other from their wrath, the child often turns aggression towards the self. This is not a new idea. Freud (1917e [1915]) wrote: "so we find the key to the clinical picture [of depression]: we perceive that the self-reproaches are reproaches against a loved object which have been shifted away from it to the patient's own ego".

This was the beginning of the conceptualization of a *punitive superego*, driven by guilt over aggressive impulses. This notion is central to much of Davanloo's work and has deep roots in psychoanalytic theory. Anna Freud, in her classic text *The Ego and the Mechanisms of Defence* (1966), suggested that defensive processes are motivated by "superego anxiety" (fear of retaliation by the superego). She viewed the superego as "a mischief-maker which prevents the ego's coming into a friendly understanding with feelings and impulses".

Particularly in highly resistant patients with character pathology, Davanloo has concluded that this self-destructive force (otherwise referred to as the "superego") within the patient is responsible for the creation and perpetuation of self-punishment and self-defeat (Abbass, 2003a; Beeber, 1999a, 1999b, 1999c). These patients are driven, albeit unconsciously, to punish themselves because of the anxiety and guilt they feel over the angry, destructive impulses they harbour towards loved ones who have neglected, hurt, abused, or even abandoned them. Such behaviour is frequently over-determined, since the internalization of sadistic impulses preserves the loved one, as well as punishing the self (see The Good Girl with Ulcerative Colitis, chapter 6, when she says that the "elegant economy" of her self-destructive symptoms is "terrible").

The goal of ISTDP is to eradicate the self-punitive system within the unconscious. We seek to free patients from symptomatic suffering and their character pathology so that they can live life to the fullest and fulfil their unique potential. Davanloo contends that the only way to defeat and eliminate this self-punitive force is to "exert gentle, but relentless, pressure on the patient by confronting any and all defences against the experience of the patient's true feelings as they arise" (quoted in Coughlin Della Selva, 2001b, p. 40). In addition, the therapist must confront the patient with all the tactics being used to keep an emotional distance from the therapist, undermining her usefulness.

How defence becomes resistance

All of the intense mixed feelings of longing, pain, anger, grief, and guilt from the past are kept under wraps by the defensive system in place when the patient enters treatment. These defences form a barrier, both within the patient (between his feelings and his conscious awareness), and between himself and others. In other words, the patient keeps himself from knowing what he feels and essentially cuts himself off from his own inner life. At the same time, in order to keep these intense mixed feelings out of awareness, he must keep others at an emotional distance, for it is in intimate contact with others that longings for connection, and the pain, grief, and anger about past losses, are stimulated. In this way, all the defences against the awareness of painful and anxiety-laden feelings combine to form a resistance to closeness (which Davanloo refers to as the patient's "wall"). Any such wall against meaningful emotional contact with the therapist must be removed if therapy is going to be a transformational experience.

If the patient cannot bear the full force of his true feelings, he will not be able to let anyone close and will present a false façade to others. The therapist will be no exception. The patient enters therapy in a state of conflict—a part of him motivated to keep the therapist out of his intimate life, in order protect the status quo, alongside the part of him longing for genuine engagement and emotional liberation. Often, patients report feeling "stuck" in their lives and are mired in an ambivalent state that shows up immediately in their interaction with the therapist (for examples see The Man Divided and The Masochistic Artist). In order to disrupt this emotional gridlock and create deep and enduring change within the personality, we must break through these resistances to emotional closeness.

Defences against emotional closeness

Davanloo (1990) has been particularly effective in creating techniques designed to identify and remove defences against emotional closeness. These innovative techniques may well be responsible for the success of ISTDP in treating character-disordered patients, who have been notoriously resistant to treatment modalities of all kinds, including medication (Magnavita, 1997). We seek to understand why these interventions are so effective.

Davanloo (1990) and others (Abbass, 2002a; Beeber, 1999a, 1999b, 1999c; Carveth, 2001) have suggested that guilt regarding aggression motivates the need for punishment and is the "perpetuator" of unconsciously driven suffering. Isolating oneself from others, and creating self-imposed exile, is considered a central aspect of the superego's retaliation against the self. The self-punitive system is unconscious and can take a number of forms—sometimes subtle, at other times quite overt. In some cases, the patient's life is replete with self-defeat and self-punishment. They may be aware that they sabotage their own efforts, while having no idea what is driving this pattern of behaviour. Others maintain the outward appearance of success but suffer from intense internal suffering and self-reproach.

While this particular dynamic (guilt over sadistic impulses) may well be responsible for the suffering experienced by that category of patients with a lifelong history of self-defeat and self-punishment, it seems doubtful that any one factor could be responsible for all psychopathology. Is it just angry, sadistic feelings that create anxiety and guilt and that drive neurotic suffering? Could it be that pain and grief, or the exquisite vulnerability entailed in opening up to love, get punished in some families and create a great deal of anxiety and chronic avoidance? In his paper on handling resistance, Davanloo (1990) wrote that resistance "is the inevitable consequence of the basic mechanism underlying neuroses, namely the repression of feelings because they are painful or unacceptable" (p. 1). This seems a far broader statement than one that suggests that it is only guilt over sadistic impulses that results in defensive processes and psychopathology.

Could it be that self-imposed suffering is the *consequence* of repression and not the cause? We attempt in this book to bring the evidence to bear on these questions, as these issues have become the topic of rather fierce debate within the field. We need to heed the words of our patients, many of whom have said things like, "The anger is easy compared to this. The pain over being rejected and abandoned is almost unbearable. Why did my mother never love me?" (see "The Lonely Businessman" in Coughlin Della Selva, 1996, pp. 60–67). Many patients presented in the current volume, including the Masochistic Artist and the Reluctant Fiancée, have suggested that feeling completely and utterly alone in the world was the most unbearable experience they have ever had, and that even anger and conflict is preferable to that kind of desolate feeling. In all cases, anger was only one of many intensely painful feelings that needed to be confronted and experienced during the course of therapy. Every patient presented here seemed to need to go through an intense period of grief and mourning for all that had been lost (for details, see the first part of chapter 10). If we maintain our focus on disrupting the defensive system and rendering resistances to emotional closeness inoperable, the anxiety-provoking feelings lying beneath will emerge in a clear and unmistakable fashion.

TECHNIQUE

Davanloo's (1980, 1990, 2000) understanding of psychoanalytic theory, his experience with both patients and teachers during his training, and his intuitive grasp of unconscious processes were all factors that influenced the development of his techniques. Impatient with the amount of time spent in traditional analysis, and discouraged by the extent of change achieved with these methods, he began to experiment with techniques designed to accelerate and condense the analytic process.

It should be noted that Davanloo was exposed to the work of Erich Lindemann (1944, 1945, 1979) during his training in Boston. That work, which involved therapeutic interventions designed to facilitate the process of mourning caused by traumatic losses, had a dramatic effect on Davanloo and his evolving technique. He observed that patients in the throes of a traumatic experience often had relatively easy access to previously unconscious feelings and memories from their childhood, which could be worked through quite rapidly. In those cases, the environmental stressor had evoked feelings of such great intensity that the patient's characteristic defences against them were weakened or rendered inoperable, creating an intrapsychic crisis and facilitating a rapid opening into the unconscious. Davanloo began to wonder if it would be possible to develop therapeutic techniques that could *precipitate* the very kind of internal crisis required to "have patients re-live and thus work through the acute stress disorder of their childhood traumas" (Neborsky, 2001, p. 17). Working largely on his own over the course of twenty years, using videotapes to study the process, Davanloo developed a technique of therapy designed to do just that. He found that the exposure of core conflicts within the patient required a high level of therapist activity, skill, and precision and involved the use of techniques designed to eliminate defence and resistance, allowing for the direct experience of previously avoided feelings and impulses. This breakthrough of previously repressed feelings seemed to be the key to "unlocking the unconscious".

Somatic experiencing

Simply encouraging patients to talk about their feelings has proven insufficient and ineffective in promoting true change (Pennebaker, 1991). The crucial factor seems to be the *visceral* experience of those feelings in the body (Levine, 1997). This insight is not new. Freud wrote, concerning abdominal noises during a psychotherapy session, that the patient's abdomen was "joining in the conversation". While Freud recognized the importance of nonverbal communications and their relation to the dynamic unconscious, it took others, such as Reich (1933) and Davanloo (1978, 1980, 1990), to develop techniques designed to make therapeutic use of them. As Davanloo experimented with techniques designed to bring buried feelings to consciousness, he found that vital memories associated with repressed feelings emerged in a clear and emphatic manner once those feelings were experienced somatically. Feelings experienced in the here-and-now, with the therapist, seem to serve as a kind of triggering event, releasing feelings and memories from the past that can be experienced directly and worked through at their source. This process enhances fluidity within the patient's unconscious, often dramatically so. Following the direct experience of the feelings that they have previously been avoiding, patients are sometimes flooded with images, memories, and dreams, which reveal the nature and genesis of their core conflicts. They often remark on how surprised they are by what emerges (e.g. see The Man Divided, chapter 4).

Basic techniques

The basic principle of Davanloo's technique, and therefore the aim of every intervention, involves an attempt to bring patients to the *direct experience*, first of conscious feelings and then of hitherto unconscious feelings and impulses—the avoidance of which lies at the heart of their neurosis. He has created a rich tapestry of techniques, referred to as the *central dynamic sequence*. This process is employed during the initial evaluation, referred to as the *trial therapy*.

Put very simply, the goal of every session is to dismantle defences against the experience of core feelings and affective contact with the therapist, releasing the buried feelings within. The experience of these feelings appears to create an opening into the unconscious in which key memories are revived, allowing for the working through of unresolved feelings and conflicts from the past. "The process of de-repression reveals the factors that have been responsible for the avoidance of strong internal feelings and close emotional involvement with others" (Coughlin Della Selva, 1996, p. 142). For example, following the experience of rage at the therapist, with the impulse to strangle and kill her, a patient ("The Woman on an Emotional Roller Coaster", in Coughlin Della Selva, 1996) suddenly got a flash of her mother's face. This was not a cognitive process or a conclusion arrived at via interpretation but was a manifestation of connections between past and present that emerged spontaneously on the heels of deeply felt emotion that had been completely unconscious prior to this session. Once the feelings towards the therapist were experienced, the connections to the past were made in an emotionally meaningful way, allowing for a re-working of feelings regarding the original trauma with her mother.

Following the experience of these core emotions, and the outpouring of memories associated with them, a period of cognitive re-analysis or interpretation follows, designed to deepen the insights obtained in the process and promote lasting change. In contrast to traditional psychodynamic psychotherapy, interpretation comes *last* in ISTDP and is employed as a means of consolidating the insights obtained via the emotionally felt experience of the patient.

Literally all of the innovations developed by Davanloo occur in the *pre-interpretative* phase of treatment and involve the handling of anxiety and resistance, as well as deepening access to the experience of core emotions within the context of an intimate relationship. He has adopted a scientific approach to this endeavour and uses the patient's response to each intervention as a diagnostic tool and guide to further intervention. He, and his trainees, also videotape all sessions, so that the therapeutic process can be studied in detail.

It is essential to understand that the central dynamic sequence is a framework for organizing the material presented by the patient and is not adhered to slavishly. Therapists must use their intuition, as well as their cognitive understanding of the process, to tailor each sequence of interventions based upon the needs, strengths, and deficits of the patient being treated.

Therapeutic stance

The ISTDP therapist takes an uncompromising stance as an advocate for the patient and his freedom. The therapist communicates the utmost care and respect for the patient as a human being, while maintaining an attitude of disrespect and intolerance for the defences that cripple the patient's functioning and perpetuate his suffering. This stance—along with the technical interventions outlined below—intensifies intrapsychic conflicts, generates complex transference feelings, and speeds the process of therapy. The therapist is deeply involved with the patient from the first moment of contact and attempts to work at the patient's highest level of capacity.

The central dynamic sequence

The central dynamic sequence can be summarized as follows:

1. Preliminary enquiry about the patient's complaints, including specific examples of the problems being reported, most notably that which precipitated the initiation of therapy.

2. Pressure towards experiencing the feelings involved in the present-
    ing complaints, leading to a rise in the patient's characteristic de-
    fences.

3. Work on defences:

    a. identification of the defence ("Do you notice you are vague?")

    b. clarification of defensive functions ("Do you see that by remain-
    ing vague you avoid your feelings?")

    c. examination of consequences ("If you continue to avoid your
    feelings by remaining vague, we will not get to the bottom of your
    problems").

4. Work on defences will lead to either a breakthrough of underlying
    feelings (in low-resistance patients) or a rise of complex transfer-
    ence feelings, with crystallization of *transference resistance* (in cases
    of moderate- to high-resistance patients).

5. The *head-on collision* with the resistance in the transference.

6. Breakthrough of complex transference feelings, with de-repression
    of feelings and memories towards significant others from the pa-
    tient's past.

7. As history is obtained, interpretations and links are made between
    past, present, and transference phenomena, consolidating insights
    obtained in the process.

"The goal of the trial therapy, and the therapy as a whole, is to get
to the bottom of each triangle" (Coughlin Della Selva, 2001a)—that is,
to gain direct access to *buried feelings* directed towards *significant others
in the past* (see Figure 2.1). However, we do not dig for these feelings
and memories regarding the past. Rather, we begin in the present,
examining the patient's difficulties in current relationships (C) and/or
dealing with the complex transference feelings (T) that get mobilized in
the process. Once these feelings are experienced in the here-and-now,
the patient himself will make spontaneous connections to people and
events from the past, which shed light on the development of the
conflicts that brought him into treatment. The response to each element
of the central dynamic sequence provides the most current and accurate data available on the patient's suitability for treatment (for more
detailed information on the assessment of suitability for ISTDP, see
The Man Divided, chapter 4; see also Coughlin Della Selva, 2001a).

THE CENTRAL DYNAMIC SEQUENCE
CONSIDERED IN DETAIL

Enquiry

We begin by taking a phenomenological approach to enquiry, and we vary our responses according to the patient's ability to give a clear and coherent account of his difficulties. In some cases, anxiety interferes with the patient's ability to think clearly, and steps must be taken to reduce anxiety immediately. In other cases, it is smooth sailing from the start. Most patients have a capacity that lies somewhere between these extremes. They bring both motivation and resistance into the initial interview and possess both strengths and areas of fragility in their functioning. The process must be tailored to each patient and to each patient–therapist pair (Osimo, 2003).

The essential feature of the process of enquiry involves an exploration of the patient's *emotional feelings* towards others, including the therapist. Davanloo has operationalized definitions of each core feeling state, so we have precise ways of assessing whether a given patient is, in fact, "in touch with his feelings". Davanloo suggests that three elements must be present for the patient to be considered in touch with a given emotion. These include the cognitive label of the emotion, the physiological experience characteristic of that emotion, and the impulse that accompanies that emotion (see Figure 2.3).

Emotions are characteristic of the species and are experienced in a similar way by all humans. How these emotions get expressed varies greatly, but the physiological experience is built in to the species (see Figure 2.4 for "a map" of the body). It is essential that the therapist be skilled in assessing whether the physiological state that the patient is experiencing is in alignment with the emotion he is labelling.

- COGNITIVE — "I feel sad"

- PHYSIOLOGICAL — "I feel a lump in my throat and a heaviness in my chest"

- MOTORIC IMPULSE — "I feel like weeping"

FIGURE 2.3.   Components of affect

- ■ ANGER: Head, neck, jaw, shoulders, arms, and hands

- ■ GRIEF and LONGING: Chest, with feelings of heaviness, pain, and ache

- ■ LOVE and JOY: Chest — light and open — expansive

- ■ FEAR: The gut

- ■ SEXUAL DESIRE: Genitals

FIGURE 2.4.   Map of the body

Working the Triangle of Conflict

Evaluation of anxiety

In all but the most exceptional cases, the therapist's rapid and direct focus on the patient's feelings triggers anxiety and mobilizes the use of the patient's characteristic defences. The therapist's first task is to assess the nature and intensity of the patient's anxiety, as this information contains vital diagnostic information. The therapist is ever vigilant for signs that the anxiety generated by this kind of pressure is greater than the patient can bear. We must follow the signals from the unconscious, which communicate via the body, to make this determination.

·As part of his core training material in Montreal, Davanloo has identified three channels for the experience of anxiety (Figure 2.5), each reflecting a certain level of ego-adaptive capacity. The *first* channel of anxiety is into the striated or voluntary muscle (see Figure 2.6A) and reveals a capacity to withstand the direct experience of core emotions (high ego-adaptive capacity). The *second* channel of anxiety goes into smooth muscle (Figure 2.6B) and often results in psychosomatic disturbances such as headaches, irritable bowel syndrome, or asthma. The *third* channel of anxiety results in the disruption of cognitive and perceptual processes (Figure 2.6C), such that the patient loses track of his

- ■ STRIATED MUSCLE

- ■ SMOOTH MUSCLE

- ■ COGNITIVE–PERCEPTUAL DISRUPTION

FIGURE 2.5.   Channels of anxiety

(A)   STRIATED MUSCLE

- Hand clenching

- Tension in arms, neck, shoulders, and head

- Sighing respiration

- Abdomen, legs, and feet tense and fidgeting

(B)   SMOOTH MUSCLE

- Bladder urgency

- Gastrointestinal — irritable bowel syndrome

- Vascular — migraine, hypertension

- Bronchi — asthma

- Localized or generalized pain

- Auto-immune disorders — lupus, multiple sclerosis

(C)   COGNITIVE–PERCEPTUAL DISRUPTION

- Drifting, dissociation, confusion

- Visual blurring or narrowing of the visual field

- Fainting, freezing, fugue state

- Hallucinations

FIGURE 2.6.   Unconscious anxiety

thoughts, dissociates, or becomes subject to alterations in the visual field, suggesting ego-fragility.

Davanloo (1990–1991) has taught us that, as long as anxiety is being channelled into the striated muscle, with notable hand-clenching and sighing respiration, the patient's body is signalling us that feelings are preconscious and can be tolerated. If anxiety is not apparent in the patient's musculature, we must enquire further to determine where it is going. This information will provide the most current and reliable data available regarding the patient's level of disturbance (mid-spectrum with character pathology or fragile ego states). Furthermore, this information will guide our subsequent interventions. Whenever anxiety is *not* being experienced in the striated muscle, preparatory work to fortify the patient's ego-adaptive capacity will be required before any exposure of core feelings should be attempted. Although a full account of all the techniques required to restructure the ego is beyond the scope of this book (see Coughlin Della Selva, 1996; Magnavita, 1997; McCullough Vaillant, 1997), examples of this kind of restructuring are illustrated in the cases to follow.

Work on defences: the patient's responses

Anxiety about feelings propels the use of defences (see Figures 2.7 and 2.8). The ISTDP therapist uses a three-pronged approach to defence work: (1) identify the defence ("Do you see that you laugh, avoid my eyes, and change the subject?"); (2) clarify the function of the defence ("That is a way you avoid your true feelings"); and (3) examine the consequences of the defence ("If you continue to avoid these feelings, you will carry your suffering with you"). It is our goal to acquaint the patient with his defences, their function, and the negative, self-defeating consequences of relying on them. This process is designed to turn the ego against its defences (see Figures 2.7 and 2.8) and increase motivation to abandon them in favour of the experience of the patient's true feelings.

The patient's response to the phase of defence analysis is also diagnostic. Patients who are highly responsive, and whose defences are largely dystonic, are able to abandon them and face their true feelings with relative ease. In most cases, however, a focus on defences intensifies the patient's conflicts about whether to reveal or conceal their true

REPRESSIVE	REGRESSIVE
■ Intellectualization	■ Projection
■ Rationalization	■ Denial
■ Minimization	■ Dissociation
■ Displacement	■ Acting out
■ Reaction formation	■ Somatization

FIGURE 2.7.   Formal defences

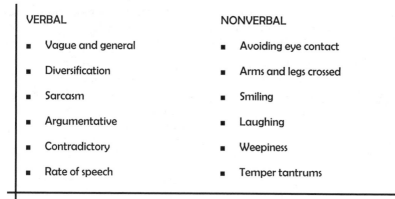

VERBAL	NONVERBAL
▪ Vague and general	▪ Avoiding eye contact
▪ Diversification	▪ Arms and legs crossed
▪ Sarcasm	▪ Smiling
▪ Argumentative	▪ Laughing
▪ Contradictory	▪ Weepiness
▪ Rate of speech	▪ Temper tantrums

FIGURE 2.8.   Tactical defences

feelings, creating a kind of intrapsychic crisis. The part of the patient that wants to face his feelings and obtain emotional freedom is available to the therapist and mobilizes an internal healing force that Davanloo (2000) refers to as "the unconscious therapeutic alliance". However, there is a counterforce in operation, fuelling the resistance. This is the part of the patient determined to avoid the pain and anxiety involved in the process of facing what they have repressed for so long. "The therapist's job is to probe for feeling and to monitor continuously the balance between resistance and the therapeutic alliance" (Davanloo, 1990, p. 3). Furthermore, the therapist must work to intensify this conflict and tip the balance in favour of the therapeutic alliance.

Rise in complex transference feelings

Anxiety about feelings leads to the use of defences. The ISTDP therapist is not neutral, but places herself squarely on the side of openness, honesty, and emotional freedom, while communicating disdain and intolerance for the repressive forces within the patient that cripple his functioning and perpetuate his suffering. This therapeutic stance will inevitably increase the patient's anxiety, which is a signal that intense and conflictual feelings towards the therapist are getting mobilized. Rather than back off in the face of anxiety, the therapist constantly monitors the patient's capacity to bear his anxiety and strives to work at the patient's highest level of anxiety tolerance. "The aim of the technique is, therefore, to enable the patient to experience his true feelings as rapidly as possible and to the maximum degree that he can bear" (Davanloo, 1990, p. 2).

Again, in highly responsive patients, these techniques alone are sufficient to mobilize the healing forces within the patient (the "unconscious therapeutic alliance") and lead to a direct experience of previously avoided feelings towards loved ones in his current and past life. More often, however, this procedure results in an intensification of complex transference feelings, along with a crystallization of resistance in the transference. The patient now begins to resist the therapist's attempts to get to know him in a deep and honest way, sensing at some level that his most painful feelings are going to be investigated (Davanloo, 1990).

The head-on collision with the resistance

Examining the negative consequences of defensive avoidance of feelings is a technique employed in almost every case and is used in an attempt to turn the patient against his defences. A common example of this, illustrated in several of the cases presented in this volume, involves pointing out that the patient becomes tearful and begins to criticize himself in an attempt to avoid the experience of anger towards a loved one. Pointing out the harmful consequences of such a strategy is essential in turning the patient's ego against his defences and increasing his motivation to face these feelings directly. In many cases, this is sufficient to shift the balance from resistance to alliance.

In more resistant cases, however, defences intensify in response to intervention and become a resistance that threatens to sabotage the working alliance and undermine therapeutic progress. In these cases, the patient begins to mobilize all his resources in order to keep the therapist at a distance and defeat her efforts. This crystallization of defences in the transference requires a head-on collision with the resistance, lest the therapy stall and ultimately fail. During the head-on collision, the therapist must point out to the patient that maintaining a defensive wall against meaningful contact with her will destroy his opportunity to get help. In some cases, the therapist must confront the patient with the futility of continuing in this manner, suggesting that they will have to say their goodbyes unless these tactics are abandoned. Often very loaded language is employed at this juncture; such as, "You can choose to maintain your wall, keep me out, and carry your suffering with you to your grave. That is up to you. It isn't up to me to say." The therapist places the responsibility for therapeutic success or failure in the patient's lap. In so doing, she also acknowledges her own limits—

that she has no magic wand, cannot be successful with everyone, and will respect the patient's choice in the matter.

The therapist must not engage in an interpersonal battle or get into a power struggle with the patient. The goal of this intervention is to increase the *internal* conflict that the patient is trying to avoid by creating an interpersonal conflict. The therapist makes her own stand on the matter very clear: she will only continue to treat him if he is willing to be open and honest. However, the choice about whether to avail himself of this opportunity is left with the patient.

In my own practice, I (PCDS) have said, on more than one occasion; "Look, there is a phone book full of therapists who I'm sure would be happy to take your money to sit and listen to you talk, even if nothing is being accomplished. However, I am not one of them." To avoid this confrontation is to collude with the patient's resistance and to pretend that some worthwhile therapy is going on. This stand also communicates the message that the therapist is not omnipotent and can't "cure" the patient without his active participation. In addition, it reveals self-respect and integrity on the part of the therapist. These interventions will flush out patients who have no real investment in change and will free up the therapist's time for those who do.

Breakthrough of complex transference feelings

In most cases the head-on collision intensifies complex transference feelings. It is important to remember that transference phenomena are not unique to the therapeutic setting, but are ubiquitous in human interactions. However, in ISTDP, we make every attempt to expose these feelings as soon as they arise, as they are the key to unlocking the unconscious system (Davanloo, 1988). Any new person who attempts to enter the patient's inner life will revive all the unresolved feelings towards important figures from the past. By helping the patient to experience and express these mixed feelings towards the therapist, long-buried feelings towards significant others in the patient's life will emerge quickly and, usually, with great emotional force. Facilitating the experience of complex transference feelings as soon as they arise also prevents the development of a transference neurosis and ever-increasing levels of resistance.

Signals from the unconscious.   The therapist waits for a signal from the unconscious that feelings are on the rise, before moving to the phase of pressure to experience them. These signals are usually nonverbal. In the case of the Cold-Blooded Businessman, for example, his tone of voice indicated a rise of feeling, alerting the therapist that the resistance was breaking down to the point where feelings could be faced directly (chapter 5). In other cases, a tightened fist, swinging foot, or tears welling up in the eyes provide the signal that feelings are ripe for the picking.

Anger is usually the first feeling to be experienced in response to defence work. Angry impulses towards the therapist are typically followed by guilt and grief over destructive impulses and the losses that have been experienced in life. Finally loving feelings, along with desires for closeness, usually emerge. "The patient becomes angry within an atmosphere in which he senses, both consciously and unconsciously, that the therapist is directing him towards his most painful buried feelings out of a genuine and compassionate concern, a determination not to spare him pain but to make him face it, with the sole purpose of freeing him from the self-defeating patterns that have spoiled his life for so many years." (Malan, quoted in Davanloo, 1990, p. 7).

The direct experience of complex transference feelings seems to create a wide opening into the unconscious. Spontaneous links are made between the feelings towards the therapist and whoever he has come to represent. Often, there is a visual transfer of images in which the patient suddenly sees the face of a significant figure from her early life. The feelings towards that figure can then be faced directly.

The phase of "pure content" and the developmental history

The process of head-on collision with the resistance, with a breakthrough of complex transference feelings, results in relief of tension and anxiety; contact with core affects; insight into links between past and present; and a sense of closeness with the therapist; as well as an internal sense of mastery and competence that comes from facing what had been avoided. Resistance is greatly reduced, while the unconscious therapeutic alliance is fortified, allowing for the phase of "pure content", in which an accurate and dynamically meaningful history can be obtained. The history that emerges following a breakdown of defences is quite fluid and dynamic—shedding light on the development of core conflicts—and bears little resemblance to the kind of formal history-taking that many of us were trained to carry out. For example, following the phase of head-on collision with The Masochistic Artist, in which the therapist repeatedly pointed out the ways the patient kept her at a distance, the patient spontaneously responded by saying, "Well maybe

I *do* want to [stay alone]. You see, I don't trust anybody, and I think that's because I couldn't trust my mother" (chapter 9). She went on to tearfully recount highly significant memories of her interaction with her mother, which helped to make dynamic sense of the struggles this woman was having in her life. The entire process is emotionally charged. Significant memories flow quite effortlessly at this point in the therapy.

THE RESULTS OF THE TRIAL THERAPY

Frieda Fromm-Reichmann (1950) said that "The patient is in need of an *experience*, not an *explanation*" (emphasis added). This is exactly what trial therapy provides. The experience of getting through defences to the direct experience of previously avoided feelings often has a profound effect. Patients typically report feeling as if they have worked hard in order to accomplish something very important. They usually leave the initial interview drained but calm, with a deep understanding of their own inner workings and with heightened motivation to continue treatment.

Caution is required

It must be remembered that not all patients are suitable for this kind of rapid uncovering of their anxiety-laden feelings, and some may be harmed by it. Davanloo has suggested that the only way to know who can benefit from this type of uncovering is to test it out via trial therapy. In other words, patients are exposed to each element of the therapy (via the central dynamic sequence) in a careful and systematic manner. Their response to each intervention will provide diagnostic information about their current capacity to bear anxiety-provoking feelings and will guide the next intervention. Most ISTDP therapists start cautiously, with pressure towards feeling and challenge to resistance, carefully monitoring the patient's responses and changing to a more supportive stance if thought-blocking, dissociation, or visual disturbances appear.

The detailed transcripts of work with the patients described in this book illustrate the variations in pace and sequence required for patients at different levels of ego-adaptive capacity.

THE THERAPEUTIC ALLIANCE

There is a large body of research literature concerned with the subject of the therapeutic alliance, with particular emphasis on trying to measure it and gauge its impact on outcome. However, as far as we know, only the literature on ISTDP takes account of the fact that the therapeutic alliance can be partly or wholly *unconscious*—that is, that the patient makes important communications to the therapist without being aware of their dynamic significance (see Figure 2.9). These communications represent a healing force within the patient that is available as an ally to the therapist. An example is a communication from The Cold-Blooded Businessman (chapter 5), who said he had a desire to do "bodily damage" to a car, which was a signal to the therapist that he was ready to face his destructive impulses towards those who had thwarted him and had got in his way. This play on words was a reflection of his unconscious wish to do bodily damage to a *person*, which became only too clear in later sessions. In the case of The Man Divided, after the therapist's comment on his mixed feelings about coming to see her, the patient spontaneously removed his coat. This was a clear signal that she had hit the nail on the head, leading to a rise in his unconscious therapeutic alliance (chapter 4).

While Davanloo pays particular attention to signs and signals of a rise in the unconscious therapeutic alliance, he also works assiduously to strengthen the *conscious* alliance by addressing the patient's will and determination to do the work at hand. In so doing, Davanloo is building consensus about the true nature of the patient's difficulties. If, for example, the patient comes in complaining about a problem with her husband, the therapist works to clarify this in such a way that this external problem is reframed in intrapsychic terms. Through a process of enquiry, the patient is helped to focus on *her* problem with her husband. Perhaps she gets anxious, weepy, and helpless in the face of her fury towards him for having an affair. Instead of joining the patient

- Healing force within the patient

- Therapist allies with this healthy force within the patient

- Alliance is in conflict with resistance

- Main function: shines light on core traumas

- Unconscious therapeutic alliance mobilized via therapeutic interaction

- In order to defeat resistance

FIGURE 2.9.   Unconscious therapeutic alliance

in externalizing the problem (that her husband is a no-good, cheating louse), we would focus on the part *she* has played in the difficulties she is experiencing. Then we gain consensus. "So, do we agree, then, that a big part of the problem for you is in letting yourself feel your anger as anger and using it to assert yourself, instead of going to a weepy, helpless state and turning it back on yourself?" By tapping into and emphasizing the patient's will to courageously face what she has previously avoided, the alliance is fortified and the treatment process moves ahead more rapidly and decisively.

ASSESSING THE PATIENT'S STRENGTHS

Since Davanloo encourages us to work at the patient's highest level of ability, attempting to facilitate the experience of feelings to the maximum tolerable degree, we must carefully assess the patient's strengths. What unique capacities does the patient bring to the task at hand? We seek to forge an alliance with the strong, healthy part of the patient in order to join forces against the defences and resistances. Assessing levels of anxiety and the nature of the patient's defensive structure is necessary but insufficient to determine the patient's ability to do the work. The balance between the patient's strengths and weaknesses will determine how rapidly and intensively he can work. For example, The Woman with Dissociation, who had been severely traumatized but possessed real personal strength, was able to make rapid and dramatic use of treatment despite long-standing and debilitating symptoms (chapter 7). In the end, it is patients' strength and resilience that brings them through the process to a successful conclusion.

MODIFICATIONS TO
DAVANLOO'S STYLE AND TECHNIQUE

Just as technique must be tailored and adjusted to fit the unique needs of each patient, so it must take into account the therapist's own style and personality, lest she become a robot or imitator of "the master". Davanloo's trainees have responded in different ways to what they have learned from him. Some follow his technique almost exactly, whereas others have introduced modifications that are better suited to their own personalities. *It is of great significance for the future of psychotherapy that many of these modified techniques are also effective.* The technique used by PCDS is but one example, and in view of the clinical material about to be presented, its effectiveness can hardly be doubted.

In the initial interview—the trial therapy—Davanloo tends to allow considerable time for the initial enquiry, whereas, perhaps surprisingly, PCDS is often more active in the early stages. She tends to embark on the phase of pressure towards feelings earlier in the session, sometimes immediately, and uses *interpretations* where indicated—something that Davanloo entirely avoids at this stage. Like Davanloo, she then goes on to clarification and challenge to the defences. However, where Davanloo often abrasively expresses his disrespect for the patient's defences, her style is much less intensively confrontational. So she sympathizes with the plight of the child, and acknowledges that the defences were adaptive—and even sometimes life-saving—in the past, while pointing out that they no longer serve the patient well as an adult. In fact, what had been a way to protect the self (e.g. withdrawing and dissociating) in childhood often becomes a way to isolate, torture, and punish the self in adulthood.

These variations in technique have important consequences. PCDS's understanding attitude tends to generate less *reactive* anger towards the therapist and, consequently, less resistance based on the defences that the patient employs to avoid the experience of anger. Given this, the interview does not necessarily proceed immediately to a head-on collision with resistance in the transference, as this is not always a major factor. In part, this is also due to her attention to building the therapeutic alliance while simultaneously fighting the forces of resistance. She works to gain consensus about the task at hand, building momentum and focusing on the positive consequences of experiencing one's true feelings, like freedom and increased energy. In cases in which the alliance is strong and the patient is able to gain direct access to the experience of his feelings towards those in his current life, an "unlocking of the unconscious", with associations to family members from the past, often emerges in an unmistakable way.

This having been said, the series of interventions that PCDS employs are derived directly from Davanloo, but put in her own words.

The different patterns of the initial interview

Because the level of anxiety and the degree of resistance vary from one patient to another, the pattern of the initial interview must also vary. Where the patient shows little resistance there is little or no need for challenge. However, in highly resistant patients, a high level of pressure and challenge is required in order to get a response and engage the patient on an emotional level. The Reluctant Fiancée experienced very high levels of anxiety, interfering with cognitive processes, but displayed relatively low levels of resistance. In that case, encouragement rather than challenge was needed. In contrast, The Cold-Blooded Businessman revealed high levels of resistance and low levels of emotional activation. This required repeated challenges and, finally, a head-on collision with the resistance in the transference, as the following example illustrates:

> *(The subject is showing resistance against experiencing anger with the therapist)*

> Th: We had an agreement to come together to have a look at the core of your problems. As we go to look at them, you tend to escape into your thoughts and avoid your feelings. What will happen if you continue to do that?
>
> Pt: If I do that, I won't be any better off than when I came here.
>
> Th: So what becomes clear is a self-defeating pattern in you.

This example makes clear that, when the situation requires it, PCDS can be almost as confronting as Davanloo.

LEARNING THE TECHNIQUE

At first sight it would seem that, as long as a therapist (1) understands the purpose of these interventions, (2) is able to sense when each is appropriate, and (3) formulates them in a fully empathic way, learning and applying them should present little difficulty. However, this is rarely the case. While appearing deceptively simple in the hands of an expert (e.g. Neborsky, 2001), ISTDP is a complex, multi-focal method of treatment that typically requires several years of training and supervision to master. Most trainees have struggled with their own anxieties and defences, as well as with the demands of this particular form of treatment. It is fairly easy to sit quietly and mumble "uh-huh", but it is a demanding task indeed to keep in mind, at every moment, where the patient is on the two triangles of conflict and person, while watching for signals from his body, as well as staying up with content and monitoring the interaction between patient and therapist. Extensive training and supervision is usually required to master these techniques. Exposure to unconscious material, via the videotaped interactions between patient and therapist used in training, can help restructure the trainee's unconscious, so that he becomes less anxious and defensive when strong feelings are aroused, especially in the transference.

CHAPTER 3

The literature:
empirical support for Davanloo's ISTDP

In a seminal book concerning the benefits of psychotherapy (Smith, Glass, & Miller, 1980), Smith concluded that "study after study has demonstrated that psychotherapy"—which includes behaviour therapy and cognitive behaviour therapy—"is an effective treatment for a whole host of emotional problems and mental disorders". Similarly, Shapiro (in Roth & Fonagy, 1996) contends that "there is more, and better quality, scientific evidence to support psychotherapy than for many other interventions in health care to-day" (p. viii). Barlow (1994) reported that psychotherapy is clearly more effective than social placebos and "in many cases . . . as effective or more effective than pharmacological approaches with proven efficacy". Luhrmann (2000) wrote that patients who are offered only medication and no psychotherapy are being subjected to "a kind of institutionalized malpractice". His research showed that such patients "do less well, are readmitted more quickly, diagnosed more inaccurately and medicated more randomly" than those treated with psychotherapy.

Yet these conclusions are not without reservations. Smith, Glass, and Miller (1980) make the quite devastating statement that "the benefits of psychotherapy are not permanent, but then little is" (p. 183), and Shapiro wrote "with notable and commendable exceptions, there has been relatively little progress in developing an evidence base for psychodynamic therapies" (in Roth & Fonagy, 1996, p. ix).

Moreover, despite the large body of evidence for the effectiveness of psychotherapy *in general* in reducing or eliminating emotional suffering, it has been maddeningly difficult to validate dynamic psychotherapy and to prove that the effects of all kinds of psychotherapy are due to anything other than non-specific factors. Many (Greenberg & Pinsoff, 1986; Havens, 1994; Hillard, 1993; Seligman, 1995, 1996, 1998) have suggested that the methods psychologists have been using to study the process of psychotherapy are inadequate. In our quest to be rigorous and scientific, we may have become too taken with a medical model, in which clinical trials are hailed as the gold standard of research tools. While providing us with some important information, clinical trials suffer from many limitations. "Conventional group comparison designs or controlled clinical trials have been relatively ineffective in identifying associations between therapy process and outcome" (Garfield, 1990, 1996; Jones, Ghannam, Nigg, & Dyer, 1993). These limitations can and must be compensated for by the addition of process research and detailed case studies. This book represents an effort to integrate findings from all these areas of research.

In this chapter, empirical support for the efficacy and effectiveness of ISTDP is presented. In addition to examining the findings of clinical trials, which have studied the treatment method as a whole, research support for each active ingredient within the model is presented. We seek to support the notion that "dynamic psychotherapy is not merely effective, but uniquely effective" (Davanloo, 1990). Davanloo has asserted that specific rather than non-specific factors are responsible for the effectiveness of this form of psychotherapy. He contends that these specific factors include: (1) breaking down defences against feelings and emotional involvement with the therapist, (2) examining the transference pattern of behaviour from the very inception of treatment, and (3) facing patients with their true feelings about the present and the past. Restructuring the defensive system and facilitating the direct experience and expression of hitherto unconscious feelings is thought to increase ego strength and adaptive capacity. Consequently, in addition to removing symptoms and pathological defences, this method of psychotherapy is expected to result in deep and long-lasting changes in personality functioning.

Davanloo's (1980, 1990) method of ISTDP consists of an elegant series of interventions, each with a specific goal and purpose. He calls this series the *central dynamic sequence*. It is a complex and sophisticated model of intervention. The therapist begins with a detailed enquiry into the patient's presenting problems, including the nature, severity, and

duration of the symptoms being reported. Following this brief overview of difficulties, the therapist asks for a recent example of the problem, in order to assess the patient's ability to communicate clearly and
to identify the feelings involved. Pressure to experience feeling typically ushers in defensive processes, which become the focus of the
therapist's work in the second phase of the evaluation. Defences are
identified and clarified. The cost of defensive manoeuvres is examined,
which leads to a phase of continued pressure to feel, combined with a
challenge to give up defensive avoidance. This combination of pressure
and challenge creates an intrapsychic conflict within the patient, while
simultaneously mobilizing a crystallization of complex transference
feelings. The patient is encouraged to express these feelings directly,
using visualization and imagination to express the impulses involved.
This process leads to a breakdown of defences and an outpouring of
previously unconscious material, linking the transference pattern of
behaviour with that observed in past and current relationships. Once
the system is open and fluid, a cognitive analysis of the process takes
place in order to reinforce the insights obtained via the process. Each
phase of the central dynamic sequence is evaluated here for effectiveness using data obtained from process research.

How do we evaluate the validity and utility of this form of psychotherapy? We will begin with an examination of the findings derived
from clinical trials, followed by process research and detailed case
studies. As an example, J. Weinberger (1995) conducted a meta-analysis
of hundreds of outcome studies in an attempt to ascertain whether so-
called common factors were responsible for the consistent finding that
psychotherapy is more effective than placebo but that no one treatment
model is superior to another. He discovered five factors that were
repeatedly and reliably associated with positive outcome. These included: (1) a positive therapeutic alliance; (2) helping the patient confront what he has tried to avoid; (3) revival of hope; (4) an increased
sense of mastery and competence; and (5) attribution of success to one's
own efforts. However, Weinberger found that most major schools of
therapy were relying on only one or two of these factors to achieve
therapeutic results. He suggested that a treatment model designed to
incorporate all five factors should result in superior outcome. It is our
contention that the combination of therapeutic factors within one treatment model which was suggested by Weinberger has already been
achieved by Davanloo (1990). In fact, the latter's method of ISTDP
includes all five of the aforementioned factors plus some additional
interventions of proven efficacy. In order to substantiate this claim, we

examine in this chapter the results of both clinical trials and process research.

It should also be noted that ISTDP, based on psychoanalytic theory, makes the assumption that much of the neurotic suffering plaguing our patients is caused by factors outside their conscious awareness. The whole issue of unconscious processes has been a hot topic of debate within our field. Recently, advances in neuroscience have allowed us to test out these hypotheses. For example, in a study reported in the *Proceedings of the National Academy of Sciences* (Knight, Nguyen, & Bandettini, 2003), investigators tested whether stimuli presented just below the level of perception could elicit a conditioned fear response. Subjects' skin-conductance responses were measured to assess level of anxiety. Results indicated that participants registered the physical response of fear even when they were unaware of hearing the noxious stimulus that produced that response. These results lend support to the value and science behind awareness of unconscious anxiety and its role in the creation and maintenance of psychopathology. For example, these findings could help us understand how survivors of trauma become susceptible to anxiety reactions to minor or imperceptible stressors (Silver, 2003). These findings also suggest that therapies that direct attention to these unconscious forces in human functioning should produce superior results to those that ignore such phenomena. What researchers termed "conditioned fear we are not aware of" certainly seems equivalent to the "unconscious anxiety" Davanloo refers to in his work (Silver, 2003). The clinical work presented in the present book will provide additional data to support the contention that unconscious factors do, in fact, contribute significantly to neurotic and characterological suffering. In addition, patients' responses to the interventions designed to uncover unconscious thoughts and feelings suggest that these therapeutic strategies are highly effective in eliminating such suffering.

CLINICAL TRIALS

A number of studies support the general efficacy of short-term dynamic psychotherapy (Anderson & Lambert, 1995; Crits-Christoph, 1992; Winston et al, 1991) and also suggest that Davanloo's particular version—ISTDP—has proven particularly effective in the treatment of personality disorders (Abbass et al., 2000; Magnavita, 1997; McCullough Vaillant, 1997). Allan Abbass (2002a, 2003b) and his colleagues (Abbass, Gyra, Kalpin, Hamovitch, & Sheldon, 2000), who have done more controlled clinical trials on ISTDP than anyone to date, report that "49 published, controlled STDP trials supporting efficacy with a range of conditions, including personality disorders, substance dependence, depression, and panic disorder" have already established the scientific credibility of the method. Abbass goes on to report that ISTDP was, in fact, developed in an empirical fashion by Davanloo, through the latter's extensive use of detailed case studies, all of which involved a full videotaped record of treatment from start to finish (including long-term follow-up interviews). While N=1 studies are coming back into vogue as a unique way of studying the process of change within an individual over time (Goldfried & Wolfe, 1996; Jones, 1993), they have been devalued for years in favour of clinical trials. It is our intention to gather data from all three sources available: (1) clinical trails; (2) process research; and (3) single case studies. The confluence of support from each separate area of research strengthens our assertion that ISTDP is highly effective and may, in fact, prove to be uniquely so.

In the most recent study completed by Abbass (2002a), 89 consecutively referred patients who accepted a trial therapy (an intensive initial interview, typically lasting 3 hours) during a two-year period were included in this study on the effectiveness of ISTDP in a real life, private-practice setting. The mean age of patients studied was 40 years, with a fairly even split by gender (52% female, 48% male). These patients were not by any means the walking well but were highly disturbed individuals with severe and long-standing impairment in their daily functioning. In fact, 25% of the sample had been out of work for over a year, and 46% had been taking a number of psychotropic drugs for over two years. This was considered a treatment-resistant group, since 83% had had previous psychotherapy and nearly half had tried psychopharmacological interventions but without clear benefit. The average length of treatment provided for the subjects was 15 sessions (60 minutes each). Patients were evaluated using the Brief Symptom Inventory; the Beck Depression Inventory and Beck Anxiety Inventory (Beck & Steer, 1987, 1990); as well as the Inventory of Interpersonal Problems. In addition to these validated self-report measures, data were collected on health-care usage and employment status. This study was conducted in Canada, where they have a single payer system of health care, allowing for easy access to data regarding cost and utilization of health-care resources. Data on health-care usage from one year before and one year after treatment allowed for comparison and calculation of cost savings, if any.

The results of this study were dramatic and impressive. Evaluation of all self-report measures revealed post-treatment changes beyond the .001 level of statistical significance. Of those taking medication when treatment began, 71% stopped taking drugs entirely by the end of treatment. "On average, medications were stopped 1.5 months after treatment began" (Abbass, 2002a, p. 229). Another 7 patients reduced their dosage. Clearly, this kind of change is clinically significant as well.

Of the 22 unemployed patients, 18 had returned to work within 9 weeks of treatment. Significantly, 17 of these 18 had been on private disability insurance, creating even greater cost savings. By the end of treatment this group had not only improved dramatically compared to their pre-treatment status, but their unemployment rate was lower than the city average (Vancouver).

In addition to the personal benefits afforded to these patients by treatment, the cost savings were substantial. "Data gathered from prescription administration, disability insurance costs, and hospital and physician service costs, suggest an overall cost reduction for these 89 patients to the system of approximately \$402,523 over the 12 month period after therapy" (Abbass, 2002a, p. 230). The savings amounted to three times the cost of the psychotherapy.

One common criticism of a study like this, using pre- and post-test data on a single sample, is that cause and effect cannot be determined. In other words, there is the possibility that some factor other than the treatment itself could have been responsible for the changes within this group. Since almost all the patients studied had suffered for many years with their symptoms and had tried multiple treatments in the past, they could be considered their own controls. What kind of independent, outside source of influence could have affected all these patients in such a way that they got remarkably better during this 15-week treatment period, when all past attempts at therapy had failed? It would require a real stretch of the imagination to come up with a viable alternative explanation for these results.

The other inherent limitation of this particular study is the fact that the same therapist provided treatment for all subjects involved. It is certainly possible that Dr Abbass possesses unparalleled skill and that his personality and particular expertise, rather than the treatment method itself, was responsible for these outstanding results. In order to control for these limitations, he has embarked on a multi-centre study with four other therapists practising in Canada and the United States. All subjects have been randomly assigned to a waiting list from 4 to 16 weeks in length. Preliminary findings (Abbass et al., 2000) for the 128 patients involved in the study, all of whom have a DSM-IV personality disorder, reveal that therapeutic gains are significant and increase during the course of therapy, suggesting a dose response. Data gathered from the first 24 weeks of the study revealed that, "the mean symptom and interpersonal scales normalize by the fourth session and remain in the normal range [thereafter]". Statistically significant improvement on all measures revealed robust effect sizes from .93 to 1.3. This study, while still not completed, adds further support to the notion that the treatment method itself is highly effective and that neither placebo nor therapist's personality could account for the changes obtained in patient functioning

Limitations of clinical trials

While the data derived from clinical trials are important, they are also limited. The most significant limitations of clinical trials include the fact that the data involve averages across a group of patients rather than change within a patient over time (which is the factor that practising therapists are most interested in understanding); variation within the groups is ignored; and there is no information provided on how the results were obtained or what specific factors were responsible for the changes observed (Garfield, 1996; Greenberg & Pinsoff, 1986; Havens, 1994; Hillard, 1993; Seligman, 1995, 1996; Strupp, 1993). The results of such studies allow us to conclude only that the method as a whole is successful. What specific ingredients in the therapy account for the changes reported remain unknown. In order to ascertain this vital information, we must conduct process research. In the following section, each element of Davanloo's treatment model is examined with reference to the scientific evidence supporting its clinical utility.

PROCESS RESEARCH

It is important to note that this shift in emphasis, from validating the method as a whole to exploring the effective ingredients within the treatment model, is in keeping with a shift within the NIMH. The NIMH is by far the largest contributor to psychotherapy research funding in the United States (and probably the world), amounting to over $40 million annually (Foxhall, 2000). As described in chapter 1, Foxhall reported that the NIMH has rewritten nearly all its funding announcements to reflect the change in priority from large clinical trials in controlled settings to research designed to "study large numbers of diverse patients in real-world settings, follow them for lengthy periods of time and measure progress by patient functioning in school, work and other areas of life" (rather than rely on symptom checklists or changes on self-report measures alone). The clinical research we present in the current volume clearly follows these guidelines. In addition to providing empirical support for each intervention included in the treatment model, in-depth analyses of therapies, as practised in a private setting, are presented in great detail in subsequent chapters. In the material to follow, evidence is provided to support each vital element of the treatment protocol, as designed by Davanloo (1980, 1990)

Phase I: Enquiry

In ISTDP, the therapist takes a phenomenological approach to enquiry and conducts a highly focused investigation of the presenting problems, in an attempt to obtain specific information about the nature, duration, and severity of the patient's difficulties. It is especially important both to understand the precipitating event that motivated the patient to seek treatment as well as to investigate recent examples of the problems being presented.

Research designed to tease out the effective ingredients in cognitive behaviour therapy (Howard, 1999; Shaw, 1989) indicated that therapeutic focus was highly related to positive outcome. In the study conducted by Shaw, ratings of therapist competence were broken down into observable behaviours. Shaw discovered that the therapist's ability to conduct the interview in a focused and structured way, while taking charge of the pacing of intervention, was highly associated with positive outcome. Of note, experienced clinicians were much more adept than their less experienced colleagues at these behaviours, which may have contributed to the low level of relapse found among their patients (Howard, 1999). Only 19% of the patients treated by experienced clinicians who followed a focused and structured method of intervention relapsed, whereas 40% of those treated by less experienced "generalists" had suffered a relapse at 2-year follow-up. It is equally important to note that, in a study of factors associated with negative outcome in psychotherapy (Mohr, 1995), a lack of focus was high on the list. It is usually assumed that only cognitive or behavioural treatments advocate this structured type of therapeutic enquiry. In fact, Davanloo advocates the use of highly structured and focused interventions, albeit in a dynamic way. In other words, the ISTDP therapist investigates feelings and emotions with the same kind of detailed, phenomenological rigor as she would the examination of symptoms or behaviours. Davanloo's ability to operationalize dynamic concepts (such as the channels of anxiety or the Triangle of Conflict) and translate them into observable and measurable behaviours has made an enormous contribution to the field of dynamic psychotherapy. (Coughlin Della Selva, 1996). Studies conducted at the Tavistock Clinic (Balint, Ornstein, & Balint, 1972; Malan, 1963) supported the notion that the dynamic therapists' ability to create an intrapsychic focus and connect the patient's current conflicts to unresolved conflicts from the past was a potent predictor of success.

In addition to conducting a tightly focused enquiry, the ISTDP therapist assumes a great deal of responsibility for pacing interventions from the first moments of the initial interview. In contrast to the humanistic tradition of "following the patient", the therapist takes charge of pacing interventions and keeping the enquiry moving along. Research suggests that this type of intervention leads to superior outcome (Shaw, 1989).

Phase II: Defence work

Once the presenting complaints have been outlined and a recent example of the patient's current difficulties has been identified, the therapist enquires into the feelings experienced by the patient in the conflictual situation being reported. In rare cases, the patient can identify and experience his feelings directly. In most cases, however, the experience of true feelings is obscured by defensive processes, which become the focus of the second phase of treatment. Defence and resistance have, from the early days of psychoanalysis, been recognized as the greatest obstacles to psychotherapeutic success (Ferenczi & Rank, 1925; A. Freud, 1966; Reich, 1933). Malan (1996) has gone so far as to write, "Of all the factors standing in the way of therapies based on psychodynamics—which of course includes psychoanalysis—resistance is the most intractable" (p. xiii). He has suggested (quoted in Davanloo, 1980, p. 13) that "in the early part of this century Freud unwittingly took a wrong turning which led to disastrous consequences for the future of psychotherapy. This was to react to increasing resistance with increased passivity".

Davanloo attempted to reverse this trend by taking an active and focused approach in the pre-interpretive phase of treatment—attacking the defences, pointing out their destructive impact, and pressuring the patient to give them up entirely. This is a radical approach akin to that of Reich (1933), who was the first to advocate an active and confrontational approach to defence and resistance. He found that defences, if not removed, would become resistances in the treatment. Furthermore, he contended that this would "form a ballast which is difficult, if not impossible, to remove" (p. 51). Likewise, Davanloo confronts defence and resistance from the first moments of interaction with the patient, with the goal of removing them and getting to the underlying feelings as soon as possible.

What does the scientific literature have to say about this issue of defence and resistance in psychotherapy and human functioning? Until quite recently, the topic of defence mechanisms was decidedly out of vogue within the experimental community (Cramer, 2000). Thankfully, this vacuum is beginning to get filled with new and striking data on the critical impact that defences have on physical as well as emotional functioning.

To begin with, there is substantial empirical evidence that defence mechanisms, defined as any number of ways in which humans keep thoughts, feelings, and memories out of awareness, do exist and are, in fact, commonplace (Cramer, 2000; Epstein, 1994; LeDoux, 1996). A recent review of the literature on defence mechanisms reveals "an extensive body of research showing that memories unavailable to consciousness nevertheless influence conscious memory and task performance" (Cramer, 2000, p. 639). Research by Baumeister, Dole, and Sommer (1998) has provided ample evidence that defences such as reaction formation, projection, displacement, undoing, isolation of affect, and denial are "pervasive" in human functioning. Furthermore, there is significant evidence to suggest that defensive functioning impairs healthy adaptation. In fact, it appears that those who rely heavily on defensive operations suffer physically as well as emotionally (Cramer, 2000; Pennebaker, 1991, 1997).

Pennebaker (1991) has amassed a tremendous amount of data suggesting that those who repress their emotions are far more likely to experience impaired immune functioning (and to become physically ill) than those who experience and express their feelings freely. His work has revealed that repression of emotion leads to suppression of immune functioning and, conversely, that expression of feelings results in a boost to immune functioning. In fact, those who express their feelings about upsetting events in their lives enjoy consistent and marked improvement in immune functioning, physical health, emotional well-being, and even competence and satisfaction in their jobs.

Pennebaker found that the more patients were able to express *negative* affect, the more relief they felt from physical pain. Given the same opportunity, those who relied on defences to avoid their true feelings derived none of the benefit experienced by the expressive group. "Studies of patients with serious medical conditions such as cancer, diabetes, kidney failure, and obesity, find that those who do not comply with medical advice also show strong use of defence mechanisms", emphasizing how damaging a reliance on these mechanisms can be (Cramer, 2000). Cramer suggested that, while defences may help patients allay their fears about their medical condition, relying on those mechanisms proved highly self-destructive, even suicidal. Denying real pain and disease is not adaptive, as it prevents patients from seeking help and following medical advice. It seems the same can be said about mental illness.

Additional research (Weinberger, Schwartz, & Davidson, 1979) has contributed to the accumulating data suggesting that a repressive coping style results in negative consequences for those who rely upon it. These include an increased risk of illness, difficulties related to a lack of assertiveness, poor empathic ability, and a decreased ability to experience joy in life (Kennedy-Moore & Watson, 1999).

The results of a study conducted by Gross and John (1997) support Pennebaker's findings that blocking and defending against the experience of emotion may afford an individual some temporary relief but costs them dearly in the long term. Specifically, they found that subjects who chronically defend against anxiety-arousing feelings ended up depriving themselves of the experience of the positive feelings, like love, joy, and happiness, that got buried beneath them.

Weinberger (1990) has found that the use of defences deadens the experience of emotion, hampers the ability to respond emotionally, contributes to passivity, and results in an inhibition of taking effective action. "Repressors maintain a view of themselves as easy-going and non-reactive, as if they experience very little negative emotion—despite the physiological and behavioural clues communicating distress. Patients can literally have tears in their eyes and say they feel good or fine." This finding suggests that the self-perception of these repressors is employed chronically, automatically, and without conscious awareness. The results of subsequent studies (Weinberger, Schwartz, & Davidson, 1979) demonstrated that repressors reported lower than average levels of anxiety and stress, while revealing higher-than-average levels of anxiety on behavioural and physiological measures. This suggests a real dichotomy between mind and body. This split was evident in facial expressions as well. While denying and minimizing negative emotions, the "repressors" overemphasized the positive. The same discontinuity between their internal experience and self-report observed with negative emotion was evident with positive feelings. These subjects put on a social smile that lacked certain crucial features of genuine happiness (they made a smile with their mouth but not their eyes, as occurs with true pleasure).

This kind of defence against the true experience of one's feelings must be removed if the patient is to get well. How is this accomplished? Researchers (Weinberger, Schwartz, & Davidson, 1997) have found that therapists who make use of nonverbal cues and bring disparities between *what* the patient was saying and *how* he was expressing himself nonverbally were more likely to get through the defensive barrier to the direct experience of the underlying emotion than those who relied on verbal material alone. This strategy is integral to the process of ISTDP and may constitute yet another feature of the model which contributes to its effectiveness.

Høglend and Perry (1998) found that defensive functioning predicted treatment outcome with depressives better than did an initial assessment of global functioning (Axis V on the DSM-IV). In fact, they found that an assessment of defensive functioning at the inception of treatment was a more accurate predictor of outcome than symptomatic evaluations. Findings obtained by Cramer and Blatt (1993) demonstrated a relationship between the use of various types of defences and level of therapeutic benefit received. Those who were rated as most improved at termination were those who showed the greatest decrease in the use of immature (also termed "regressive") defences. At the conclusion of their article, the authors suggested that clinicians assess the level and nature of patients' defences, as well as their symptoms, in order to predict response to treatment. Subsequent research (Cramer, 2000) found that "clinicians' ratings of defences also predicted adequacy of interpersonal and global functioning, with immature defences being a negative indicator" (p. 642). Studies have shown that responses to self-report measures that do not assess defensive functioning are likely to come to highly distorted and erroneous conclusions about the nature and severity of psychopathology present. Vaillant (1993) has asserted that "no mental status or clinical formulation should be considered complete without an effort to identify the patient's dominant defence mechanism". Malan has gone even further, suggesting that pathological defences must be removed and replaced with adaptive coping strategies for patients to be considered healthy. This stance coincides with that taken by Cramer (2000), who has suggested that therapeutic efforts should be aimed at changes in the defensive system as well as a reduction in symptoms.

In order to dismantle the defensive system, Davanloo (1980, 1990) advocates an approach in which the therapist confronts the patient with the self-defeating consequences of his defences. Research conducted by Cloitre, Koenen, Cohen, and Han (2002) supports the notion that such an approach, with a focus on negative consequences, is positively related to outcome. However, these authors make the erroneous assumption that such behavioural analysis is the sole purview of cognitive-behavioural methods. Perhaps the authors were unaware of Davanloo's work, which views this process as essential to facilitating change in the defensive system.

Strupp and Binder (1984)—two other short-term dynamic psychotherapists who have done a great deal of research on the method—have concluded that when defences are not removed, they become a resistance in treatment, preventing the emergence of unconscious conflicts and the painful affects associated with them, subverting therapeutic gains. They went on to suggest that the therapist's role needs to be that of a technical expert whose task it is "to penetrate the defences in order to gain access to the major conflict lying beyond" (p. 23). In a similar vein, Hamer (1990) urges therapists to "tell it like it is" rather than collude with patients' tendency to beat around the bush when it comes to confronting difficult truths about themselves. The therapist's intention must be to "break through the barrier of the surface noises people ordinarily make to fend off relating" in an emotionally real and open manner (p. 40).

Phase III: Breakthrough of feelings

Nearly all those who have attempted to make psychodynamic psychotherapy more efficient and effective have placed the experience of emotion at the very centre of their treatment model (Alexander & French, 1946; Fosha, 2000; Greenberg, 2001; Greenberg & Safran, 1987; Malan, 1976a; Malan & Osimo, 1992; McCullough Vaillant, 1997; Reich, 1933), though none more emphatically so than Davanloo (1978, 1980,

1990). Once defences against the experience of core emotions are removed, Davanloo advocates the use of fantasy and visualization to aid in the process of deepening the experience of affect and facilitating its expression. Rather than relying solely on verbal means of expression, he has developed techniques that tap into the nonverbal aspects of emotion. He urges patients to "listen" to their bodies and use their imagination to picture how their visceral feelings and impulses want to be expressed. In so doing, he is likely working in a way that helps activate both right (visual, spatial) and left hemispheres (verbal) of the brain, aiding integration and supporting growth. Recent advances in neuroscience strongly support the notion that "mental processes are grounded in the brain's mappings of the body" (Damasio, 2003, p. 12). The integration of mind, emotion, and body—so central to the clinical work of all who practice ISTDP—seems to be gaining empirical support from the basic sciences.

Given the absolute centrality of affective experience in the theory and practice of ISTDP, a good deal of data is presented here that supports the hypothesis that the full and direct experience of previously avoided feelings is the key to healing in psychotherapy. We examine data on the role of emotion in mental and physical health, review the results of process research, and outline the relationship between emotion and attachment, as well as looking into the most recent results of the neurobiology of emotion. We will begin with a brief review of the literature on the neurobiology of emotion.

The neurobiology of emotion

It is now well established that the human brain processes emotion in two essential ways: one involves the visceral experience of emotion, the other involves the regulation and expression of it (Damasio, 1994, 1999, 2003; LeDoux, 1996). These two processes occur in different parts of the brain. This means that one can experience emotion without being consciously aware of it or reflecting upon it. Conversely, one can think *about* feelings without experiencing them. What seems to be required for optimal functioning—and what we attempt to promote in psychotherapy—is the combined ability to experience and express feelings in such a way as to maximize health and happiness.

Research in cognitive neuroscience (Damasio, 1994, 1999, 2003; LeDoux, 1996) suggests that we have little, if any, control over *what* we feel. However, we can and do learn *how* to regulate and express (or suppress) what we feel. In fact, the ability to regulate emotion appears to be crucial for physical as well as emotional well-being and can either facilitate adaptation or interfere with optimal functioning. In an interesting study on the process of emotional regulation in depressives and those considered "normal", it was found that both groups responded to loss with an initial dip in mood. The difference between the two groups was not in their initial experience of sadness and grief, but in how they regulated the emotion over time. Those in the normal group were able to go through the sadness and rebound to previous levels of well-being, while those rated as depressed stayed in the sad, grief-laden state for prolonged periods of time.

The limbic system, often called the "emotional brain", is not capable of reasoning (Damasio, 1994). The structures within the brain that constitute the "emotional brain" are ancient and operate with lightning speed. This system has been selected for its contribution to our survival. The amygdala, an essential component of this system, picks up information about danger or safety and transmits it to the body before conscious awareness is possible (LeDoux, 1996). It is the neocortex (the most recent development within the brain), sometimes called "the rational brain", that allows us to evaluate and reflect upon our feelings and impulses (Damasio, 1994). However, neocortical processing takes time and is relatively slow compared with limbic functioning. When people act on limbic impulse, disastrous consequences can follow. In an all-too-common scenario, someone hears a noise in the night, assumes a predator has invaded the house, grabs the gun in the nightstand, and shoots, before taking time to assess the situation—discovering, after the fact, that she has killed a family member. What seems to be required for optimal functioning is conscious reflection on the feelings and impulses experienced in the body. Once the feeling has been identified and reflected upon, a conscious determination can be made about when, where, and how to express it.

Can feelings be unconscious?

Some still question the existence of unconscious feelings, but new techniques for studying the brain give us an unparalleled opportunity to test out these assumptions. Work by LeDoux (1986, 1992, 1996) suggests that there are neural pathways for feeling emotions that bypass the neocortex and go straight to the amygdala. Therefore, the brain circuitry within the amygdala begins to process this information before it is consciously perceived by neocortical structures. Many consider this to be neurobiological evidence of the "unconscious". Even mainstream publications, such as *Newsweek*, are presenting articles (e.g. Gutrel, 2002) on the scientific credibility of Freud's theories about unconscious phenomena and their effects on human behaviour. Gutrel (2002) quotes Damasio, who wrote that "Freud's insights on the nature of consciousness are consonant with the most advanced contemporary neuroscience views" (p. 50). In particular the hypothesis that unconscious drives shape our behaviour without conscious awareness has been substantiated by research suggesting that "these drives really do exist, and they have their roots in the limbic system, a primitive part of the brain that operates mostly below the horizon of consciousness" (p. 50).

Paul Whalen and his colleagues (1998) have conducted research demonstrating that the amygdala can, in fact, respond to visual stimuli presented so quickly that subjects could not consciously detect them. Even more amazing is the research finding that "emotionally competent stimuli" (e.g. angry or happy faces) nevertheless "break through" the barrier of blindness or neglect (when blindness is caused by lesions to the occipital and parietal lobes) and are indeed detected (Vuilleumier & Schwartz, 2001) by the brain.

Once again, there is evidence that the emotional system in the brain can, and does, operate independently of neocortical functioning—on occasion. It looks as though the amygdala is almost fully developed at birth, well before the capacity for language emerges. Early affective experience can be imprinted in this area of the brain, without any verbal labels or conscious memory of it. LeDoux (1992) has suggested that this understanding of the brain and its development "lends support to a basic tenet of psychoanalytic thought: that the interactions of life's earliest years lay down a set of emotional lessons based on the attunement and upsets in the contacts between infant and caretakers". When the amygdala is aroused, signals are sent out to activate neurochemicals (e.g. adrenalin and noradrenalin), imbuing these emotional memories with strength and intensity. These "emotional blueprints", embedded in the nonverbal, emotional brain, can be very potent and influence behaviour well into adult life, without any conscious awareness or cognitive understanding of their impact. "We have seen how a nonconscious conditioned memory can lead to current emotion" (Damasio, 2003, p. 57). Given this, verbal psychotherapy alone may prove ineffective in accessing these feelings and memories. Conversely, therapies—such as ISTDP—that focus on the *experience* of feeling in the body, and pay attention to the visual images that are associated with these feelings, may be more effective in accessing this kind of material.

Memory and emotion

Despite the ways in which the emotional and cognitive centres of the brain can function independently of one another, there are many neural connections between the amygdala and neocortex, which allow for integration of thoughts and feelings. In fact, self-awareness—a central component of "emotional intelligence"—involves the ability to make sense of one's emotional signals and to translate this understanding into adaptive action.

It is this very kind of self-awareness that we attempt to promote in dynamic psychotherapy. First we seek to evoke the emotional response, then to help the patient make sense of it.

Just as there are two centres in the brain responsible for the experience and regulation of emotion, it seems there are two memory centres as well. One stores the facts—what has happened to us—while the other stores the emotional experience involved in the events. Consequently, it is possible to remember an event without accessing the emotions involved. Conversely, we can suddenly be seized with the physical experience of an emotion without any conscious awareness of what triggered it. In order to make sense of one's inner experience and the world, remembering the crucial events in one's life and their emotional consequences seems essential.

Feelings and memories are inevitably linked and become dependent upon one another over time. Damasio (2003) has explained it this way:

> When the emotion sadness is deployed, feelings of sadness instantly follow. In short order, the brain also brings forth the kind of thoughts that normally cause the emotion of sadness and feelings of sadness. This is because associative learning has linked emotions with thoughts in a rich two-way network. Certain thoughts evoke certain emotions and vice versa. Cognitive and emotional levels of processing are continuously linked in this manner. [p. 71]

While specific parts of the brain appear to have particular functions related to emotion, Siegel (1995) contends that "emotion is found throughout the entire brain" (p. 122). Going a step further, Dodge (1991) states that "all information processing is emotional, in that emotion is the energy that drives, organizes, amplifies, and attenuates cognitive activity and in turn is the experience and expression of the activity" (p. 159). Again, the message seems to be that awareness of the experience of emotion, along with conscious reflection, is required for physical and emotional health. There is a wealth of scientific data from disparate sources that supports this conclusion.

It has been suggested (Neborsky, 2001) that Davanloo's method of psychotherapy, which is designed to stimulate the experience of intense and conflictual emotions, taps into the emotional centre of the brain, where memories of early attachment traumas are stored. In this way, the ISTDP therapist gains rapid access to the core emotional problems besetting the patient. Then, in the here-and-now between patient and therapist, these primitive feelings can be experienced and understood. In the end, the patient feels both tremendous relief and greater understanding of themselves and others. Just how this is done within the model of ISTDP being practised here, along with the scientific evidence to support these interventions, is discussed later in this chapter.

Emotional experiencing

In the past decade or so, the notion that facilitating in-session emotional experiencing can render therapy more potent and effective has gained widespread support (Clark, 1995; Fosha, 2000; Mahoney, 1991; Wiser & Goldfried, 1993, 1998). Emotional experiencing has been associated with the emergence of repressed material, increased insight, decreased resistance, and a strengthening of the therapeutic alliance—all of which contribute to positive outcome (Hill et al., 1992; Kiesler, 1971; Mahrer, 1989; Silberschatz, Fretter, & Curtis, 1986; Weiss, 1990, 1993). In addition to the results of psychotherapy research, there is a growing consensus from such disparate fields as neurobiology, immunology, child development, and the optimal functioning of adults suggesting that these theorists have been on the right track. In fact, these complementary sources of data suggest that the experience of emotion does a great deal more than just facilitate therapeutic change. An examination of the accumulated data suggests that the key to a happy, healthy, productive life is the possession of "emotional intelligence" (Goleman, 1995).

It is also increasingly clear that mind, body, and emotion all affect one another and cannot be viewed as functioning independently of one another. Davanloo's focus on the experience of feelings in the body is a strategy now supported by neuroscience (Damasio, 2003). Damasio has written: "I am convinced that mental processes are grounded in the brain's mappings of the body, collections of neural patterns that portray responses to events that cause emotions and feelings" (2003, p. 12). Furthermore, he has suggested that feelings and emotions are essential ingredients in the regulation of life processes, promoting survival and well-being. "In all emotions, multiple volleys of neural and chemical responses change the internal milieu, the viscera, and the musculoskeletal system . . ." (p. 63). Again, all these systems are activated and involved in the experience and processing of emotion. By extension, our efforts to increase patients' conscious awareness of their feelings, grounding them in the physical experience of core emotions, can only increase their adaptability and enhance life experience.

Emotional intelligence

Very briefly, emotional intelligence is defined as the ability to accurately identify and adaptively express one's own feelings. Additionally, the ability to "read" others' emotions and respond empathically seems essential to optimal functioning. In fact, studies on longevity (Danner, Snowdon, & Freisen, 2002) have found that emotional factors are far more potent predictors of a long, healthy life than factors such as diet and exercise. Those who remain actively involved in life, and possess a sense of hope and personal agency, live far longer and healthier lives than their pessimistic cohorts.

Emotions provide us with vital information about our experiences and seem to work as a kind of signal-detection or internal-guidance system. Goleman (1995) has suggested that "our deepest feelings, our passions and longings, are essential guides" in life and concluded that "our species owes much of its existence to their power in human affairs" (pp. 3–4). As Leigh McCullough Vaillant (1997) so eloquently puts it, "the more one can laugh when happy, cry when sad, use anger to set firm limits, make love passionately, and give and receive tenderness fully and openly, the further one is from suffering. And the fuller one is with the joy of existence, the more generous one can be toward others" (pp. 1–2). Emotions help us to organize action; monitor our internal state and the state of our relationships; enhance learning; facilitate decision-making; and give meaning to life. For those fortunate enough to enter adulthood with these abilities intact, life is good (Goleman, 1995). Those with deficits or impairment in the detection and regulation of emotions seem to suffer on every level—physically, emotionally, and even occupationally. These people are much more likely than their emotionally intelligent counterparts to end up in the hospital, therapist's office, unemployment line, or even prison. By designing techniques that help enhance the emotional intelligence of those who are impaired, we can dramatically alter their life course for the better. In so doing, we also have a positive impact on all who come into contact with them.

There is a good deal of research support for the contention that the experience and understanding of emotion is essential to the process of change in psychotherapy. Bohart (1977) found that patients who were helped to experience unresolved angry feelings and then reflect upon them had more successful therapeutic outcomes than those who either experienced their feelings alone or were asked to simply reflect upon them. Both processes were required for health and well-being. Stanton and colleagues (2000) found that women with breast cancer reported less distress and greater health and vigour when they were encouraged to experience and express their feelings about the illness. In this study, emotional expression was found to be particularly important in facilitating a sense of hope and personal agency in the subjects studied. In other studies with breast cancer patients, the effects of emotional expression were even more crucial. Derogatis, Abeloff, and Melisarato (1979) found that breast cancer patients who failed to express negative emotions had a shorter life-span than their expressive cohorts.

Emotion and immune functioning

There is a great deal of evidence that those who experience a lot of intense emotion as the result of some very trying or traumatic event, but do not express how they feel about this event, have increased levels of anxiety and physical illness (Pennebaker, 1991, 1997). In other words, it is especially important to express emotions in highly arousing situations. Failure to express emotions that have been evoked has a decidedly negative impact on overall well-being (Pennebaker, 1991, 1997). Some have even suggested that post-traumatic stress disorder (PTSD) develops when the overwhelming emotions associated with trauma are suppressed rather than experienced directly (Levine & Frederick, 1997). The debilitating symptoms associated with PTSD can last decades without intervention to facilitate the experience of the emotions that were avoided at the time of the trauma. This confirms the work emerging from studies on "resilience", which strongly suggests that it is not trauma *per se* but the inability to talk about and process the feelings involved that results in physical and psychological impairment.

Pennebaker and his colleagues (Pennebaker, 1991) have conducted a large number of experiments designed to study the relationship between emotional expression and immune functioning. Across many different groups studied—including college students, Holocaust survivors, cancer patients, victims of sexual abuse, parents of deceased children, and executives who have lost their jobs—a clear and persistent finding emerges: inhibition of the emotions evoked by upsetting life events leads to stress and impaired immune functioning, while the free expression of these feelings leads to a decrease in physiological reactivity and improved immune functioning.

It is important to note that the subjects involved in Pennebaker's research did not constitute a psychiatric population. For example, in one study of 200 employees of a major corporation who agreed to participate in a study of the relationship between stress and health, 65 had experienced at least one childhood trauma they had not disclosed prior to the study.

This suggests that the experience of trauma, and its aftermath, may be very widespread. Regardless of the nature of the trauma experienced by these research participants, had the trauma not been discussed the consequences for the individual were dire. The 65 participants who had experienced trauma but never disclosed it "were more likely to have been diagnosed with virtually every major and minor health problem that we asked about: cancer, high blood pressure, ulcers, flu, headaches and even earaches". The researchers hypothesized that the repression of the feelings associated with trauma resulted in the suppression of immune functioning, rendering the individual susceptible to all kinds of illness.

In another study by this group, subjects were instructed to spend 20 minutes per day for 5 successive days writing or talking about either trivial and superficial matters or their thoughts and feelings about the most traumatic events of their lives. Many significant findings emerged. Before the study was conducted, records of health-care usage revealed that all groups attended the same health centre at approximately the same rate. After the study was complete, those who had disclosed distressing feelings about traumatic events in their lives evidenced a 50% drop in doctors' visits for the following 6 months. In addition, disclosers revealed that they felt awful as they expressed their upset feelings but experienced improved mood and a more positive outlook thereafter. Participants attributed their improved sense of well-being to having come to terms with what had happened to them. In fact, 80% of those who disclosed upsetting thoughts and feelings about traumatic events in their lives explained the value of the experiment in terms of insight gained. Yet, of great significance, only high emotional disclosers achieved this benefit. Participants who were rated as "repressed", and who did not get emotionally involved in the process, got none of the physical or emotional benefits of the experience.

During disclosure, those who were emotionally involved revealed heightened heart rates and elevated blood-pressure readings (Pennebaker, 1991, 1997). Following disclosure, both heart rate and blood pressure were lowered significantly. Low emotional disclosers showed no evidence of change on these physiological measures of arousal and gained no benefit. These results suggest, once again, that it is the visceral experience of emotion that is mutative. This level of emotional experiencing is what we aim to achieve in ISTDP. All defences against this kind of visceral experience of emotion are challenged and removed to allow for the full experience of feeling, which seems so essential for healing. Research conducted by McCullough and her colleagues at Beth Israel (McCullough et al., 1991) found that patients being treated with ISTDP became more anxious and disrupted early in treatment when previously avoided feelings were being activated, but they became markedly less anxious afterward—a finding that parallels those reported by Pennebaker (1991, 1997). Some patients dropped out during this early phase, suggesting that neither patient nor therapist was prepared for such emotional upheaval.

Another study by this innovative group of investigators (Pennebaker, 1991, 1997) found that emotional expression had a profound impact on employment, as well as on immune functioning. Following a major corporate restructuring in which 100 senior engineers were "downsized" (a polite word for being fired), Pennebaker and his colleagues were asked to become involved in the process known as "outplacement". This process has been designed to help displaced workers secure new employment. Those workers who agreed to participate were divided into two groups. One group, who served as controls, was given a typical "outplacement" intervention, consisting of keeping a journal of their job-seeking activities and learning "time-management" skills. The experimental group was asked to write about their thoughts and feelings regarding the lay-off for 30 minutes a day for 5 consecutive days. The men who wrote about their experience in depth—detailing their rage and humiliation, as well as the emotional, financial, and interpersonal problems that followed the lay-off—reported feeling significantly better than those who were not offered this opportunity or were unwilling to take it on (i.e. to get emotionally involved in the process). In addition, the researchers discovered large differences in their rate of employment following the lay-off. Of the expressive group, 27% had a new job within 3 months. By the 6-month follow-up, 53% of this group had secured employment. In contrast, only 5% of the control group had obtained a job within 3 months and an additional 13% within 6 months, despite the fact that these groups were essentially identical in terms of education, job experience, and number of interviews for new jobs. The investigators hypothesized that those who took the opportunity to express their feelings were able to resolve them and enter interviews for new jobs in a calm and appropriate manner. Conversely, those who were still holding onto unacknowledged anger and resentment about being fired may have communicated this hostility and bitterness in interviews, making them less likely to be offered a new job. Data collected by Abbass (2002b) demonstrated a dramatic increase in employment levels in those patients who had been treated with ISTDP, confirming the findings of these other studies.

Goleman (1995) has written an entire book on the effects of emotional intelligence in the workplace. All the data he has accumulated amplifies that already reviewed here. Those who can identify and express their feelings appropriately, as well as being responsive to the feelings of others, do better in the workplace than those who do not possess these abilities. Also, they do better in every way, from leadership to cooperation and ability to motivate themselves and others to achieve set goals. Those considered "superstars" in their field invariably had high emotional intelligence (EQ), as well as traditionally assessed IQ. Conversely, those with exceptional intelligence, who frequently graduated first in their class, did poorly socially and occupationally if they had low EQ scores. If you cannot regulate your own emotions or get along with the people around you, it looks like you won't be happy and successful in life, no matter how intelligent you might be.

Techniques designed to facilitate emotional experiencing

Given all the evidence supporting the notion that emotional intelligence is essential to a long, healthy, happy life and that facilitating within-session emotional experiencing is associated with positive outcome in psychotherapy, it is surprising (and distressing) to note how little research has been designed to investigate methods that will reliably create an emotionally charged atmosphere within psychotherapy.

Wiser and Goldfried (1993, 1998) have attempted to fill this gap by examining the effects of therapeutic intervention on the elicitation and maintenance of high levels of emotional experiencing in cognitive-behavioural and psychodynamic psychotherapies. Of interest, they were not able to identify *any* interventions that reliably elicited emotion within therapy sessions, regardless of the therapist's theoretical orientation. Initially this finding may seem alarming, as one would tend to assume that psychodynamic therapists would be more focused on emotion than their cognitive-behavioural counterparts. When examined more closely, however, these results should be sobering rather than surprising. Traditional dynamic therapists may pay lip service to the importance of emotional activation within sessions, but it is often a fairly cognitive process, relying almost exclusively on interpretation (Alexander & French, 1946; Reich, 1933).

Despite the lack of differences observed between the two groups in their ability to reliably *elicit* emotion in their patients, researchers (Wiser & Goldfried, 1993, 1998) were able to identify crucial differences in their respective abilities to maintain high levels of emotional involvement once it was activated. Two specific types of therapeutic episodes were studied: those in which there was a switch from high to low levels of emotional experiencing and those in which the switch within session was from low to high. As previously stated, no therapist behaviour observed in this study was reliably associated with moving patients from low to high levels of emotional experiencing. However, when the patient was already experiencing high levels of emotion, therapist interventions had a marked effect on whether emotional activation was maintained or decreased. Therapists who responded with affirming or reflective statements intended to reveal their understanding and acknowledgment of the feelings being expressed were able to create an atmosphere in which a high level of emotional experiencing was maintained. In contrast, when therapists responded with behaviours defined as protective and nurturing, patients tended to shift to low levels of emotional experiencing. In addition, therapists who responded with a high level of verbal activity or were rated as "interpersonally controlling" also interfered with the maintenance of high levels of emotional experiencing. Therapists in the cognitive-behavioural group were most likely to be rated as controlling and highly verbal (comments such as "Your thinking is incorrect here," or "Don't let that kind of comment get to you") and, consequently, more likely to squelch patients' experience of high levels of emotion than their psychodynamic colleagues. This had a dramatic impact on outcome.

Sudden gains and "significant" sessions

High levels of emotional experiencing have been associated with "significant" sessions (defined as those in which clear and rapid changes within the patient followed immediately), which have been highly predictive of positive outcome (Tang & DeRubeis, 1999; Wiser & Goldfried, 1993, 1998). In one such study (Wiser & Goldfried, 1998), both patients and therapists were asked to rate their perceptions regarding the significant factors affecting outcome. The great majority of patients studied rated emotionally charged sessions as particularly important *and* most responsible for positive outcome. Psychodynamic therapists agreed with this perception, resulting in a high level of agreement between patient and therapist. In contrast, the cognitive-behavioural therapists tended to rate low-experiencing sessions as more productive than those in which the patient was deeply involved in the experience of emotion. One can only wonder what effect this difference of opinion had on outcome, as research has confirmed the observation that achieving consensus on the rationale for treatment is predictive of positive therapeutic results (Ilardi & Craighead, 1994).

Another study (Tang & DeRubeis, 1999) found that, in many cases, the severity of patient depression improved suddenly and dramatically in only one between-session interval. The authors concluded that these "critical sessions" seemed to account for a surprisingly large portion of the patient's total symptom improvements. Discovering this, they investigated the phenomenon further to ascertain whether these sudden gains were random or were the result of therapeutic breakthroughs in the session preceding the sudden improvement. The results revealed that these changes were not random but followed emotionally dramatic sessions. Half of the dramatic sessions identified occurred in Sessions 4–10 and accounted for 51% of the total improvement over the course of therapy. Furthermore, those who experienced these sudden gains had significantly better outcomes than those who did not, and these improvements were maintained at follow-up. So it appears that these sudden and dramatic shifts have significant and long-standing positive effects for the patient.

Since ISTDP is designed to create a highly emotionally charged environment in which change is expected and promoted in-session, this form of treatment should consistently produce positive outcomes. A number of recent studies provide impressive support for this hypothesis (Abbass, 2003b; McCullough, 2003; Piliero, 2003). McCullough has found that facilitating emotional experiencing at even low to moderate levels (30–50, as assessed by the Achievement of Therapist Objectives Rating Scale), was sufficient to achieve considerable therapeutic change in patients treated with short-term dynamic psychotherapy. Abbass (2003) has discovered a clear dose-response relationship between level of emotional activation and outcome in ISTDP. Low to moderate levels of emotional experiencing reliably lead to symptom reduction or removal, while higher levels of activation seem to be required for character change to occur.

McCullough Vaillant (1997), who has been involved with research on ISTDP for decades now, has conceptualized defences and symptoms as manifestations of "affect phobias". Simply put, she contends that our patients have learned, through experience, to fear their emotions. The pairing of an expressed feeling with negative outcome often leads to avoidance of that very feeling. Furthermore, if non-expression of feelings is reinforced, the tendency to avoid expressing emotions will become stronger and more entrenched. By encouraging our patients to face the very emotions they have learned to avoid, they have a new and frequently healing experience. Patients discover that their feelings no longer lead to negative consequences. In fact, quite the opposite usually occurs: the experience of feeling is often both liberating and enlightening. Miller (1996) put it this way:

> Consciously experiencing our legitimate emotions is liberating, not just because of long held tensions in the body but above all because it opens our eyes to reality (both past and present) and frees us of lies and illusions. It is therefore empowering without being destructive. [p. 115]

It seems as though the experience of facing what we have feared and avoided is crucial in expanding and consolidating a sense of personal mastery and competence. Weinberger (1990) found that increasing a sense of mastery and competence is one of the essential ingredients in successful psychotherapy. There is little that does more to facilitate this than facing what had been avoided. These findings are discussed further when we consider the evidence to support the consolidation phase of therapy.

Much process research involves an analysis by therapists. An in-depth analysis of *patients'* experience in ISTDP (Piliero, 2003) has shed light on their unique perspective of the process. These patients were anxious (78%), depressed (87%), and in considerable distress when they entered therapy. An overwhelming number of patients participating in this study rated their functioning as poor (47%) or extremely poor (50%). After an average of 30 sessions, two-thirds of these patients rated themselves as significantly improved and extremely satisfied with their experience in therapy. Not only were they functioning in the "very well" to "extremely well" range, but they reported feeling as if deep and lasting change had taken place in their "sense of self".

How were these impressive results obtained? Ninety percent of this sample concluded that *in-session emotional experiencing was the key factor* in their recovery. The "emotion cluster" included the following state-ments: (1) "affect focus was key"; (2) accessing "bottled-up feelings"; (3) "unlocking buried feelings"; and (4) an "intensely emotional" expe-rience. This cluster was related to the change index at the .001 level of significance. In particular, this group recognized the role of the thera-pist's *technique* as the factor most responsible for achieving these ends. In fact, technical expertise was viewed as more important than thera-pist warmth. Only 11% described their relationship with the therapist as "extremely warm and close", while 36% characterized the therapist as "somewhat reserved". This finding has been replicated elsewhere (J. Weinberger, 1995). Despite this, therapists in the more humanistic camp continue to focus almost exclusively on the effects of a warm, caring relationship on patient improvement.

In any case, it is clear that more work is required in this field. It is essential to discover and validate therapeutic techniques designed to elicit, facilitate, and deepen patients' access to emotional experiences and consequently to facilitate deep and lasting change. It is our intent to expand our knowledge in this vital area of research. One area of re-search has focused exclusively on the experience and expression of anger, which is often considered a very troubling emotion (Tavris, 1989).

Anger and "negative" emotions

Accumulating evidence suggests that there are particular benefits to the expression of negative emotion, when it is aroused. Studies by Gross and John (1997) and Pennebaker (1991, 1997) have found that blocking and defending against the experience of negative emotion may afford an individual some temporary relief, but costs him dearly in the long run. The notion "that what you resist, persists" seems to be true. In other words, when the conscious experience of anger and resentment is blocked, it remains within the person and continues to affect him long after the incident that aroused the anger is over. In contrast, those who are able to freely express negative feelings report feeling liberated and are subsequently able to express more positive feelings than those who keep such feelings to themselves. Clearly, the old adage, "If you don't have something nice to say, don't say anything at all" is seriously off the mark. It seems as though negative feelings have to be expressed to clear the way for the experience and expression of positive feelings, untainted by unexpressed resentments. The importance of this finding cannot be overestimated, as the ranking of positive emotion, from the earliest time in life, has been associated with significant decreases in mortality. Results from the Nuns Study (Danner, Snowdon, & Freisen, 2002) have confirmed that positive emotions in early life were strongly associated with health and longevity six decades later! So the ability to express and receive positive emotion has profound and long-lasting effects on health and well-being.

This very liberation of positive emotion, described in the research literature, is often observed in the process of ISTDP. Following the full and direct experience of the previously avoided feelings of rage, guilt, and grief, patients often experience strong feelings of relief, along with surges of love, joy, tenderness, and happiness (see chapter 9 for examples of this). A nun I was treating, who had always considered anger to be a sin, experienced an outpouring of love, compassion, and openness each time she acknowledged and faced her anger directly. Accompanying these emotions was a deep sense of acceptance of herself and others, which had previously eluded her. She noted that this was one of the great surprises of our work together.

Mainstream psychology is only now catching on to the adaptive value of the experience of anger (De Angelis, 2003). For years, researchers have failed to make the crucial distinction between the internal experience of anger and the various ways, often defensive, that this emotion is expressed. Typically anger has been equated with hostility and violence. It is essential to differentiate between the *experience* of anger—an emotion like any other—and the *expression* of it.

Because anger often gets associated with anxiety, this emotion is frequently expressed in defensive ways. Some avoid the experience of this anxiety-arousing emotion by internalizing it and becoming depressed. Others discharge the emotion via action and act out in destructive ways. In any case, it is not the *experience* of anger that causes the trouble, but the defensive ways it is often handled. In the literature on anger and heart disease, these distinctions are not made, and the emotion of anger is equated with the defensive discharge of the emotion through angry outbursts. Perhaps this is why Carol Tavris (1989) entitled her book on the subject, *Anger: The Misunderstood Emotion*.

The internal experience of anger is usually described as heat and energy running through the body, with mobilization of energy in the muscles in the jaw, neck, shoulders, and arms, preparing the individual to take aggressive action. Anger is an energizing emotion and is the adaptive, built-in response to threat, violation, or trespass (Hendricks, 1999). Again, neuroscientific studies suggest that we cannot determine or control what we feel. However, we can control and determine how we deal with and express our feelings.

The ways in which feelings, including anger, are expressed can be either healthy and constructive or pathological and destructive. Some (e.g. McCullough Vaillant, 1997) have suggested that constructive self-assertion, limit setting, and the definition of boundaries are adaptive ways of expressing anger. The constructive use of anger helps promote change on both personal and interpersonal levels (De Angelis, 2003). Averill (in De Angelis, 2003) found that the direct expression of anger helped strengthen relationships. Tafrate, Kassinove, and Dundin (2002) found that 40% of a community sample they studied reported that the direct expression of anger had positive long-term effects in their lives. Kassinove, Sukhadolsky, Eckhardt, and Tsytsarev (1997) suggested that "anger may serve an important alerting function that leads to deeper understanding of the other person and the problem".

Lerner and colleagues (Lerner, Gonzalez, Small, & Fischoff, 2003) have found that the experience of anger results in a feeling of empower-ment. (See chapter 9 for a confirmation of this.) Those who allow themselves to feel anger and outrage at injustice seem to feel they can do something to avoid being victimized. Would it have been possible for women to get the vote or for civil rights reforms to take place without the emotion of anger as the fuel for change? As Malcolm X suggested, there are times when no other emotion will do. Those who do not have ready access to the experience of their anger do not set limits and often get taken advantage of by others. As discussed else-where, those who suppress anger also get sick more often than their more expressive counterparts.

The relief experienced following the expression of previously warded-off feelings seems to free up creative processes as well. Patients tend to become quite eloquent in describing their inner experience following the breakdown of their defences against the experience of intense emotion (Fosha, 2000). In fact, many of my patients have left emotionally charged sessions to go home and write music, poetry, or prose or take a whole new approach to their painting. In one case, a patient who had come up with the title for a novel ten years prior to starting therapy was able to complete the novel in a matter of months, once she freely experienced the anger she had been stifling nearly all her life (see The Good Girl with Ulcerative Colitis, chapter 6).

Emotion and the therapeutic alliance

All the findings reported thus far suggest that it is in the best interest of our patients to learn how to gain access to their emotions and to express them appropriately. How do we, as therapists, facilitate the deep experiencing of feeling, so necessary to emotional and physical health? Research suggests that within-session emotional intensity is a strong predictor of positive outcome in the treatment of depression (Beutler, Clarkin, & Bongar, 2000). However, this was only the case when depth of emotional experiencing occurred within the context of a strong working alliance. This link between a strong working alliance and depth of within-session emotional experiencing has been corroborated in other studies (Iwakabe, Rogan, & Stalikas, 2000) and exists at the very heart of a treatment model developed by Diana Fosha. She has suggested that the seeds of psychopathology are sown "when reliance on defences against emotional experience becomes chronic as a result of the failure of the emotional environment to provide support" (Fosha, 2000, p. 5). In order to promote healing and development within treatment, she contends, "the experience of vital affects in the context of an attached relationship is the primary agent of emotional transformation" (p. 5). In particular, facilitation of emotional sensing and experiencing on a visceral level within the body is viewed as essential for change to take place. This insight dates back to William James (1902), who wrote that emotionally charged experiences "are extremely potent in precipitating mental rearrangements". Going a step further, he asserted that "emotions that come in this explosive way seldom leave things as they found them" (p. 198).

It is important to note that intense emotional experiences can have negative, as well as positive consequences. In the absence of emotional support, affects can be experienced as overwhelming and have a toxic effect on the patient (Fosha, 2000; Levine & Frederick, 1997). The consensus seems to be that facilitating a deep, visceral experience of core emotions within the context of an emotionally supportive relationship has the power to heal.

Transference and the therapeutic alliance

Just how is a strong therapeutic alliance developed? Perhaps it is too naïve to assume that this is simply a matter of being empathic and caring. Research suggests that the more active and challenging the therapist is in interpreting the transference pattern of behaviour, the more likely the alliance will strengthen and improve (Horvath & Luborsky, 1993). Conversely, those who did not address the patient's feelings towards them were less effective. These differences were especially pronounced if the patient had a negative emotional reaction to the therapist. If the therapist addressed the negative feelings directly and encouraged their expression, the patient improved. If the therapist avoided these negative feeling and stayed focused on content or figures in the patient's past or current life, patients fared less well. This research also found that training and experience in working with feelings within the transference had a marked impact on increasing competence and effectiveness.

This research supports findings reported decades ago by Malan and his colleagues at the Tavistock clinic (Malan, 1963). They found that dealing with negative feelings in the transference as soon as they arose was absolutely essential in forming a working alliance. Failure to address these feelings often led to early and abrupt termination of treatment, whereas a direct examination of these feelings helped otherwise resistant patients to engage in treatment in an authentic manner.

Research suggests that there are two crucial time periods for this work in the transference—at the inception of treatment, and again during the phase of therapy in which the therapist is challenging the patient's ingrained patterns of behaviour. Therapists who are comfortable dealing directly with their patients' emotional reactions towards them clearly provide a therapeutic experience that is deeply affecting. In ISTDP, the therapist is always on the look-out for signs of feelings in the transference and endeavours to get them out in the open as soon as possible. Transference reactions unexpressed become a resistance in the treatment. Therefore, by dealing with transference feelings directly, we remove any resistance they could mobilize and provide a corrective emotional experience to boot (Alexander & French, 1946).

While there is evidence, as just reported, supporting the notion that dealing directly with transference is essential to positive outcome, the way in which this is done seems crucial. A study by Salerno, Farber, McCullough, Winston, & Trujillo (1992) on ISTDP suggests that confrontation is not an effective tool in eliciting transference feelings. In contrast, an approach that combined a graded and empathic approach to defences resulted in more positive outcome. Foote (1992) demonstrated that confrontations accompanied by supportive and empathic statements were more effective than confrontation alone. In other words, an integrated approach led to a greater likelihood of emotional expression, a strengthened therapeutic alliance, and greater improvement, especially among the more impaired group.

Data on the effects of countertransference feelings is also relevant here. In a recent study on countertransference and working alliance, it was found that negative countertransference feelings were associated with a poor working alliance, while positive countertransference (by definition, a distortion—as opposed to a positive therapeutic alliance) was associated with a weak attachment bond (Ligiéro & Gelso, 2002). These findings seem to suggest that the therapist has to be willing to deal with all of their own mixed feelings towards patients lest they introduce a positive or negative bias into the process. These findings suggest that having any kind of distorted picture of the patient, even a positive one, will undermine therapeutic progress. Obviously, if the patient is able to pull the wool over the therapist's eyes and seduce her into some sort of idealization, he will not be helped. Therapists must be aware of false façades and get through them in order to facilitate an authentic interaction.

The use of visualization

Once we break through the repressive barrier of defence and resistance, and the patient is in touch with the visceral experience of emotion, we need to provide a therapeutic pathway for the expression of these feelings. Since internalizing feelings is destructive to the individual, and discharging them is often damaging to the other and their relationship, Davanloo suggests an intermediate course, using visualization to create a vivid portrait of the patient's feelings and impulses. While this is a mental process, it is only encouraged once the patient is in touch with the visceral experience of emotion. There is some evidence from process research that just such a strategy can be very effective (Clark, 1995; Mineka & Thomas, 1999). Therapeutic methods designed to arouse and channel feared emotional states in new ways via visualization and imagination have been demonstrated to promote a positive therapeutic change process. Use of visualization and imagery seems to provide an intermediate stage between suppressing emotion and discharging it via action, which allows for an active reworking of conflictual emotions. Venting alone, without conscious processing and reworking, is of no lasting therapeutic value.

Davanloo (1990) advocates an approach in which emotion is evoked and then channelled into a vivid portrait of the expression of these feelings in an imagined interpersonal context. It is very important to recall that feelings exist not in a vacuum but in relation to others. Rather than urging a patient to simply verbalize how he feels in general, he is encouraged to imagine expressing very specific feelings to the particular people these feelings involve. This includes, and intensely focuses on, expressing the bodily impulses mobilized within the patient. The patient feels the impulse and imagines what would happen if he expressed it. It is very clear to the patient that the therapist is focusing on the use of imagination to come to terms with feelings and impulses that

d not actually express in physical form. Acting out of any kind
__ ....raged and is considered defensive.

When it comes to studying the expression of feelings, research suggests that nonverbal communication is highly influential. "The study of
emotion suggests that nonverbal behaviour is a primary mode in which
emotion is communicated. Facial expression, eye gaze, tone of voice,
bodily motion, and the timing of response are each fundamental to
emotional messages" (Siegel, 1999, p. 121). In order to "speak" the
language of emotion, we must attend to the body and nonverbal communication. In ISTDP all these signs of feeling are identified and fed
back to the patient via the interaction with the therapist.

These techniques are especially well suited to the goal of facilitating
affective involvement in the treatment process. Often the body gives
clues to emotion that are not available on the verbal level. Siegel (1999)
contends that "emotions are primarily non-conscious mental processes
which create a state of readiness for action" (p. 132). This "readiness for
action" is often observed in a patient's movements. For example, when
expressing anger, a patient might make a fist or shake his foot, even
though he is not aware of it. The ISTDP therapist will bring this to the
patient's attention so he can be more aware of how his body speaks.
Furthermore, this aids integration of body, mind, and emotion.

Emotion and attachment

The expression of emotion is especially important in forming and sustaining secure attachments (Goleman, 1995; Greenberg, 2001; Siegel,
1999). By helping our patients accurately identify and adaptively express their emotions, we are helping them acquire the skills necessary
to create intimacy and closeness in their most important relationships.

There is a great deal of evidence that intimate relationships are a
balm, reducing stress and enhancing satisfaction in life (Gottman, 1994;
Gottman & Silver, 1999). Conversely, those who are not able to create
sustaining relationships suffer from a whole host of physical and psychological symptoms, and even die earlier, than those with solid support from others (Goleman, 1995). It follows, then, that we will do our
patients an enormous service if we help them experience and express
their feelings in a non-defensive manner. Yet it is often the experience
and free expression of feelings within the context of close relationships
that is so problematic for our patients.

Davanloo (1990) has suggested that unresolved feelings from the
past can intrude in current relationships to create vicious, repetitive
cycles of interpersonal conflict. These interpersonal conflicts then con-

stitute a projection of unacknowledged and unresolved intrapsychic conflicts, involving intense mixed feelings towards attachment figures from the past. In order to stop this repetition and acting out of conflicts, the therapist must help the patient to experience all his true feelings directly. This can be accomplished by examining the transference pattern of behaviour, as well the feelings in current relationships. Experience has proven over and over again that getting through defences to the direct experience of mixed feelings in the here-and-now creates an opening into the unconscious. The figures from the past that are being represented in current time, come to the fore, where they can be reworked directly. This re-working breaks the repetitive cycle and frees the perception of projections.

Neborsky (2001), following Davanloo, "conceives of the central problem of neurotic psychopathology as the aggression that occurs when the nurturing bond between caregiver and child is disrupted" (p. 19). Perhaps it is more accurate to say that it is the *guilt* over aggression, along with the need to punish oneself for it, that is the culprit in psychopathology. The impulse to want to hurt or destroy someone who is also loved and desperately needed creates enormous tension within the child. If these feelings are intense and there is no outlet for their direct expression, the entire complex of feelings can be repressed. Guilt over destructive wishes towards loved ones also gets repressed and is often translated into self-punitive behaviour. Conceptually, this is referred to as "superego pathology" (Davanloo, 1990). Davanloo has suggested that patients who are self-defeating are driven to self-destruction by this unconscious guilt and the need to suffer. While patients suffering from superego pathology employ defences to ward off the conscious experience of guilt, "the unconscious superego nevertheless demands its pound of flesh in the form of the unconscious need for punishment (for patricidal, matricidal and fratricidal impulses)" (Carveth, 2001). In order to be released from this need to suffer (sometimes referred to as superego retaliation), the patient must face and experience all the intense mixed feelings towards others, including the guilt over his own aggression. Learning how to "face and bear one's guilt is the road to freedom from the grip of the unconscious need for punishment".

It is also essential to understand and to point out to the patient that guilt feelings are related to love. When the patient experiences rage and imagines expressing it, feelings of guilt and grief typically follow. Grief and guilt are evoked because the figure in question is also loved. To imagine hurting, killing, or torturing someone we love is uniquely painful. When all the feelings are acknowledged and understood within the context of the rupture to the attachment bond, compassion for self and other replaces guilt and the need to suffer.

Davanloo (1990) has suggested that, when the reservoir of rage, guilt, and grief from the past has been drained, relationships can begin afresh. No longer afraid of his intense mixed feelings towards others, or guilt-ridden about aggression towards loved ones, the patient is freed to create close and satisfying relationships in his current life.

In summary, the ISTDP therapist encourages the direct experience of emotion by challenging the patient to remove all defensive barriers against his experience. Once the patient is in touch with the experience of feeling, the therapist suggests verbalization and visualization of the feelings and impulses in order to facilitate their full expression. Special attention is paid to nonverbal manifestations of emotion, as well as any reference to transference feelings. This multi-focal approach has empirical support and may help to explain the high rate of success reported with this method of psychotherapy.

Phase IV: Re-analysis of the process

Once the survey of the patient's difficulties has been completed, the therapist focuses on a specific recent example of the problem at hand and explores the feelings involved. This process typically stimulates anxiety and the use of the patient's characteristic defences. The therapist works to acquaint the patient with his defences and the negative consequences of continuing to use them for progress in therapy, as well as life. As the patient relinquishes defences, the underlying feelings emerge and are expressed via word and imagery. Following this emotional outpouring, new memories, dreams, and associations are produced which shed light on the origin of the patient's conflicts. In the next phase of the therapy, all that has happened is reviewed in order to consolidate the insights obtained. Once again, we look to the psychotherapy literature to support the use of this vital therapeutic strategy.

To the critics who confuse the kind of emotional experiencing advocated by Davanloo with catharsis, Greenberg and Safran (1987) have pointed out that "they fail to see that the true therapeutic purpose of this form of expression is to validate the feeling and produce change in the meanings" they have. Pennebaker's work (1991, 1997) substantiates the notion that it is the shift in meaning and understanding of self and other that takes place *after* the experience of hitherto avoided feelings that has lasting therapeutic value. While the actual experience of feelings is clearly essential, what seems to stay with patients, after the fact, is the new perspective and understanding of self and other they achieve via this process.

Humans seem to have a need to understand themselves and create meaning out of experience (Frankl, 1959). By processing aroused emotion in a symbolic way and clarifying its source, the patient is helped to make sense of his experience (Kennedy-Moore & Watson, 1999). These authors have suggested that this process is essential to breaking the cycle of automatic processing that underlies the tendency to repeat old and destructive patterns. In ISTDP, for example, it is fairly common for patients to use their understanding of depression as a defence against anger to help them intervene in the depressive cycle. In other words, they use the symptom of depression as a cue and ask themselves, "Am I angry with someone?" In this way, they can continue the work from their therapy sessions in their own life. By using depression as a clue to the underlying feeling they may be avoiding, they have conscious choice about whether to stay in that position or face their feelings directly.

In many cases, unacknowledged and undigested feelings create incoherence in one's sense of self and life narrative (Main, 1991). Neborsky (2001) has suggested that the process of ISTDP aids in the consolidation of a coherent life narrative, as the breakthrough of previously repressed emotion also leads to a de-repression of memories, which helps them to make sense of their experience and development. Research data obtained by Main and others (Main, 1995a, 1995b, 1996; Main & Goldwyn, 1984; Main & Hesse, 1990; Main & Morgan, 1996; Main & Solomon, 1990) suggests that coherence, or lack of it, in a mother's life narrative is the single greatest determinant of the nature and quality of the attachment that she is able to establish with her baby. It follows that mothers who have incoherent life narratives put their children at great risk for attachment disorders. Conversely, helping mothers work through all the intense, mixed feelings about their own attachment failures will help succeeding generations to form healthy attachments and halt the intergenerational transmission of psychopathology.

Warwar and Greenberg (2000) have also found that the combination of high emotional arousal along with conscious reflection distinguished good from poor therapeutic outcomes in their emotion focused therapy. This is just what Davanloo advocates in his model of ISTDP. Following the direct experience of previously unconscious feeling, the therapist initiates a cognitive re-analysis of the process to deepen self-understanding. This process allows the patient to (1) make sense of his experience; (2) make distinctions between defensive avoidance and the direct experience of feeling; (3) examine the consequences of each strategy; and (4) create a coherent life narrative.

Rationale for treatment

Other research (Frank & Frank, 1991; Greenberg, Elliott, & Lietaer, 1994; Ilardi & Craighead, 1994) has demonstrated that, while a confidential relationship and an emotionally charged environment were critical to success, other key ingredients included helping patients to understand the meaning and source of their symptoms, while being provided with a rationale for treatment. Furthermore, when patient and therapist had some belief in the importance of what they were doing, the therapy itself was more successful than in situations where the patient neither understood the rationale for intervention nor believed in the methods being used. The treatment model being examined here, ISTDP, incorporates all these elements. The relationship is confidential and is certainly emotionally charged. The patient is helped, from the very beginning of treatment, to understand that the cause of his suffering lies in his reliance on defences designed to avoid painful and anxiety-laden feelings. Given this, the treatment rationale—that of facing the feelings directly and expressing them openly with the therapist—flows directly from, and is consistent with, the understanding of the patient's problems. Patients leave the first session having had both a powerful emotional experience and a good cognitive understanding of how they have created and perpetuated their own suffering. They also have a clear understanding of how to alter that pattern. Research confirms our clinical experience that patients' response to the rationale for treatment is predictive of their response to therapy as a whole (Ablon & Jones, 1999; Ilardi & Craighead, 1994; Malan, 1976a) and tends to have a lasting effect in promoting self-esteem (Ablon & Jones, 1999). Furthermore, the practitioner's active involvement in the process communicates her belief in the process.

Maladaptive beliefs frequently accompany anxiety-laden affects. Patients have been taught, for example, that certain feelings are dangerous or sinful. It is not enough to encourage the experience and expression of these feelings, but to re-examine the pathological beliefs that come to light as this process takes place. McCullough Vaillant (1997) reminds us that "learning principles can also apply to the representational behaviour of intrapsychic functioning. Not only can behaviour, thoughts, and feelings be reinforced, punished, and extinguished, but so can their intrapsychic models and their meanings" (p. 50). In our endeavour to free patients from anxiety and inhibition, these pathological beliefs must be modified. We may find out, for example, that a patient has learned to view tears as a sign of weakness or that the sharing of emotions is a burden to others, rather than an opportunity for closeness. Having these pathological beliefs disproved in therapy has been demonstrated to have a striking impact on positive outcome (Weiss, 1993). Weiss (1990, 1993) contends that our patients will test out their pathological beliefs with their therapist. His research data support this notion and underscore the role of the therapist in disproving old and maladaptive beliefs. For example, a female patient who has been taught that, to be liked and accepted, she must be quiet and subservient may test the validity of this belief by behaving in an assertive manner with the therapist. If the therapist responds by violating her old assumptions and reinforcing her new and more adaptive behaviour, she will tend to take leaps in development, becoming increasingly bold and forthright. It is the patient's response to the therapist's intervention that determines outcome. In Davanloo's teaching, he stresses that we must stay tuned to the patient's response to our intervention and use it as a guide every step along the way.

Summary

In this section, a review of the scientific literature on the efficacy of each phase of treatment recommended by Davanloo has been presented. The results suggest that this method of treatment does, in fact, incorporate many highly effective techniques into one integrated model of psychotherapy. It is our contention that this multi-modal approach to treatment, with an emphasis on encouraging emotional experiencing, is highly effective. The case studies presented in part II illustrate these principles in great detail.

EXPOSITION:
FOUR DETAILED THERAPIES

PRELIMINARY NOTE

All patients described in this book were treated by Patricia Coughlin Della Selva. Sessions were conducted face to face for 50–60 minutes once a week. The length of follow-up is always measured from termination. In the interest of confidentiality, all names have been disguised.

CHAPTER 4

The Man Divided

Initial interview and therapy

The Man Divided (teacher, age 44) offers an excellent illustration of one of the most important functions of the initial interview—namely, the dynamic assessment of a patient's suitability for ISTDP. The therapy consisted of 24 sessions.

Th: So, what brings you?

Pt: What brings me here is, I was depressed. I say was, probably still am, because I feel a bit differently now than when I first called you (*there was a 6-week wait for this appointment*). There's probably a term for people who reconsider at the last moment, but I didn't trust that reconsideration. I wanted to see how it went, but also to know the nature (*clears throat*) of the differences in the feelings I had then (*clears throat*) from the way I have for the past two, two-and-a-half years. As I think I told you on the phone, my wife and I have been seeing a marital therapist, and, at the termination of our sessions with him, the therapist, my wife, and myself thought I should go see someone myself. I got a couple of recommendations from people, but my therapist said, "Fine, but I would rather have you see Patricia Della Selva". So I said, "OK". Early this September I was riding on the train and reading a Personal Health column by Jane Brody. It was an article on depression, and it had a list of 8 things and I answered all 7 and then the eighth was that, if you answered in such a way, you should go see someone, like TODAY! So, I said, I guess I better move on this and I did. As I say, that was early in September, and since then there's been a slow but significant change in my feelings about things and it's been more positive for the most part.

Th: So, your primary reason for coming here is depression, which you say dates back two, two-and-a-half years.

Pt: Approximately.

Th: And it's abated some in the last month or so (*since calling for an appointment*).

Pt: Yes, and that's not a very long time. Plus, there have been some complications over the summer, which make me really not clear. I don't feel so much *de*pressed as *op*pressed by a number of things that I have to address and find answers for, but I, uh, in describing the depression, when you ask me how long it's been, I say two, two-and-a-half years and I get a pang of guilt when I say that because that's the age of my second child and I think that a lot of . . . a lot of it, well . . . it doesn't have so much to do with the second child, but . . . it does, it's more than a coincidence.

Let us examine these initial interchanges between patient and therapist to begin the process of assessing suitability for treatment. While the patient is very wordy and tends towards intellectualization, he has waited 6 weeks, arrived on time, and responded to the therapist's opening query with a direct and detailed statement about the nature of his presenting problem with depression. He makes a link between the birth of his second child and the onset of depression and, in so doing, reported a "pang of guilt", revealing an intrapsychic focus. He also displayed a fair amount of motivation to get to the bottom of his difficulties by waiting a considerable amount of time for the session and casting doubt on the slight improvement in mood he has experienced since making the appointment. These are all positive signs, suggesting he would be a candidate for ISTDP. The therapist can proceed confidently and can do so with some increased pressure on the patient to be in touch with his true feelings.

ANXIETY IN THE TRANSFERENCE

Th: OK, we are here to look at what the problems are and what kind of help you are looking for, but I'm wondering, because you make some reference to having mixed feelings about coming here today. I think we need to address that.

Pt: Yes (*removes his coat*). I do have mixed feelings about being here. I feel a little bit better and less depressed.

Th: OK, and how did you feel about coming here today?

Pt: A little nervous, a little apprehensive, but not terribly.

Th: OK, let's look at that. How do you experience this anxiety?

Pt: I experience it as nervousness because . . .

Th: Not why, how? Let's look at how you experience this nervousness. . . . are you aware?

Pt: Of?

Th: How do you feel the nervousness?

Pt: I experience it as butterflies.

Once again, this enquiry into his feelings reveals that both resistance—there is a sarcastic tone and a tendency to intellectualize and explain things rather than feel them—and unconscious alliance—acknowledging mixed feelings and removing his coat—are in operation. This indicates the presence of an intrapsychic conflict. Our job as therapist is to intensify this crisis and use it to gain access to the unconscious and resolve the conflicts buried there. The patient is aware of his anxiety and can tie it to the interview, which suggests a high level of ego-adaptive capacity. Given this, the therapist will continue to exert pressure on the patient's feelings.

Pt: This is not easy, and I, I kind of feel distrustful of this sense of order and wholeness that I'm getting a glimpse of now in my life. I feel like, if certain aspects of it shift, I'll be right back where I was.

This response reveals that the alliance is in place and that the patient is doubtful of this recent "flight into health". He goes on to reveal some even more meaningful material.

Pt: I've managed to complicate my life dramatically over the course of the summer by getting involved with another person.

Th: Another person? (*challenging vagueness*)

Pt: Another woman.

Th: Uh-huh.

Pt: So, on the face of it, while I have this kind of divided loyalty, the marriage seems stronger and more satisfying and I want to understand that. Whether the other relationship has sensitized me to the value of what I have with my wife and children and family, or whether it was really external things. This is all in the way of explaining I'm a little less *de*pressed about the surface of my life and about functioning on a day-to-day level, but I feel *op*pressed about ways to disentangle myself.

BEGINNING WORK ON DEFENCES

Th: You use a lot of words—are you aware of that? You explain a lot.

Pt: I'm a teacher.

The therapist completely ignores this defensive statement.

Th: It's interesting. I ask you about feelings and you'll even say, "I feel" but it's not a feeling at all—it's a thought. You get caught up in your head with thoughts and explanations, but it's not at all clear you're in touch with what it is you're feeling.

Pt: Yeah.

Th: You're aware of that?

Pt: It'll take a while to sink in, but yeah . . . no, actually I'm not aware of it.

Th: But you were ready to agree with me (*speaking to his compliance*).

Pt: Well, I was thinking that it's a reasonable response and I'll think about it . . . maybe that's so, but I guess . . . clearly, I'm not aware of it. You're saying I'm out of touch . . . I'm using a lot of words and thinking my way through things.

This is another mixed response. At first he responds with increased defensiveness—vagueness, rumination, and compliance. However, at the end he comes to realize that he is, in fact, out of touch with his feelings. This needs to be explored further.

Th: Even when I asked you about the *experience* of your anxiety, you looked at me like I was speaking a foreign language. Then you were able to say "butterflies". Then you went on to tell me what you thought that was about, but it gets complicated—you diversify and on and on we go. So, clearly there is anxiety here. When did that start?

Pt: Driving over—not before. I wanted to see somebody and you were recommended, but, frankly, a lot of what I have to talk about is of an intimate and sexual nature, so when I saw you I thought, "Oh God, she's not old enough" (*laughs*).

Th: Not old enough? You mean you had an emotional reaction when you saw me—which was what?

Pt: Which is this rather confessional fear. The fear which, it seems to me, is normal . . . that I'm talking to a stranger about problems of an emotional and even physical nature, and I'm being videotaped, and you're my peer or younger and an attractive woman.

Th: So your emotional reaction?

Pt: Well, anxiety, sure.

Th: So there's some anxiety about this whole process of opening up, to

let someone else get to know you and, perhaps, particularly someone you consider young and attractive. So, again, we see that there
are mixed feelings about being here.

Pt: Yes, I do have mixed feelings.

Th: A part of you wants to come to someone to open up and talk about
all this so you can get some help, but another part of you is scared to
do that.

Pt: Yeah.

Th: And are you aware of the ways you're dealing with that anxiety?

Pt: By throwing up these word-screens or something?

Th: You're guessing or you think that's one of the ways you avoid . . .

Pt: I think that's what I'm doing with *you*. I think what I'm doing with
myself is not digging deep enough.

The preceding dialogue reveals a shift from defence and resistance to
openness and alliance. He reveals anxiety about opening up to a young
attractive woman about his intimate thoughts and feelings and begins to
see how he is putting up barriers that would undermine his goal of
getting help. This seems to increase his motivation, as he ends by taking
himself on and declaring that he has not dug deeply enough. Since he
also has some tendency to comply, this declaration of motivation needs
to be tested out immediately.

EXPLORING THE PATIENT'S EXTRAMARITAL AFFAIR

Th: Could we look at this recent incident?

Pt: I was visiting this family, with whom we've been close for years. I
went up to the country house 6 weeks ahead of my family to get it
ready. During this time I began to be attracted to the sister in the
family. I'd known her for years and was never particularly attracted
to her. A friend was helping me on the house, and, as he was single,
I urged him to take her out, confessing that I had a bit of a crush on
her. I realized I was starting to go over there in the evenings after a
day of work, not so much for the family as to see her. I was wary of
it, though. My wife and kids came back and nothing had happened.

Th: You didn't act on those feelings?

Pt: Right, I didn't act on them. My family returned and about a week
went by. It was great. We were enjoying being together again. Then,
after another week or two, we had another terrible, terrible fight like
so many we've had before, and something in my head snapped. I
said to myself, "I'm not going to close myself off to any intimacy
that comes my way".

Th: What do you mean something snapped? (*challenging vagueness*)

Pt: I felt that the fury we were feeling . . .

Th: You felt fury.

Pt: We both did. There's no right or wrong when these things happen, but you *feel* right. The fury that came out of her over this very inconsequential thing, to me, was just putting us back to square one.

PRESSURE TO FEEL WITH CHALLENGE TO THE DEFENCES

Th: Let's look at this, because all this time we are together (about 35 minutes into the interview) there's been much talk and explanation. Some of it is important, but obviously what is missing are your feelings. It's very much from a detached point of view. Now, for the first time, you mention the feeling of fury, but then you go to *her* fury and so on.

Pt: It wasn't fury on my part.

Th: I'm sorry?

Pt: It wasn't really fury. I know I said it, so obviously that's important, but . . .

HEAD-ON COLLISION WITH THE RESISTANCE IN THE TRANSFERENCE

Th: Well, we don't know what you feel, and that is the issue. I am sure you have a tremendous amount of feeling about what has happened in your life regarding your marriage, the loss of jobs, and so on, yet you never mention it. You go on to talk about *thoughts*, ideas, and explanations, but these are ways of avoiding the experience of what you're feeling. Now you come here to get help—to have a clear and honest look at what you're feeling—but a part of you, very strong, is running and avoiding that very thing. . . . Now you look away.

Pt: Well . . . I . . . OK (*laughs*).

Th: And now there's a chuckle. You have a reaction to what I've said?

Pt: No . . . yes. I accept it. I think you're right. I'm glad to hear it. I have to weigh it through, every time you say something like that. I have to ask myself, "Is it true?"

Th: Have you ever thought of this before—that you actually have a difficulty knowing what you feel, with a tendency to go to your head, or, now you're telling me you can also go to action and act on those feelings, which, I'm assuming from what you're saying, has negative consequences and ends up being quite self-defeating.

Pt: It is self-defeating, in the sense that it never leads me out of the situation.

Th: It's not a solution.

Pt: No, it's not.

Th: You attempt an *external* solution (*the affair*) but it doesn't resolve the issue. It covers up the emotion. So, do you want to have an honest look at this?

Pt: I think I need to, but I don't know where it will lead me.

Th: Part of what is driving this behaviour is *feeling*, and if you're not aware of those feelings, you are blind to what's behind your behaviour. You have to decide if that's the way you want to live or whether you want to have an honest look at your feelings so you can decide where, when, and with whom to express them.

The preceding series of interventions was designed to acquaint the patient with his defences, assess their rigidity or flexibility, and determine whether he could relinquish them in order to have an honest look at his feelings. Examining the negative consequences of maintaining a defensive position helped to turn his ego against these self-defeating strategies. The therapist tied his defences to a presenting complaint of his: not being able to make a clear decision and act on it with conviction. If he doesn't know what he's feeling, he can't make decisions about the important things in life.

Initially, as the therapist probed for feelings, anxiety and defence increased until these defences began to crystallize into resistance. As long as there are no signs of disruption and the patient can tolerate this increased level of anxiety, the therapist continues to up the ante until there is a shift in favour of the alliance. In this case, the patient was able to see that by obsessing or acting out he was avoiding the direct experience of his honest feelings. Furthermore, he could see that these strategies were self-defeating and only perpetuated his suffering. Finally, he declared his will to have an honest look at his feelings, even though he did not know where that would lead. Again, this declaration must be tested out.

DEFENCES AGAINST EMOTIONAL CLOSENESS

Th: You see, the other question I have is, whether you have a difficulty with intimacy and closeness?

Pt: I think I do, I really think I do, and I think it's about the same difficulty my wife has.

Th: OK, but you're here by yourself, so let's look at this incident where you said something snapped, so we can examine your true feelings.

Pt: When I say something snapped, I didn't mean it was fury on my part. She's the one who was furious. I mean, she was literally frothing at the mouth and out of control.

Th: She was enraged with you.

Pt: Totally enraged and out of control.

Th: Out of control how?

Pt: Out of control in that she was screaming and screaming and screaming in the presence of the whole neighbourhood, and I had a lot of trouble with that.

Th: What do you mean?

Pt: I mean, maybe she has a right to scream, no matter who's around, but it bothered me tremendously.

Th: And "bothered" means what? Clearly you have a feeling towards her—what is the feeling?

Pt: The feeling is an aspect of a bigger and more important feeling. You see, I'm used to my wife having tantrums in front of people.

Th: But that doesn't say how you feel about it.

Pt: The anger is a dimension of it, but what really bothers me is what happens in reaction to other intimacies. In the past two, two-and-a-half years, we almost never make love. By that I mean, maybe once a month. When it happened, the next day I would feel laid bare. I would feel in touch with her. I would feel that some level of contact had been re-established.

Th: You felt close to her.

Pt: Yes, and then, inevitably, something would come up the next day to get into a row about—and the speed with which that intimacy would just disappear would deeply hurt me (*getting choked up with emotion*) and I would withdraw even more. It's like being slapped for extending yourself. *So*, that time, when she started screaming and I had spent 6 weeks anticipating their return and being able to say, "Look at what I've done" and hoping for "Isn't that wonderful", well, in the same way, I just felt like withdrawing.

The patient's responses suggest a fusion between his feelings of pain and anger and the defence against it—in this case, withdrawal. He confuses his avoidance (withdrawal) with the feelings themselves. Feelings must be distinguished from the defences against them, lest pressure to feel results in an exacerbation of symptoms and defences. He needs to become aware that he withdraws in order to avoid these distressing emotions and that, in the end, this only undermines his goal of preserving intimacy and closeness in his marriage.

CLARIFICATION OF A MAJOR DEFENCE

Th: But withdrawing is not a feeling. Let's slow down here, because this is very important. You had been anxiously awaiting their arrival—working hard and being proud and happy about the work you'd done. There was a longing to be reunited and initially there was a feeling of closeness. But then she suddenly lashed out in public, which has become a pattern. Now, clearly you have a lot of feeling about this. I could see tremendous pain on your face and hear it in your voice, but when I asked you about it you said you felt like withdrawing. Withdrawing is not a feeling but a way to avoid your feelings.

Pt: I don't get it.

That statement makes clear the level of fusion between feeling and defence.

Th: The feeling inside is a deeply painful one.

Pt: Then or now?

Th: Both. But you avoid the full experience of that painful feeling inside, as well as the feeling towards her, by withdrawing. Do you see that?

Pt: OK. I follow.

Th: And what effect does that have on your life?

Pt: It endangers it. Perhaps there is a wish to destroy it.

Th: I don't know if that is your wish, but the fact is, to deal with your feelings by withdrawing and going to another woman is very self-destructive.

Pt: Yes, I could lose everything.

The purpose of these interventions—namely, to differentiate feelings from defences against them and to help turn the patient against these destructive defences, while encouraging him to face his feelings—had been accomplished. The patient finally saw how withdrawing and going to another woman could lead to massive loss. This was not just a cognitive realization, but something deeply felt. He went on to detail other ways in which he was behaving self-destructively, signalling to the therapist that there was a self-punitive mechanism in operation. Since all this acting out (as well as the depressed affect) had happened since the birth of his second son, it was hypothesized that angry and destructive impulses towards the son—who had taken his wife away (they had not made love much since the birth)—were stimulating guilt and driving self-punishment. The therapist attempted to check this out by enquiring whether he wanted his children.

FURTHER ENQUIRY

Th: We've got about a half an hour left. I wanted to ask you a few other questions. Did you *want* the children?

Pt: I wanted the first child. I didn't feel so intensely the wish for the second, but it was always acceptable to me. I grew up with lots of brothers and sisters. I have three brothers. I always say that. I have two brothers. There was one who died.

This kind of slip, like the nonverbal signal he gave early in the interview when he took his coat off, is a sign that the unconscious therapeutic alliance is in ascendance.

Th: So what is the line-up?

Pt: I'm the second in line, with one older brother and two younger brothers and a much younger sister. The second brother after me only lived two weeks. It's funny, I always say three brothers. (*He gave the names and ages of his siblings.*)

Th: So you must have been 9 or 10 years old at the time of his death. Do you have any memories of it?

Pt: I have a memory of my mother telling my brother and me about it, and I remember being distracted. We were watching TV or something and didn't want to be bothered (*that word again*). My mother was very upset. My brother and I heard it but went on with what we were doing (*becoming tearful*).

Th: You look upset now.

Pt: Yeah, I am (*very choked up*). I do have this . . . when I think of children dying (*crying*) . . . I think about children dying all the time.

Th: You've been aware of worrying about that?

Pt: I guess the kind of final fear is that their death would be a punishment for my transgressions (*more tears*), because if I project to my wife finding out . . . I don't know if she would leave me . . . it's entirely possible, but I suppose what's in that is the fear of having the children taken away from me and, beneath that, perhaps their dying . . . somehow connecting the two.

The phase of "content"

From this point on, his defences were much less in evidence. The therapist therefore largely switched her attention to reiterating her perception of the deep and painful feelings lying underneath (the lower corner of the Triangle of Conflict, Figure 2.1). The following sequence emerged:

1. He is deeply attached to his grandmother and her sister (his great aunt, who is 91), both of whom consider him quite special. His grandmother is ill and frail and likely to die soon. He told of a recent incident in which he bent over and kissed her, and his mother said that it reminded him of a photograph, of his grandmother bending over and kissing him as a little boy. The therapist said that he obviously feels a lot about this (his eyes filled with tears) but doesn't allow himself to cry.

2. In response, he said that he *had* broken down on several occasions when he visited his childhood home, with the feeling that this was the last time he would see "them", which referred to his mother as well.

3. The therapist then spoke of the transference, pointing out that he was able to share his pain with *her*.

4. He showed his new-found insight by saying that the issue of not being in touch with his feelings was crucial. At the same time, he can be watching something apparently mundane on the TV and be unable to hold back the tears.

5. She pointed out how deeply sensitive he is, and again she spoke of the transference, asking him what it was like to be sharing these feelings with her.

6. He said it was good, and it then emerged how much he would like to establish true communication with his *father* before it was too late; but if he tried to do so—here he made a gesture of looking at his watch—his father would say, "Sorry, I've got to run".

7. There then emerged crucial information about his relationship with his *mother*. He said that recently he had managed to establish a "plane of communication" with her, but that, from an early age and up to the age of 35, "he couldn't bear to be in the same room with her". She is "bizarre, over-protective, wacky, ridiculous". She is controlling and wants everything "orchestrated" to fit in exactly with her ideas. This is also what *the patient himself* is like.

8. He went on to say that he was never rebellious, and he managed to escape from her by winning a scholarship to a private boarding-school. This was a thousand miles away, but he had to travel there by train because his mother had a phobia of flying.

9. Finally, he said, "There was nothing that I was allowed to do that wasn't a reflection of my mother's fears about things."

10. The therapist pointed out that he still has a tendency to be "compliant and submissive" and to go along with the woman's wishes,

and that this had been present with her, the therapist, from the beginning. It was also clear that he had established a pattern of flight to escape these pressures.

It is clear that the patient began the interview in a state of resistance but ended with free access to deep feelings and attendant memories, all of which shed light on the nature of his psychopathology. Therefore he appears to be highly suitable for ISTDP. His reaction to the initial interview, as revealed in the next session, will shed further light on whether this provisional judgement is accurate.

FORMULATION
(BASED SOLELY ON THE INITIAL INTERVIEW)

The videotape of the initial interview was viewed independently by two judges. One of these was Jennifer Malan (JM), an educational psychologist—not trained as a therapist but thoroughly familiar with ISTDP. The other was one of the present authors (DM). Both were entirely blind to all subsequent events.

Each judge independently wrote a "Formulation", consisting of (1) a list of the Disturbances in the patient's life, (2) a Dynamic Hypothesis to explain them, (3) a Prediction of the Issues that would need to be dealt with in therapy and would be likely to lead to therapeutic effects, and (4) a list of the Criteria to be looked for at follow-up which would indicate an "ideal" therapeutic result. As stated in chapter 1, a fundamental rule is that *every known disturbance must not merely disappear, but must be replaced by the corresponding aspect of "positive mental health".*

The aim of this procedure, which was used on all seven patients, is twofold: (1) to be able to match the findings at follow-up with criteria already laid down, thus rendering highly subjective judgements far more objective; and (2) to explore the degree to which dynamic psychotherapy can be treated as a scientific experiment—the question of whether it is possible to predict the important events of therapy and, thus, to obtain evidence for the validity of psychodynamic theory and practice.

It is important to state that this procedure possesses all the properties of a *prospective study* without the necessity for waiting many years for long-term follow-up.

For brevity, in the formulations of all the following patients the Disturbances have been omitted, since they are clearly implied in the Hypotheses and Criteria.

Dynamic Hypothesis by DM

1. The patient appears to have blanked out most of his feelings, using defences that include emotional withdrawal, rumination, and intellectualization.

2. In the interview the main underlying feeling that emerged was a deep longing for emotional closeness.

3. His background reveals obvious causes for the arousal of painful or anxiety-laden feelings: (a) his mother's extreme neurosis and the way in which she used her neurotic anxieties to control him; and (b) the lack of true contact with his father.

4. It is clear that in his more recent life something goes wrong in his relationship with women (he said his first wife hated him, and his current wife regularly picks a quarrel after what seemed to him to be satisfactory love-making). In his two marriages he has been unable to resolve this and has responded by emotional withdrawal and turning to another woman. I suspect that, in fact, he suffers from intense buried hostility against women, derived from his mother, and that their hostility is a reaction to his.

5. It seems likely that the main feelings against which he is defending himself consist of distress and anger—especially anger—at not receiving the love that he craves. This applies to the people involved in all the above situations—that is, his current and his previous wife, and his mother and his father in the past.

Dynamic Hypothesis by JM

1. He suffers from repressed anger towards his mother, who was rigid, domineering, and controlling. He coped as a child by detaching himself emotionally, and later physically when he went to boarding-school.

2. He is caught up in an antiquated pattern of compliance with women. Submission and passivity lead to a sense of self-defeat and inadequacy.

3. He longs for intimacy and closeness, but he married his first wife who "really hated him"; and then his second wife who can be nurturing and loving, but can also be cold and distant, often unavailable sexually, and lashes out verbally and publicly, thus reminding him of his mother. He escapes into affairs.

4. He feels guilty about his affairs and punishes himself by not allow-

ing himself fulfilment in any part of his life, and by becoming depressed.

5. He is a very sensitive, creative person, capable of making warm relationships, but has become detached from his feelings. He uses the defences of withdrawal, vagueness, intellectualization, and running away from situations. This is an early pattern of coping with his mother.

6. Therefore (a) he has no idea of his true needs and feelings that would enable him to make informed decisions, remaining in conflict with no commitment in relationships; (b) he is underachieving and not using his potential in painting or in developing family life.

7. He must have unacknowledged feelings about his baby brother who died at the age of 2 weeks when the patient was 9 or 10 years old.

Predictions of Issues to be dealt with in therapy (DM)

The main issues are unacknowledged and unexpressed grief and anger about loss of love. Throughout therapy, links need to be made between the *present* and the *past*—that is, between loss of love from his *wife* and loss of love from his *parents*.

Predictions of Issues to be dealt with in therapy (JM)

1. To recognize his defences and avoidance strategies, their origin, and the role they have played in his life, and to understand the self-defeating consequences of avoiding deep, often painful feelings.

2. To enable him to experience fully the rage towards his mother,

3. To become aware of, and to experience, the true nature of his feelings towards his father. This may be crucial and enable him to become closer to him.

4. To recognize the inappropriateness of continuing to be compliant and submissive with women, rather than honestly expressing his feelings and needs. Although the patient had little choice as a child, he should now negotiate as an equal and become more self-assertive.

5. To explore the feelings about the death of his brother and to understand the relationships with his siblings.

6. To learn to value his positive qualities—sensitivity, creativity, and ability to form close relationships.

7. To recognize his need for emotional closeness and intimacy within his marriage, rather than channelling it into extramarital affairs about which he feels guilty.

8. To understand the projection of his guilt about his extramarital relationships onto others. And to recognize that he is punishing himself by not allowing himself any gratification in his life, at times becoming so depressed that he cannot function effectively, and fearing that his children may be removed or die as a punishment for his infidelity.

Predictions of Issues likely to lead to therapeutic effects (DM & JM)

DM: Since his therapist will be a woman, hostility is likely to emerge in the transference and will be quickly related to his mother.

DM & JM: It is the experience of intense anger against his mother that is most likely to lead to therapeutic effects.

Criteria for a successful outcome (DM & JM)

[1] *Feelings and defences*
DM: The ability to face his true feelings and use them constructively in all situations, without using the defences enumerated above.

JM: To be in touch with his whole range of feelings.

[2] *Self-destructiveness*
DM: The replacement of self-destructive behaviour by constructive behaviour.

[3] *Symptoms*
DM & JM: To lose his symptoms, mainly depression and excessive drinking.

[4] *The relationship with women*
DM: Whatever it is that goes wrong between him and women should no longer occur. To end his pattern of extramarital affairs and develop a mutually fulfilling, emotionally close, and committed relationship with his wife or—if his marriage breaks up—with another woman.

JM: To develop a committed relation with one woman within marriage, based on intimacy and closeness, and to end his pattern of extramarital affairs.

[5] *Anger and self-assertion*

DM: To be able to experience anger and to use it to assert himself constructively.

JM: To be able to be more assertive with women, especially his wife and his mother, expressing his feelings and needs honestly.

[6] *His children*

DM: To develop true caring and closeness with his children.

JM: To develop a more satisfying and closer relationship with his children.

[7] *His parents*

JM: To be able to share a greater depth of feeling with his parents and siblings.

[8] *Creativity and enjoyment*

DM: Depression to be replaced by happiness and enjoyment of life, with an increase in creativity.

JM: As he becomes more in touch with his emotional needs, to allow himself gratification and freedom to have them met. To be more productive and fulfilled in his painting.

[9] *Attitude to himself*

JM: To be less demanding and controlling of himself and to accept himself more comfortably—increased self-esteem and self-confidence.

[10] *Work*

JM: To be more productive and fulfilled in his work.

Comment on formulations, including hindsight

From a practical point of view, the part of the formulation that matters consists of the Criteria. As the reader will see, "Self-destructiveness" was included by DM and not JM; and "His parents", "Attitude to himself", and "Work" were included by JM and not DM. The other six Criteria were essentially identical.

We write not only as scientists, but as fallible human beings, and we publish these predictions "warts and all". What was missed in the Hypotheses, by both judges, was the link between the patient's *second son* and his *second younger brother*. With hindsight this should have been clear, but the issue of *unconscious hostility and death-wishes* never became explicit in the first interview on which the formulation was based (though it did in the second). In the first interview the patient spoke of guilt, but he immediately went on to speak of guilt about his *affairs*, avoiding the issue of guilt about his brother.

The prediction—made by both judges—that the main issue in therapy would be *anger with his mother* turned out to be completely wrong. Here one can only say that most probably anyone reading this account would have predicted the same. The therapist herself made the same prediction, writing that he needed to be helped to face mixed feelings towards his *parents* in the plural.

In fact, the correspondence between predictions and actual events turned out to be the least satisfactory of all these patients—in the others, the majority of the predictions were fulfilled. An analysis of the evidence in all seven patients is given in chapter 8.

Session 2

It is standard practice to conduct a 1-hour follow-up within a few days of the initial 2- to 3-hour session, in order to evaluate how the patient managed the feelings and memories that emerged during the first interview. The following are the highlights.

Insight about his defences

Th: What stayed with you?

Pt: First and foremost, that I was throwing up screens with words and not really connecting with the feelings I have on a deep level, and, connected with that, my inability to make decisions about things because I haven't been building in my feelings.

This is insight into part of the mechanism responsible for obsessional indecision. It was spelled out by JM in her Hypothesis: "he has no idea of his true needs and feelings that would enable him to make informed decisions".

Pt: Then, a number of things, like talking about the brother who died and my response to my mother's upset. . . . Well, the surprise of that.

Thus, instead of showing further resistance, the patient immediately describes genuine insight into two of the most important—and formerly unconscious—issues that emerged from the initial interview: namely (1) his main defence, and (2) the factor that precipitated his depression. This gives the patient the ability to do the work himself rather than remaining dependent on the therapist.

Th: It's really important for us to look into this.

Pt: The other thing was about my father.

Th: The longing for closeness with him—all the feelings about that and how it affects your relationship with your boys?

The patient goes on to describe two male friends, both of whom have risen above the absence of a good relationship with their father and made their family central to their lives.

Pt: This is in contrast to my ambivalence about family life. The contrast is so vivified (*he gets choked up*). . . . For me, family was something to get away from, but the experience with these other people is very satisfying and makes me feel very attached to my wife and children.

This is very significant. He's known these people for years but has never been able to use the experience to feel nurtured. Now he describes, with great emotion, that the visit to one of these families was "like a warm bath". This family closeness is what he craved and sought through alcohol in the past.

Pt: The thing about my father. I was surprised at how emotional I got about my brother. The thing that was significant was remembering my mother being upset and my father hovering in the background. When she came in to talk about the death of the baby it was a "family moment"—a time for all of us to deal with it, but she got left to deal with the emotion of it, all by herself.

(JM wrote of the need to explore his feelings about the death of his baby brother and to understand the relationships with his siblings.)

Pt: (*Continues, with tears in his eyes*) When I think of one of my children dying, it doesn't have so much to do with the life not lived as how destroyed I would be, and how suicide would be the only option (*now crying*). I think this thing about really wanting to punish my-self for all these seeming transgressions takes that form. I see the child dead *and how I make it happen*. So the only conclusion is for me to kill myself (*big sigh*). I just want to understand that.

This is a major manifestation of the unconscious therapeutic alliance. The patient is actually asking the therapist to open up one of the central, most guilt-laden, and most completely unconscious areas of all— namely, the fulfilment of his death-wishes towards the baby who died, together with the link with his second son, and thus his severe sense of guilt and the reason for his self-destructive behaviour

Th: Absolutely. It's essential that we understand this, because we can see that you behave in a highly self-destructive manner, and, in a sense, you have been playing around with this (*i.e. suicide*). You could kill yourself in a variety of ways. You're destroying yourself. So, when you say, "I would feel destroyed", it's not a feeling at all, but something you're doing to yourself in the face of all these strong feelings you have. It is essential for us to get to the bottom of this if you are not, *in fact*, going to destroy yourself. We have some evidence that this is connected, at least in part, to all these feelings about the death of your brother.

The patient reveals the intensity of the feelings that emerged from his unconscious.

Pt: I hear that, and I believe it, because I remember what it felt like to suddenly *disgorge* that—that's what it felt like, like *vomiting* or something, it came up so strong. It seemed to come up out of nowhere.

Encouraged by this intensity, the therapist leads him towards the link between the past and the present

Th: Right. And if we follow your train of thoughts, it went from these feelings about your mother and brother to the current situation, and how you would feel if one of your children died. You say you couldn't bear it, that you would feel guilty and have to kill yourself. The question is, how are you responsible for your brother's death or the imagined death of your son? What comes to mind?

The patient speaks of one of the sources of his guilt, but not the one most relevant to the issue at hand, which the therapist immediately challenges.

Pt: I'm responsible for my son's death because of my inability to do the right thing, to be a good boy, to be faithful . . .

Th: But, why is that? Your unfaithfulness is just another way in which you're self-destructive. So what drives that self-destructive behaviour? It goes back to the birth of your second child, which you weren't thrilled about.

Pt: I *was* thrilled. I'm not denying what I said. I dated the depression since then. I had suppressed these feelings.

It is not enough for him to feel and express these previously suppressed emotions, but to understand how this has affected his life past and present. This is not a cathartic treatment, but one aimed at helping patients relinquish self-defeating defensive patterns so that they can experience their true feelings and face the truth about themselves and their lives.

Pt: I'm. . . what perhaps you're getting at and I'm starting to see (*laughs*) is that he is, in some ways, the younger brother. He either is the younger brother I have and push away, or the one who died.

Th: Right. The second son comes along and you don't feel so close to him and now you realize his birth has stirred up a lot of unresolved feeling from the past. So he represents your brothers, towards whom you have a lot of mixed feelings.

Pt: Absolutely—lots of mixed feelings! My older brother and I have a stormy but decent relationship, but I've given up on my younger brother, who is impossible. I don't know what to call him. He suffered from deafness and was bounced around from school to school and has had lots of difficulty. I remember urging my parents when he was 12 or 14 to get him help.

Th: He was a terrific pain in the neck.

Pt: Yes, a terrific pain in the neck.

Th: When your mother got pregnant, you already had a brother who was a big pain and here she is, pregnant again. So how did you feel about that?

Pt: My older brother had stronger feelings than I did. But I must say, having yet another brother to contend with was very difficult to entertain.

Th: That's a polite way to put it.

Pt: Right—I hated it.

Th: You hated it, and you needed another brother like a hole in the head. You hadn't been aware of these feelings ahead of time, so we can only imagine what this would do to a 10-year-old boy. You don't want another kid around, and then the baby dies. You get your wish but . . .

Pt: It doesn't go down very well.

Th: Do you think, perhaps, you have felt guilty and responsible all this time?

Pt: It's certainly possible, yeah . . . I have a need to clarify something. You see, I dealt with all this by leaving (*the patient had left home at the age of 13 to attend boarding-school a thousand miles from his home*).

Now it becomes absolutely clear how he was repeating the past by suppressing feelings of anger and jealousy, and withdrawing—an action that was entirely appropriate in the past but is not appropriate now, especially as it involves going to another woman.

Th: A lot was going on there, and now having two boys of your own has stirred it all up.

Spontaneous return to the subject of his father, with insight about his defences

> Pt: I also thought about the drinking, how it was a way to get close to my father, but now it's a way to get away from all the feelings and just numb it out.

> He now understands that all these complex mixed feelings from the past got re-stimulated by the current trigger of his son's birth. Now that he is aware of all this he can deal with it direct.

Comment

These two interviews demonstrate how much work can be accomplished during the trial therapy. Following the initial contact, the patient spent the weekend with two married male friends and reported a significant change in the way he perceived them. In addition to this shift in perception of others, he experienced a renewed feeling of closeness with his wife and a new-found sense of connection with his second son. In the second interview, he remembered all the salient points that had arisen in the first. He demonstrated insight into his defences against his feelings, his obsessional indecision, and his drinking. As predicted by both judges, he began to recognize the importance of his feelings for his father. Finally, he enabled the therapist to open up one of the crucial issues in his psychopathology, which was indeed the reason why he had sought treatment—namely, the guilt-laden link between the birth of his second son and the brother who had died.

THERAPEUTIC STRATEGY AS FORMULATED BY THE THERAPIST AT THIS POINT

The results of the initial evaluation clearly revealed that this man was punishing himself with depression and self-destructive acting out due to guilt over aggressive and destructive wishes towards his younger son. In addition, the initial evaluation revealed that this current conflict has re-stimulated unresolved feelings towards a brother who died when he was a boy. Given this, the therapeutic strategy involved getting through defences to the direct experience of his mixed feelings towards his son and his wife, who insisted on having another child. Furthermore, he should be helped to face similar mixed feelings towards his parents and siblings.

SESSION 3

The patient began by reporting feelings of empathy for his wife, who was upset because her father was ill. He felt good about the support he was able to provide for her and reported feeling a sense of genuine closeness with her. She went away over the week-end to take care of her father, while the patient stayed home to look after their boys. The younger child got sick with the 'flu, so he brought him into bed with him. He asked, "Where's Momma?" "She's taking care of Grandpa, and I will take care of you", he replied. At this, his son opened his arms to him and they enjoyed a deeply touching embrace. As he spoke, tears came to his eyes. He felt deeply moved by the affection expressed by his son and sad for the lack of closeness he experienced with his own parents or, in fact, with that son prior to starting treatment. The work on his feelings about his brother who died fulfilled one of the Issues formulated by JM, and the above incident fulfilled one of the Criteria formulated by both judges—that he should develop a closer relation with his children.

We see significant change occurring already, particularly in the patient's ability to give and receive love—the very thing that had been blocked prior to treatment. In addition to feeling good about being a loving and capable father during the preceding week, he also got in touch with anger and frustration when he was unable to contact his wife.

Temporary relapse

Instead of taking a passive position, he put that energy into finding her. However, once he did, he found himself behaving in an irritable and withdrawn fashion. He started drinking and went out on his motor cycle. This current conflict was used as an example to place us on the Triangle of Person and then focus on the intrapsychic processes that this experience had set into motion. In particular, this example was used to help him distinguish between the direct experience of anger and the mechanisms he was using to avoid it (withdrawing, drinking, and driving too fast on his motor cycle). *This, and his drinking reported in Session 15, were the only two examples of "acting out" found in all seven patients.*

Th: We have to wonder why you are so afraid of your own anger.

This reveals an entirely new aspect of his father.

Pt: I get a picture of my father, who was a very frightening figure. We were always told, "Wait until your father gets home". I literally had to stand there, waiting for him with my pants down, and he would walk in and take off his belt.

Th: I'm sure that stirs up lots of feelings.

Pt: Yeah, fear and pain.

Th: But you leave out your anger at your father—just as you remain unaware of your anger at your wife—it is a blind spot, ah?

Pt: Well, yes and no. I can see what you're saying, but I *was* angry with my wife and I told her so when she got home on Saturday night. She was actually quite responsive and, interestingly enough, I no longer felt any need to drink.

The patient was able to make sense of his own behaviour once he allowed himself to experience his true feelings. He was also standing up to the therapist and setting her straight, rather than behaving in a compliant fashion, as he would have in the past. Apparently, he had done the same with his wife. Here we find a good example of constructive self-assertion taking the place of defensive processes (drinking). Again, it is more than symptom removal (passive-aggressive manoeuvres, in this case), but new and constructive behaviour in its place, which is what we seek.

Session 4: The mixture of longing for love from his father and anger with him [essentially predicted by both judges]

The patient came in saying that while he has been dealing with his wife quite differently since starting treatment, he kept wondering about the relationship with his father. He got in touch with his longing for closeness and reported a clear memory of sneaking in under his father's arm while his father was sitting on the couch with his whiskey and newspaper. As he recalled the feeling of warmth and smell of the alcohol, he wondered if he was using drinking as a substitute for human warmth and contact.

Pt: I think it also helps me cover up feelings of insecurity. When I went away to boarding-school at 13, I was small and skinny and very self-conscious. I hadn't started puberty and was worried something was wrong with me. I got up the courage to ask to see the doctor about it before going to school, and my father said, "Just don't smoke cigarettes—they stunt your growth".

Th: Again, the question is, what do you feel towards your father?

Pt: Angry. What a bastard. He didn't help me at all. I was then sub-jected to all kinds of bullying when I got to school. This one charac-ter tried to force himself on me sexually. I stood up to him and didn't let it happen.

Th: So, although you're angry with your father and wish he had been more understanding and supportive, you were not about to become a victim of some bully. You could stand up to this kid, just not your Dad.

Pt: Yeah, but I didn't care about *him*. . . . It has affected me adversely with women, and it was a big problem in my first marriage—my own insecurity about masculinity and my own sexuality. I've really only been comfortable being sexual with a woman in the last ten years.

Pattern of withdrawal and substitution in the face of anger

Th: So again, you manage to work it out yourself, but you're still angry that you didn't get what you wanted from your father.

Pt: So I went to other people instead. I developed a really close relation-ship with a teacher, who was like a substitute father—and I let my Dad know about it.

He thus shows insight into his mechanism of dealing with an unsatisfac-tory relationship by turning to someone else, as predicted by both judges.

Th: What was going on there, then?

Pt: That's a pattern, I see. I don't tell the person I'm angry with and disappointed in—I let them know in an indirect way, by going to somebody else. It's a kind of "fuck you". There's also something about competition and jealousy, I think, because I remember seeing my mother bathe my brother and hold his penis. I used to mastur-bate with a towel. I think I was jealous but settled for a substitute, rather than show those feelings.

Th: It sounds like this is all starting to fit together and make a lot of sense.

Already the patient is doing most of the work and is, in fact, guiding the process. This is what happens when defensive operations cease to func-tion and the unconscious is open (it is also a reflection of a strong therapeutic alliance). Memories surface in a meaningful way, which helps to make sense of what seemed confusing in the past.

Session 5: New-found ability to experience and express anger directly

Pt: The only thing that really happened this week was related to the problem with my wife I was telling you about last week. Yesterday we had a big argument about something that may sound silly, but the quality of the anger I felt was different. By different I mean better—it felt better and I dealt with it better and worked through it more constructively.

Th: Tell me about it.

Pt: It's always driven me crazy that when we're involved in something—like, in this case, we were making dinner for the children—if someone calls on the phone, she is seemingly incapable of putting them off. I asked her, in this case, if she could call them back. This is reflective, at least to me, of this public self that is always extremely accommodating to others, to a fault. It's always angered me, and I don't know why—if it's envy or what.

Th: OK, but in that situation, her being so accommodating and polite on the phone means who suffers?

Pt: Me. And it happened twice that day. In both cases—you see, this thing is going on with her father—so she was just updating people on her father's progress, but, nevertheless, I asked her to call her sister back and get the kids fed, because clearly this wasn't an emergency.

Th: So you were clear, then, that you were angry.

Pt: Yes, and it had happened earlier in the day, too. A dear friend called, and while I understand she works hard and doesn't get to socialize as much as she'd like, after a half hour or so with her on the phone and me holding down the fort with the kids, I started to get angry. So . . .

Th: So you were already angry.

Pt: I did feel it earlier in the afternoon, but I was carrying it around. I really had the sensation of carrying it around, and it gradually dissipated, but when the second call came, the anger came up again.

Th: So it came up again and was even stronger then?

Pt: Yes, stronger in the evening.

Th: So how do you experience that anger towards her?

Pt: I'm not sure I'll be able to describe the experience of it as much as how I dealt with it. That is to say, we had a fight and I said it was clear there was no emergency. I said these issues with her father are very important and she needs to concentrate on that at a time when we're not also involved with getting the children dinner (*patient clearly activated, with hands in motion*).

Th: And it looks like you're feeling it right now, as you go back to that ... how do you feel that inside, if you pay attention? What gets mobilized?

Pt: What gets mobilized?

Th: In your body.

Pt: A kind of urgency or rush inside.

Th: So you feel that and then tend to channel it into arguing?

Pt: In this case, more than arguing. I just told her, "You know, whatever I believe about this, just assume I'm wrong and tyrannical, and just do this for me. If we're involved in something as a family and you get a phone call, if it's not an emergency just tell them you'll call them back because your abusive husband can't stand it." I just didn't care how she framed it or saw me, I just wanted it to stop. I was able to get my point across. Just do it for me. The long and the short of it is, she said, "I'll do that". It was resolved. It just felt so good. It felt different from anything else I've felt. The only thing I can liken it to is how you feel after sex.

This man, who had always relied on what Schnarch (1991, 1997, 2003) calls an "other-validated" sense of self, was beginning to define himself and stand up for what he believes in. He was no longer going to kowtow to his own fear that his wife might not like him at that moment. He was able to say, "I didn't care how she framed it or saw me". He wasn't going to allow himself to be held hostage to his need to be liked. He took a stand, and she could feel the difference in him immediately. This is how couples develop respect for one another, grudging as it may be. This was included in Issues by JM—"to recognize the inappropriateness of continuing to be compliant and submissive with women", and it fulfilled the criterion on self-assertion formulated by both judges.

Th: You mean, to stand up and declare yourself?

Pt: Yes, just to say, "Don't do it". Just to say, "Do this for me".

Th: So that was really different, then, to channel your anger into direct communication, to asserting yourself and setting limits.

Pt: It felt really good, and she seemed to get it. I think she understood. But it just felt so good to be liberated from this fear of speaking frankly about it.

Extremely violent impulses against his wife
[predicted by DM in terms of "hatred of women"]

Later in the session we went back to the experience of anger, and aggressive impulses got mobilized. He recalled how he smashed his own hand once, while in a rage with his wife. He realized that he had wanted to smash *her*, and he could see how he had diverted the impulse and punished himself for it by smashing his own hand instead. He was able to feel the impulse mobilized in his hands but became anxious about facing what he wanted to do to her, trying to get the therapist to beg off. Rather than engage in a power struggle about whether he would or would not face these impulses, I put the conflict back in his lap and let him decide. In other words, it is up to him whether he would continue to deny these impulses or face them honestly. Each choice has its own consequences. At that point, he took himself on and decided to face it.

The impulse consisted of slapping her, pushing her down on the ground, "fucking" her, and throwing her down the stairs. We were able to see how he had used "fucking" to express anger, which allowed him to make greater sense of his past affairs. Rather than express his anger directly towards his wife, he "fucked" her over by "fucking" other women. No interpretation from a therapist about this dynamic would have the same emotional wallop and therapeutic impact that his own realization had.

SESSION 6: Anger in the transference [predicted by DM], with the impulse to deal with it by his characteristic defence of turning to someone else

The patient had become highly engaged in the therapeutic process and began each session without hesitation. This is a common phenomenon observed in ISTDP. The therapist displays high levels of activity in the early phase of treatment in order to eradicate defence and resistance. As the resistance abates and the therapeutic alliance takes over, the patient does more and more of the work on his own. The therapist becomes a guide and participant in the process, rather than the engineer.

He began this session by reporting some lingering discomfort about the mixture of sexual and aggressive impulses towards his wife that had been experienced towards the end of the last session. He reported some anxiety that these feelings would somehow be damaging to the relationship. He reported having no confidence that "relationships can weather a storm". He had imagined calling me to cancel our session or just not showing up at all. Furthermore, he imagined calling his old therapist instead. We were able to use this transference pattern of behaviour to re-work the Triangle of Conflict (Figure 2.). He was angry (I/F) with the therapist for encouraging him to face feelings that are anxiety-provoking. He imagined acting it out (D) in his characteristic way, by withdrawing from me and going to a substitute. The good news was that he came in and told me about the feelings and impulses instead of defending against them by acting out. Furthermore, taking it apart as it was happening between us deepened his level of awareness of his own internal processes and the links between transference feelings and those towards significant figures from his past and present life.

Thus, in contrast to the previous incident in which he gave way to his impulse to act out (reported near the end of Session 3), this time he stopped himself and instead talked about it to his therapist.

SESSIONS 7–9: Therapeutic effects

The patient reported wonderful feelings of closeness with his family over the holidays. He called his mistress long-distance and told her he was ending it with her once and for all, as he intended to preserve his marriage. Now that he had closed that exit, he was dealing very directly with all his mixed feelings towards his wife.

SESSION 10: Insurance problems.
Further therapeutic effects

A notice from his insurance company indicated that his coverage might be running out soon. While he was feeling much better and felt the therapy had been extremely helpful, he did not feel finished and wanted to continue. He decided to take an active stance on his own behalf, advocating for a continuation of treatment, which was, in fact, granted. This kind of self-assertion was new on his part and was a clear therapeutic gain.

He reported a real change in the nature of his relationship to his wife, in which intimacy was no longer followed by distance or rupture. The closeness they were feeling sexually was extended beyond the bedroom. They were physically affectionate and speaking to one another in an intimate way. He decided not to drink during the week, as he came to think of that as a way to avoid closeness or seek a substitute. Now that he was feeling more deeply connected to his wife, he could not imagine going outside the marriage for satisfaction.

The patient was getting ready to return to his childhood home for his brother's wedding. Mixed feelings towards his brother were the focus of the hour. He recounted an event from the previous summer that had repeated an earlier trauma. His brother had left a space-heater on in the guest-room, and it caught fire. The patient sprang into action and put the fire out, but later he found his brother reconstructing the site to take pictures of it. This triggered a memory of a highly traumatic event from his childhood. There had been a gas leak in his home, which exploded late one night. It was a huge story in the local newspaper, with reporters and photographers coming around to document it. His father had been thrown out of the doorway with such force that he broke both his legs and his back, requiring months of hospitalization. While the patient had always been aware of fear and anguish around this event, he had not been aware, until now, of how angry he felt towards the people (including his brother in the recent incident) who were getting some kind of voyeuristic satisfaction from his trauma. Again, he saw his repressed anger as the missing piece and was able to put it all together.

SESSION 15: Major breakthrough of longing and grief concerning his childhood [predicted by DM in terms of distress about loss of love]

This was an extremely intense session that the patient later referred to as a "watershed". It is almost impossible to describe the emotional intensity and exquisite poignancy of the hour, as the patient was in touch with deep feelings of grief throughout the session. The patient's beloved grandmother was dying, so he returned "home" to say good-bye.

Pt: I had a devastating time at home. I don't know where to start. I thought I had gotten rid of a lot of the sadness but I haven't. I woke up crying in the middle of the night. My wife woke me up and we had a long talk about it, which was really nice. She knew I was having a hard time. I'm glad I've had a day to think about it, because I need to make sense of it (*breaks down and starts weeping*).

Th: Yes, of course.

Pt: You might have guessed it would be like this but I didn't.

Th: No, I wouldn't have guessed this.

Pt: (*Crying.*)

Th: Obviously there is a tremendous amount of pain here—do you know what it's about?

Pt: It's mixed up, but I have some ideas. Seeing my grandmother (*who is at death's door*) was very hard. It didn't seem at the time as hard as I thought it would be, because she was, in fact, more presentable than I thought she'd be, but it was still hard. I saw her every day and I think . . . well, one day she was asleep and couldn't be roused, but on the other days, when she could muster the energy, her speech was garbled from the strokes, but I was aware that *she* was aware of my being there. She had clearly anticipated my coming, and others were surprised that she spoke as much as she did when I first arrived, but I think that's really just the baseline of the whole thing.

If one remembers the patient's lack of any true emotion when he first came, the following sentence, and several later statements (here put in italics), show how far he had come since then—even though one of his major defences reasserted itself immediately.

Pt: *I was so sensitive and sensitized to everything going on,* and I started drinking while I was down there. Even my mother noticed and said something to my wife. She told my mother that I've been seeing someone and have been much better, actually. In the course of the days, I realized that the drinking is a function of this kind of need to get comfort but to do it in a self-destructive way. My thought about it was that I was doing it on both levels. I was remembering my father and drinking to absorb it but, at the same time, drinking to distance myself from the *intensity of the feelings I was having about everything.*

Th: You were trying to numb yourself while you were there and didn't quite realize until you came home?

Pt: No, I knew it all the time I was there. I said to my wife, "This is very difficult for me".

Th: So you were feeling a lot.

Pt: So many things going on and everything seemed pertinent to my life and what we've been dealing with here. I mean, *you name it, and I had a feeling about it.* The weather was 65 degrees and sunny—and people are sunny. That part of the world is so incredibly beautiful and restful and desirable, and so I think I was really experiencing, for the first time, a kind of wish for it all again instead of pushing it out, as I've done all these years.

Th: Letting yourself feel the longing for that—to be absorbed in the warmth of it all.

Mixed feelings for his father
[essentially predicted by both judges]

Pt: Yes. I ran into my sister while my mother and I were getting something. They had pulled out this big piece of newsprint that was pasted together of a drawing my sister had done. It was of a man who had a shirt and tie on. It said—which was searing to me—"My Daddy sells insurance. My Daddy travels a lot. My Daddy reads the newspaper." And on the bottom it said, "My Daddy is a nice Daddy". This was something my sister had made, and I stopped in my tracks. My mother said, "Isn't that cute". This is the way I experienced my father, too—there was nothing else.

Th: So what was the feeling that welled up inside when you saw that?

Pt: I don't know. It wasn't really anger or sadness as much as surprise to see that image. I've mentioned this before about newspapers and my associations. I even said the last time I was down there, "Dad, you must be the most informed man on the earth". Now I realized this is this physical thing he throws up in front of people—in front of his family. Even when he asks you a question, before you can answer it, he throws up the newspaper. It's just very clear to me now that it's a barrier.

Th: And your feeling about these barriers that he puts up?

Pt: I have mixed feelings about it. I have *anger and longing*, I suppose, but at the same time, I realize *I really do love him* and I'm trying to reconcile.

Th: There are intense mixed feelings towards him. There's love, and longing for closeness, which is why his putting up this barrier causes so much pain and evokes so much anger. For some reason, you still have a hard time facing all these feelings and have ended up identifying with him and doing the same thing—throwing up barriers to closeness.

Pt: I realize that. It all makes a kind of sense to me now. We went to my brother's house, where my grandmother used to live. The boys were there, and I went up to his wife's study. She's a brilliant woman who did a complete career change, which I really admire. We were up there and looking out the window. I saw her son crossing the yard. I almost lost it right there. I had to turn around and walk away. There was this weird combination of me being the child who was alone and a sense of failure of not being the parent I've wanted to be to my own child (*becomes very tearful*). And it was clearly tied to the fact that it was my grandmother's house. When it was first becoming clear that the house was too much for her, they asked if I would consider coming back. I mean, she would have just given me the house. I, of course, said no, and it just, it was so. . . (*tears*)

Th: Overwhelming feelings of grief.

Pt: And loss. I walked across that yard as a child and did the same things. I kept having these dual kind of reactions—like drinking to connect to feelings of warmth and drinking to avoid feeling and get distance. It was just really rough.

It is as if all the defences against the experience of his own sadness and grief had come down, allowing for the full experience of what he had always avoided. This is a good sign, in that he is able to tolerate the feelings without resorting to symptoms or defences of any kind. It can be borne. When emotions are considered unbearable, then there is trouble.

Th: I can see that.

Pt: Another thing that came up was that I felt . . . oh yeah, I feel really close to and dependent on my wife. I felt needy but really good to be able to rely on her. I felt very, very close to my kids. I did something I felt terrible about. I was babysitting for a while and my brother had brought over an old Disney movie. I had seen it as a child but didn't really remember. I asked my brother if there was anything in it that would be frightening or inappropriate for a five-year-old and he said no. I forgot that he also thought *Robin Hood* was appropriate for them to see, which was, in fact, quite violent. I was off doing something when a very scary part of the movie—which had scared me terribly as a child—came on. There was a banshee, and my boy was petrified, and he was wandering around a house that wasn't his own, calling for me. He finally found me, and I told him I had been scared of it too when I was his age. I told him I was so sorry I wasn't there for him. He wasn't crying or anything, but I feel like I really screwed up.

Th: But you did what you could. He wasn't alone and you told him you had been scared too. That's much more than you ever got.

Pt: I just don't want to do what my father does. I know I don't. I've done better than that but I want to do *a lot* better than that.

As mentioned previously, his attack of drinking reported in this session was the second of only two episodes of acting out that occurred in all seven patients.

Session 16: Work

The patient reported feeling much better after the last session. In addition to a sense of emotional release, he was able to make sense of his life, and what had happened to him, in a deeply meaningful way (constructing a coherent life narrative).

Now he wanted to tackle the psychological issues involved in his work life, especially as it pertains to competition and his tendency to assume the position of the loser. He had just received an invitation to apply for a new job and wanted to get clear about whether to compete or duck out. Most importantly, he wanted to operate in such a way that would further his own self-interest and was not self-defeating.

As I enquired into the nature of the job, it became clear that he wanted to compete in the process and win the position. To duck out of the competition would be to avoid all his feelings about winning and losing. One of the people involved in the interview process was a woman he knew and viewed as "needy". In the past he had been drawn to "needy women", as a way to bolster his flagging ego. He could have fallen into this pattern and sucked up to her in the hopes of winning her over, but he could no longer live with himself for behaving in such a way. He wanted to conduct himself in a straightforward manner and win the job on his own merits.

Session 17

The patient came in reporting broad improvement in his internal state, the quality of his relationship with his wife and children, and a heightened sense of possibility for more intimacy and closeness within his family of origin. He described himself as feeling "empowered" by access to his own feelings and desires, no longer putting himself in the helpless, reactive position, which he now viewed as a holdover from childhood. He described feeling like an adult, who could have an effect on relationships and his life's trajectory. He decided to apply for the job and pursue it to the best of his ability.

He had been sick over the weekend and found his wife was wonderfully nurturing. That relationship had been deepening considerably as the result of his new-found ability to speak up about his feelings. He also reported feeling closer to his sons, and even to his brothers. He even hoped for the possibility for more genuine contact with his mother, who was quite fragile emotionally, now that her own mother was dying. He realized that he had followed his father's lead and trivialized his mother's feelings, regarding her as "ridiculous".

Session 18: The death of his grandmother

The patient's grandmother died during the previous week. His parents called to inform him of her death, but they urged him not to come to the funeral, since he had just been down for a visit and saw her while she was still alive. He stood up to them as a man, rather than allowing himself to be treated like a little boy, and declared his wish to be there. He would not just retreat and feel rejected, as he would have in the past.

These changes suggested real character change. In other words, he was not only symptom-free, but behaving in a way that clearly suggested that self-defeating defences were being replaced with healthy alternatives.

He had also found out during the previous week that he had not been selected for the job he had applied for a few weeks ago. This raised some feelings of dejection, similar to those he felt in high school. The therapist questioned him about where his feelings of adequacy had gone. He began to realize that he was angry about the selection process. The person who got the job had fewer credentials, but was "a woman of colour", so she was chosen. He could readily see how going to the position of "poor me" was a way to avoid the anger and outrage he felt about the unfairness inherent in the process.

Given the healthy ways that he had dealt with some very difficult situations, the patient wondered about ending therapy. He had exceeded his own expectations and felt capable of going out on his own. We agreed to work towards termination.

Session 19

The impending termination of therapy was stirring up a lot of feeling towards the therapist. The patient became aware of a tendency to sexualize his attachments in the face of loss. He had not felt any sexual attraction to the therapist since the first session, and he became wary of it when it began to surface. He wondered if it was a way of staying attached in fantasy, rather than dealing with feelings regarding loss. He went on to say that he had always done that in the past—hooked up with one woman before separating from another. This pattern went all the way back to his earliest life, when he turned to the housekeeper to fulfil the emotional needs that were neglected by his mother. He told me about a painting he was working on, in which there was a little boy and two women—all in the same room (not split, as they were in an earlier painting). He spontaneously reported, "I know that little boy represents me. There I am between two women but looking for my father."

Sessions 20–23

Sessions 20–23 were spent consolidating the gains achieved in the therapy. His new-found ability to assert himself, both at home and in the work place, resulted in increased confidence and a sense that he was no longer living his life from the position of a helpless, inadequate boy. The sense of closeness with his wife and family were major achievements. He reported feeling especially good about his ability to experience the pleasure of giving—particularly, how nice it is to feel vital and needed. This dynamic also emerged in the transference—that it felt good to have me appreciate the work he has done. His other therapist had been very important to him, but when he went back to see him after termination, the therapist hadn't remembered him! He recalled that, at the time, he felt "small and insignificant". Now he feels angry about it and realized that this would help him tell the difference between those who really care about him and those with whom he has only a superficial connection. He knew I would not forget him.

SESSION 24: Last session

We began by reviewing the status of his presenting complaints. All of his symptoms had been removed, and his self-defeating defences had been replaced with healthy alternatives. He no longer distanced himself from his own feelings and, consequently, from others. Instead, he was freely in touch with his feelings and was able to express them in order to solidify important relationships. He reported feeling especially close to his wife and children.

He also attained benefits he had not imagined when he first came to therapy. For example, he reported that this process has resulted in a much greater sense of self-definition. In other words, he now knows who he is, where he stands, and what is important, and, furthermore, he is willing to fight for it (as he did to be at his grandmother's funeral or to be included in the running for the job).

At the start of this session, the patient noticed that I seemed shaken by the previous session, and he made an empathic comment about how difficult it must be to go through this with people. He expressed his gratitude for all I had done for him and said it didn't feel like a sad goodbye. He has me with him and he won't lose that.

THE RELATION BETWEEN
PREDICTIONS AND ACTUAL EVENTS

Predictions that were fulfilled

1. Both judges predicted that mixed feelings about his father would become an important issue (Sessions 4 and 9)
2. DM predicted hostility against his wife (Session 5)
3. DM predicted hostility in the transference (Session 6).
4. JM predicted the importance of exploring his feelings about his younger brother who had died.
5. DM predicted his distress about the lack of love in his childhood (Session 9)
6. In her Hypothesis, JM foresaw the issue of obsessional indecision being due to an inability to be in touch with the true feelings that would enable decisions to be made (Session 2).

Predictions that were not fulfilled

Both judges predicted that hostility against his mother would be the most important issue in therapy, and DM predicted that this would lead to therapeutic effects. DM also predicted (in different words) that it was necessary to complete the Triangle of Person in terms of hostility towards his wife, the therapist, and his mother. In fact, hostility towards both the *therapist* and his *wife* became abundantly clear, but—most surprisingly—neither was linked with his *mother*. Hostility towards his mother was never mentioned.

It remains a mystery how such a complete therapeutic result could be achieved in a therapy that made no reference to this apparently crucial issue.

Follow-up

The therapist interviewed The Man Divided for follow-up at 1, 2, and 10 years after termination. The following assessment is based on an amalgamation of the Criteria formulated by DM and JM, both of whom were entirely blind to events subsequent to the initial interview.

We will leave the two most general Criteria, [1] and [2], to the end.

[3]   To lose his symptoms,
         mainly (a) depression and (b) excessive drinking

(a) *Depression*: At 10 years follow-up, the patient made clear that he had not been depressed at all during the intervening years, even under the stress of his mother's death or failing to get hired for jobs he applied for. As will be seen, it is also clear that his depression has not merely disappeared, but has been replaced by pleasure in every aspect of his life.

(b) *Drinking*: At all the follow-up interviews, he said that drinking consisted solely of wine with meals. His cardiologist told him that drinking wine was good for him. He no longer drank to excess or got drunk. In fact, he reported that drinking with a meal was part of the pleasure of life and was not a way either to numb his feelings or to discharge rage in a self-destructive manner, as he had in the past.

[4]   To end his pattern of extramarital affairs
       and to develop a committed relation with one woman,
       based on intimacy and closeness

At 6 months follow-up, he said that he was no longer distracted by fantasies of other women. He feels that he is developing a deep level of intimacy and closeness with his wife and children, and that they are now at the centre of his life. This was evident as he spoke about them and also as he expressed his gratitude to the therapist—in each case, he had tears in his eyes and was clearly comfortable about sharing these feelings with her.

At 2 years follow-up, he spoke of "the deep closeness I now feel with both my wife and kids".

At 10 years follow-up, he said that the only problem now is that he does not see enough of them, because his job is many miles away and he only comes home at weekends. However, "The summer is a very important time for us. We go to our home in France and spend the whole of the summer together. It's a life-saver. I'm very happy about the time we spend together, and I feel very close to my wife and the children." "After the summer I find it very difficult being separated from my wife."

Extremely significant is his ability to resolve strains. He said that if they begin to drift apart, he speaks about it. Over the winter they were both so caught up with their own affairs that he began to feel distant from her. "I said, 'Hey, it's starting to feel like we're just sharing space', and that did it—we were able to re-connect. Then we had the summer together and it was delightful. I want more of that and I don't want to keep having it interrupted by me having to go off to work during the week."

The therapist pointed out that, in the past, the effect of being away from home during the week would have been to make him very vulnerable to having affairs:

Pt: I'm not doing that and I don't want to—quite the contrary. I won't say there haven't been opportunities and even temptations, but I'm not looking for another woman. I value what I have with my wife. I feel a sense of wholeness within the family.

[5]   To be able to experience anger and use it
       to assert himself constructively

At 10 years, he described two situations. The first was that his mother has died and within three months his father remarried. Since then his father has both been thoroughly uncooperative and has been entirely neglecting his family. He was extremely dilatory over releasing money from the patient's mother's estate, which made the patient very angry. "I held back these feelings for some time after my mother's death, but I finally blew up at him. I started to express it very directly in a series of letters." He said that his anger had been welling up and he just had to express it. This self-assertion was effective, since his father finally gave in.

The second situation involved a man who betrayed him over a job that he wanted. "I had a real blow-out with him and took him to task. I didn't speak to him for some time after that, but now I am civil if I bump into him."

[6]   To develop true caring and closeness with his children

The fact that this has been entirely fulfilled must already have been made clear under [4] above. Here are some further details (at 6 years follow-up):

Th: What about your son? You had gotten depressed after the birth of the second child and you found it difficult to attach to him.

Pt: Right. I was able to get to what that was about early on in our work together, and there's been no problem with it since. I feel very close and connected to both the boys.

At 10 years he said, "The children are doing so well and I'm very proud of them."

[7]   To be able to share a greater depth of feeling with his parents and siblings

As far as his mother is concerned, at 10 years this was fulfilled:

Pt: "I'm really at peace with my mother's death. I feel very sad about it—you remember the conflicts I used to have with her—but it's an amazing thing, having gone through all that here, I was able to have a good relationship with her. It's not that I've forgotten the problems and grievances with her, but I dealt with my feelings and I have forgiven her.

At 6 years it really seemed that this criterion was fulfilled with his father as well. He had gone to his father for advice about how to invest his money:

Pt: This was the start to what has become a real solid connection between the two of us. I was so distraught at the idea that he would die without my ever have gotten to know him.

Th: I can see how moved you are and how much this means to you. So what helped you to come to terms with it all?

Pt: Well, being able to feel what I felt about it.

This is one of many an examples of a patient being able to describe accurately what was important in therapy (see also below, and chapter 11, for a full discussion of this issue).

At 10 years it turned out that the apparent closeness to his father was illusory. He said that he had had hopes that it would be the beginning of something real, but this never developed, and in fact true closeness was never achieved. Apparently money was the only subject his father was ever willing to discuss. Clearly his father's intolerable behaviour after remarriage was not caused by anything in the patient's behaviour.

The patient ended by saying, "He's going to die and I will be for ever without the love and affection of my father. I try to make things up with my own kids, but there's nothing more I can do with him."

As far as his brother and sister are concerned, he is still in touch with them:

Pt: Even though we're at a distance and my brother can be difficult to deal with, we've banded together and often talk on the phone.

My sister and I get along fine, but she's really exasperated with my father and the fact that he doesn't pay any attention to any of her three children. He hasn't even seen her 6-month-old baby.

[8]   Happiness and enjoyment of life, with an increase in creativity

As far as happiness and enjoyment are concerned, it should be obvious that these criteria are fulfilled. As for creativeness, the trouble is that his job is so far away that during the week he has to stay nearby and can only come home at weekends.. He said it was only during the summer that he had time to do his own work as a painter. "If I quit the job, I'll be able to spend more time on my own creations and more time with my wife."

[9]   Increased self-esteem and self-confidence

It should be absolutely clear from all the above that both of these criteria are completely fulfilled. In connection with self-esteem and quitting his current job, he said, "I don't need that kind of validation any more."

[10]   To be more productive and fulfilled in his work

The fact that the job mentioned under [5] fell through was a blessing in disguise. At 6 years he reported that he had now got a full faculty position and that it was going extremely well. At 10 years, he said of the same job, "I feel part of a community, making a contribution and being productive—and making a nice salary."

THE TWO ESSENTIAL GENERAL CRITERIA

[1]   To face his true feelings and use them constructively in all situations, without such defences as rumination and intellectualization, or emotional or physical withdrawal

As far as defences are concerned, there is an immense contrast between his somewhat convoluted and intellectualized way of expressing himself in the initial interview, and his direct, simple, and often deeply felt communications from later in therapy, up to the final follow-up.

This change is reflected in all his relationships with the people close to him—that is, his wife and children—where he is clearly entirely free with his feelings, and therefore experiences intense emotional closeness and fulfilment.

It is worth noting that these changes have enabled him to repair the relationship with his wife completely—a relationship that was under serious threat when he first came.

[2]   The replacement of self-destructive behaviour by constructive behaviour throughout his life

Originally his two main areas of self-destructiveness were (a) his affairs with other women, and (b) his drinking, including driving his motor cycle too fast while under the influence of drink.

a.   He has abandoned his tendency to having affairs and says he no longer wants them. Obviously they have been replaced by a really close and warm relation with his wife.

b.   He has replaced excessive drinking by moderate drinking of wine with meals. He has an extremely responsible attitude to this, including its effect on driving.

HIS COMMENTS ON THERAPY

During the first follow-up interview, 1 year after termination, he reported that the therapeutic factors of greatest importance to him were the therapist's willingness to focus on difficult feeling and to "ride the roller-coaster" with him. He said, "That made all the difference."

POSTSCRIPT

Towards the end of the 10-year follow-up interview, two things happened that shed light on the patient's current personality and his relationship to the therapist.

In the first, he mentioned that he had been held up by a traffic diversion while driving to the therapist's office and had begun to get really upset that he might be late. "Then I said to myself, 'What are you so upset about? Even if you miss the interview she'll understand and re-schedule it.'" This is an example of natural rather than obsessional anxiety, which was most un-neurotically overcome and is a measure of his emotional maturity.

In the second, he spoke of a difficult situation that he had learned about, related to the therapist and her private life. His concern about her welfare was that of a close friend, wholly genuine, and was in no way tinged with what may be called "transference". More details of this are given in chapter 11.

ASSESSMENT OF THE THERAPEUTIC RESULT

No trace of his original disturbances can be detected, all having been replaced by "positive mental health". The only possible judgement is "Total resolution".

LEVELS OF EVIDENCE

There are many levels—really, a continuum of levels—on which the information that a patient gives at follow-up may be assessed. These may be illustrated by considering answers to the therapist's question about this patient's depression.

At Level 1, we may take the first sentence of the patient's reply: "I'm not depressed and I haven't been in a long time." This is important evidence, but "not depressed" does not describe what his state of mind is like. We need to know whether his depression has been replaced by the corresponding aspect of positive mental health, which is essentially the capacity to enjoy life.

At Level 2, therefore, the therapist might ask about this capacity and might receive the answer that, yes indeed, the patient is able to enjoy life. This is not enough. The patient could be consciously or unconsciously concealing the truth, or simply idealizing the situation. It does not reach Level 3, which we may call the "level of authenticity". This, though subjective in the extreme, consists of *authentic elaboration, obvious genuine emotion, or the living and detailed description of specific examples*, conveying unmistakable conviction.

Here the patient spoke first of his work: "I have a very good job that I like very much. . . . I feel part of a community, making a contribution, and being productive." He then went on to speak of his family: "We go to our home in France and spend the whole of the summer together. It's a life-saver. I feel really happy about the time we spent together this summer and feel very close to my wife and the children."

This is the lower end of Level 3, obviously genuine, and entirely acceptable. But it does not reach the upper end, an extreme example of which was given in chapter 1—namely, the experience of joy between The Self-Loathing Headmistress and her daughter.

POSSIBLE CRITICISMS

A criticism that has been made of this method of assessing outcome is that it is impossible to obtain good agreement on the Hypotheses between one judge and another. This can be answered very simply: no doubt it is true if all you have in your possession is a question-and-answer interview, in which case you can do no more than speculate about the psychopathology. With a good dynamic interview, however, in which a view of some depth is obtained into the patient's unconscious, there is no difficulty—the evidence is direct. We hope to have demonstrated this with the material already presented.

A second possible criticism is that the follow-up interviews were conducted by the therapist rather than by an independent observer. This might mean that the information was distorted by residual feelings about the therapist, particularly that the therapeutic result was idealized in order to please her.

This criticism can be answered as follows:

• A point that is never considered in the literature on follow-up is that an interviewer only learns the real truth within an atmosphere of *maximum rapport*. It is quite clear that no one is more likely to achieve this than the therapist herself. The absence of rapport with another human being is the most serious deficiency of all paper-and-pencil tests and, indeed, of all purely question-and-answer interviews, no matter how "reliable" and "validated" the results may appear to be. This issue will become especially relevant with some of the other patients, in particular The Woman with Dissociation, where the therapist was able to obtain highly intimate details both of the improvements, and of the deficiencies, in the sexual relation with her partner.

FURTHER DISCUSSION

At the beginning of his therapy, this patient showed (1) inhibition of all feeling, (2) the use of wordiness or rumination as a defence, and (3) difficulty over taking decisions. This means that, psychodynamically speaking, he could be regarded as suffering from an *obsessional personality*, though his condition was nowhere near being severe enough for him to fulfil the DSM-IV criteria for that diagnosis.

One way of looking at many obsessional phenomena is that they consist of mechanisms unconsciously designed to avoid the dangers of *spontaneity*, such as emotional involvement leading to ambivalence or the pain of loss, or anger leading to destructiveness. Such mechanisms can pervade the whole of a person's functioning, which is what had happened to this particular patient.

One of the major issues with which this book is concerned is the search for *specific* changes that indicate that a neurotic state has been truly *resolved*. It follows from the above considerations that the essential criterion indicating true resolution of these obsessional mechanisms is the development of *emotional spontaneity*.

It might well be thought that such an all-pervasive state would be extremely difficult to change at all, let alone resolve completely, but clearly it has happened here. In other words this patient has been entirely cured of his obsessional personality, which can be set alongside the equally complete cure of the narcissistic personality of The Cold-Blooded Businessman (chapter 5) and the masochistic personality of The Masochistic Artist (see chapter 1).

The Cold-Blooded Businessman

Initial evaluation

The Cold-Blooded Businessman (married, age 58) came to therapy complaining of depression and high levels of anxiety, which had been precipitated by a move and had been on-going for the past 12 years. He reported experiencing anxiety as "a lot of physiological inner turmoil", with persistent diarrhoea, sleep disturbance, erectile dysfunction, and work inhibition. In fact, enquiry revealed that most of his anxiety was around the issue of performance—both at work and in the bedroom. Depression was experienced as dysphoric affect, low energy, and a helpless/hopeless attitude towards life. He was so despondent, in fact, that he had a detailed plan for suicide if this therapy did not work.

During these 12 years, he had undergone a series of treatments, including two fairly long psychodynamic therapies, one behaviour therapy, and several rounds of medication. He was referred to me by one of the nation's leading cognitive behaviour therapists, who had rejected him from inclusion in a study on the treatment of anxiety and depression because his Minnesota Multiphasic Personality Inventory (MMPI) revealed a "narcissistic personality disorder" (though I did not know that at the time).

The patient arrived on time and engaged readily in the process of enquiry, providing useful factual information and cooperating with the therapist. However, when the enquiry turned to an examination of his feelings, characteristic defences against emotional involvement came into view. As we focused in on the emotionally sensitive area of eating and weight gain, the following emerged:

Pt: I am so anxious in the morning before going to work that I can't eat. Then, later, I overeat at lunch, dinner, and after dinner. I'm trying to watch what I eat. Up until the time I was 35 years old my biggest problem with weight was trying to put it on. Now my biggest problem is trying to keep it off (*big smile, for the first time, indicating some rise in feeling*).

Th: And you smile. Are you aware of that?

Pt: Yeah, it's strange. I became aware of it just a fraction of a second before you mentioned it.

Th: So what's the feeling about gaining weight?

Pt: Relief in being able to verbalize.

Th: But that doesn't tell us what your feeling is about gaining the weight.

Pt: I wish I didn't have a weight problem. I'd like to lose weight and keep it off.

Th: So you know what you think and what you want to do about it, but you avoid the feeling about it.

Pt: I'm not following you.

This interchange reveals the extent to which this man employs isolation of affect as a primary defence. He mistakes his thoughts and actions for his feelings and is unaware that emotion is being avoided altogether. This had to be pointed out again, until he could see it. Following this new awareness, the following emerged:

Pt: I don't like it—I'm unhappy about it because it detracts from my physical presence.

Th: It's a sore spot?

Pt: Yes, I'm having trouble ageing. (*Moves in his chair and gets physically activated for the first time in the session*) I've always taken a great deal of pride in how I look and how I dress. A great deal of it had to do with the art of attracting women. The fact that I've aged. Suddenly, I'm not as attractive to women as I used to be.

Th: What makes you think that?

Pt: There was a time when I could establish eye contact with a woman and develop a relationship with her. It hasn't happened, basically, since I've been here (*a move to Albany, which precipitated his anxiety and depression*).

Pt: Now they just look at me like I'm an old man. There was a time when I was very active sexually outside the marriage.

Th: So you had lots of affairs.

Pt: Not lots of affairs, lots of sexual contacts.

Th: You had lots of one-night stands?

Pt: Yes, one-night stands and ongoing relationships that there was no commitment or anything ... it was just purely sexual, and that happened with a lot of people.

Th: Did your wife know about this?

Pt: Initially no, but eventually yes. We ended up having a very open relationship.

Th: So she was unfaithful too?

Pt: I hate to use that word—that's not a good word. I don't like to think that we were unfaithful to each other. If I was sexually exclusive, but verbally or physically abused my wife, would that be faithful? Just because there are outside sexual relationships doesn't mean there is anything wrong with the relationship.

Th: But something was going on there—not a full commitment.

Pt: I don't think so.

Th: There is no need to quibble about it, but it looks like you are able to act on sexual feelings and impulses while staying divorced from other feelings.

Pt: That's right.

This information, obtained via the dynamic interaction between patient and therapist, also sheds light on the origin of his disturbance. It looks like he managed to keep his mixed feelings towards his wife separate by having two separate lives—one at home with her and the children, and one on the road while travelling for work, which was full of sexual conquests. When he moved to Albany and took a job that involved no travel, his external solution was eliminated. He was not able to contain his mixed feelings and became symptomatic. He was unable to achieve erections and have intercourse with his wife, and he became anxious, depressed, and suicidal.

This understanding of the genesis of his problem guides the interventions that will be required. First and foremost, the defence of detachment must be removed, so that the feelings he has been avoiding can be experienced.

Examination of the transference pattern of behaviour

Pt: I have a tendency to want to stay aloof.

Th: So you are distant and detached.

Pt: Yeah.

Th: Are you aware of that happening here with me?

Pt: No, I don't feel that. I feel that you are antagonistic.

Now we see that having his defences challenged will arouse hostility, which is also defended against. In this case, he begins to project his own hostility onto the therapist. This will be used as a vehicle to work on the Triangle of Conflict in the transference.

Pt: It's almost like you want me to lash out or something and I don't.

Th: So you experience me as antagonistic. And now you are smiling, so what is the feeling towards me?

Pt: I sat here and thought to myself, "Do I want to put up with this?" and I thought, maybe this is just what I need to help me with my anxiety and depression. So, unless I can't cope with it, then I would drop.

Th: What is your way of coping? (*examine defences*)

Pt: My way of coping is to accept you as you are. Maybe this is what I need.

Th: But you remain aloof and detached, yet you're having a lot of reactions here—thoughts and feelings about me that you've kept to yourself. If you do that, how I can help you?

Pt: I'm telling you.

Th: But you were not about to volunteer this and I had to ask you. Now if you stay detached, we won't get anywhere. So let's look at what this feeling is towards me.

Pt: OK. We're saying this is how I perceive you (*suggesting he recognizes some distortion*), so how do I feel towards you? . . . Ambivalent . . . I don't know, I can't find a feeling . . . OK—I find you pouncing, and so I feel angry.

Th: How do you experience this anger towards me.

Pt: I don't understand the question.

Th: You say you feel anger towards me, so how do you experience that inside? You are biting your finger, and now you avoid my eyes.

Pt: I'm thinking. I don't want to be distracted.

Th: But it's also a way to avoid me and this angry feeling towards me.

Pt: I don't want to avoid you. I really don't. I understand what we're trying to do but I'm having trouble verbalizing (*speaks to the unconscious alliance*).

Th: Which is one of the problems you have.

Pt: OK, so I have this anger towards you, and I just feel like, I'm pissed or something.

Th: So how do you experience it?

Pt: I experience it internally as a kind of mental anger rather than a . . .

Th: You don't feel it in your body?

Pt: No.

Th: So you are cut off from the feeling inside?

Pt: I'm not feeling anything physically. Maybe if I were hooked up to monitors . . . I suspect there may be changes in my breathing or pulse rate.

Th: Are you aware of it?

Pt: No, it's a form of mental anger. I feel angry, and so what—I'm not going to let it get the best of me. I feel angry and I'm going to withdraw.

Th: So you go to withdrawal and a certain kind of defeat.

Pt: Yeah!

Th: In the face of anger you take a helpless, limp position, which is what's been happening in your life.

Pt: Yeah, I see that. Other times I can become very bitchy and nit-picky.

Th: But here, what we saw happen was that anger got aroused and you avoided the experience of that by going to thoughts and, finally, collapse and defeat.

Pt: My thoughts are a refuge.

Th: But what will happen as long as you escape into your thoughts and avoid these feelings? What will happen to your goal?

Pt: If I do that, I won't be any better off than when I came here.

Th: So what becomes apparent is that you have a self-defeating part of you in operation.

This sequence contains an enormous amount of information regarding this man's defensive structure and his ability to give up deeply entrenched patterns of withdrawal, helplessness, and acting out. His responses to interventions suggest that his defences are quite syntonic, but that they can be rendered dystonic with therapeutic focus. He begins to realize two crucial things: (1) that his avoidance of anger via passivity and withdrawal are directly connected with his presenting complaints of avoidance at work and in relation to his wife; and (2) that continued reliance on these defences will destroy his potential for cure in the therapy and happiness in his life. This work is employed in order to solidify the unconscious alliance and turn the healthy ego against its self-destructive defences. We can see that movement was achieved in both arenas. There were several communications to the therapist suggesting that she was on the right track. Therapeutic gains were achieved by investigating the transference pattern of behaviour. Had the anger towards the therapist been avoided, it would have fostered further defence and resistance.

Triangle of conflict in his current life

As we examined the pattern of anger and withdrawal with his wife, the following material emerged quite spontaneously and with a great deal of activation (in contrast to his earlier limp, detached manner):

Pt: Speaking of anger, when we drive down one street by our house we have the right of way. The other people have a stop sign but they don't bother to stop. I feel like I'm just waiting for somebody to cross me so I can get really angry (*arms mobilized*) and I visualize going to the trunk and getting the tyre jack and smashing the guy's car.

Th: So, again, you want to smash the car, which is a displacement. Who crossed you?

Pt: The other guy.

Th: Right, this man. So if the angry impulse came out towards him—if we are honest about it—who do you want to go after with the tyre jack?

Pt: No, I'd be afraid if I did something like that.

Th: In reality, obviously, we are not talking about acting on these impulses, but even in your fantasy you don't allow yourself to face honestly what is inside of you.

Pt: I want to vent my anger, but I don't want to hurt anyone.

Th: Obviously, in reality, but you have the impulse.

Pt: I want to smash his headlight, the windshield, the boot, to do body damage.

Th: To whom?

Pt: The car—that's body damage. (*Smile*)

Th: But whose body do you want to damage? There's a smile and a big sigh.

Pt: Well, I have been fighting what you have been driving at, and obviously I'm starting to see it now. Am I unconsciously wanting to hurt somebody, but I don't do it?

Th: You beat yourself up instead, getting depressed and anxious (*speaking to depressive mechanism*).

Pt: The thought just came to me. I've heard that depression is anger turned inward, but until this moment, I never understood what that meant. (*Big smile*) I'm glad I came here, you know that.

After much hard work, therapeutic progress has been made. The patient is now acutely aware of how he has created and maintained his own suffering. By having at least a partial experience of the angry feelings and impulses he characteristically represses, he leaves the evaluation feeling energized and hopeful. He was also able to directly express his gratitude towards the therapist. Had the therapist failed to examine the transference pattern of behaviour and extract his anger towards her, this would not, in all likelihood, have happened. Despite the long-standing nature of his disturbance and his entrenched character pathology, his response to the trial therapy suggested that he would, indeed, be able to benefit from a course of ISTDP.

Developmental history—follow-up to the initial evaluation

Because it took almost the whole of the first interview to break through his resistance, most of this historical information had to be obtained in the second interview. Both his mother and father were immigrants to the United States. The patient was the eldest by 7 years of two boys, born to his parents late in life.

His father worked 6 days a week. He was educated, intelligent, and caring but suffered from tremendous feelings of inadequacy owing to a physical disability about which he was very self-conscious. The patient loved his father and used to long for his father's one day off each week. These were special times, and he and his father used to go out together while his mother stayed at home.

In contrast to his positive and three-dimensional view of his father, he portrayed his mother as "stupid and vile" and had nothing good to say about her. He expressed intense hatred and contempt for her. It turns out that she never learned the English language and depended on the patient to be her interpreter and mediator in the outside world. No matter how hard he tried or how well he did, she had nothing but criticism for him. She called him a Nazi and was verbally abusive. The following memory was of great importance in understanding the origin of his conflict.

Traumatic childhood experiences

One day, while walking home from synagogue with his father, the patient was overcome with the smell of lamb coming from his mother's kitchen. As a fairly direct 7 year old, he told his mother he didn't like lamb and wouldn't eat it. She flew into a rage, grabbed his hands, and held them against the stove until they burned and blistered. Following this incident, the patient refused to eat anything his mother cooked. He lost weight dramatically, and at the age of 10, reduced to skin and bone, he was sent to a "health camp", where he remained for the next three years.

His parents rarely visited him during this time. Even as a child, the patient was able to understand and forgive his father's relative absence, due to work constraints and physical disability. However, he never forgave his mother, who didn't seem to want to make the effort to travel on her own to see him.

He spoke of the "loneliness and isolation" of his childhood. It is no coincidence that a discussion of his appetite and eating pattern at the beginning of the trial therapy stirred up so much feeling.

Later history

He did well in high school and joined the military immediately after graduation in order to escape from home (again). While overseas he met and married his wife. They have been married for 35 years and have four children. He seemed to function relatively well as long as he was separated from his wife by his work duties and could maintain two separate lives. However, all that changed 12 years prior to treatment, when he moved and got a new job that involved no travel. He was no longer able to have extramarital affairs and became symptomatic. It was also revealed that he had no close friends and was distant from both his children and grandchildren. There was a palpable sterility in his life, inside and out.

HYPOTHESIS BY DM

The formulations by DM and JM were the same in all essentials, so those by DM are given in detail.

There were the following potential sources of emotional trouble in his background:

1. His father's ineffectiveness, physical disability, and failure to protect him from his mother.
2. His mother's ill-treatment of him, particularly the incident over the cooked lamb, resulting in major conflict with her (refusing to eat anything she had cooked).

3. A prolonged period of separation: being sent to a health camp for 3 years.
4. His description of the "loneliness and isolation" in his childhood, which presumably referred mainly to Source 3, but possibly to times before this as well.

There is no evidence for any effects of Source 1.

There must have been a great deal of *distress* about these factors, but hardly any direct evidence for this appeared in the interviews. What did become abundantly clear was that he had "an immense reservoir of *anger*" about them, presumably mainly directed against his mother, and possibly currently expressed against women in general.

There is some evidence that underneath his aloof and arrogant exterior he is a sensitive man; however, he defends against his buried feelings by *avoidance of emotion and emotional closeness,* with a compensating preoccupation with his own attractiveness and sexual prowess, leading to a pattern of sexual relationships without emotional involvement or commitment.

His defences have broken down into depression and anxiety, which coincided with his move to a new job in Albany. Here his opportunities for his sexual pattern of one-night stands were at first reduced and then—when his wife joined him—eliminated altogether.

This set up a vicious circle of (1) depression, (2) a falling off in sexual performance, which he attributed to ageing, and (3) anxiety about this, leading to further loss of performance, and so on.

ISSUES TO BE DEALT WITH IN THERAPY (DM)

1. Resolution of all his defences against emotions.
2. Bringing out the full extent of his anger and tracing it to its source in childhood, presumably largely directed against his mother.
3. Bringing out his distress about the events of his childhood, especially his separation.
4. Mourning for the loss of his enjoyment of life caused by his defences and his self-destructiveness.

It is Issue 2 that is most likely to lead to therapeutic effects.

CRITERIA

Criteria are covered in the follow-up section.

FORMULATION BY JM

Additional factors in JM's Hypothesis

JM included anger with his father, particularly for his passivity and collusion in his being sent to a health camp. She also queried resentment against his younger brother, who was born and "replaced" him when he was 7 years old and who stayed at home while he was sent away at the age of 10.

His angry feelings were too painful and frightening for a 6- to 7-year-old child, so he coped by withdrawal into himself and passive resistance and refusal to eat.

His anger at his mother may be linked to detachment from all women, including his wife, and from all close emotional relationships.

Additional issues to be dealt with in therapy

1. Discover emotional closeness with his family—wife and children.
2. Get a positive feeling of self-worth—stop feeling "the bad child".

Therapy

The therapy for The Cold-Blooded Businessman, which consisted of 58 sessions, illustrates the need for extreme persistence in challenging resistance.

ADDITIONAL HYPOTHESES BY THE THERAPIST

In addition to interventions aimed at dismantling defences and activating feelings, the therapist hypothesized that work would be required to integrate feelings he had split and actively kept apart. In particular, he seemed to separate his loving feelings from sexual feelings. He also split, rather than integrated, sexual and aggressive impulses. Consequently, he "preserved" his wife by distancing from her sexually and "fucked" women he neither knew nor cared about. His history suggested that he used acting out to discharge feelings that could not be directly expressed in his primary relationship. When the opportunity to act on these feelings outside the marriage was no longer available to him, he became symptomatic. The therapist hypothesized that work would be required to integrate these feelings once they became activated and available to consciousness.

THE PROCESS OF TREATMENT

The first block of sessions focused on restructuring the patient's defences against impulse/feeling, which were highly syntonic and would pose an enormous obstacle to treatment if not removed. He mistook his defences, such as intellectualizing, for the feeling itself. Furthermore, he saw these defensive operations as an expression of his identity—"that's just the way I am"—rather than a means of avoiding anxiety-laden feelings. In order to render these defences dystonic, specific interventions were required. The first stage of treatment focused on defence work, involving a three-step process, including: (1) the identification of defences; (2) clarification of their function; and (3) the elaboration of the negative consequences of their continued use.

In this case, the patient clearly mistook his thoughts (defence) for feelings. He was helped to see that he used intellectualization as a way to *avoid* the experience of his feelings. Once the defence (intellectualization) was identified, and its use clarified (in order to avoid feelings), we could proceed to an exploration of the consequences of a continued reliance on defences. It is essential that patients come to acknowledge the self-defeating nature of their defences, so they will be motivated to relinquish their use. This patient needed to be able to see—and viscerally experience—that his reliance on defences was responsible for his presenting complaints. His tendency to avoid the visceral experience of his feelings left him feeling numb and depressed. These defences robbed him of energy and left him detached and uninterested in life. It was of critical importance that he make the connection between his repressed sadistic impulses towards others and the symptoms of anxiety and depression he was suffering. He achieved some insight into this mechanism during the trial therapy ("I beat myself up instead. Some say depression is anger turned inward. I never understood what that meant until this moment"), which greatly improved his motivation and strengthened the unconscious therapeutic alliance. While that was an important start, many repetitions would be required to produce deep and lasting change in what had become a characterological style of cynical detachment.

This first phase of treatment, lasting approximately 15 sessions, resulted in rapid symptom removal. The patient stopped taking anti-anxiety medication within weeks of the trial therapy and tapered off antidepressants completely by the third month of treatment. Despite symptomatic improvement, his problems with intimacy and closeness remained largely untouched. In order to facilitate character change, all his defences against emotional closeness needed to be tackled. This required a phase of pressure and challenge to the character defences.

In response to the interventions of pressure (to feel) and challenge (to relinquish his defences), resistance increased and crystallized in the transference. He took a passive, victimized stance with the therapist, occasionally peppered with defiance. The ways in which these defences would sabotage therapeutic efforts were elucidated, culminating in a "head on collision".

In ISTDP, we seek to conquer the resistance and solidify the alliance towards health. I refer to this sequence of interventions as the one–two punch—pointing out both the self-defeating consequences of avoidance as well as the potential for liberation and growth in facing one's true feelings honestly. Rather than take a "neutral" stand, the ISTDP therapist is an advocate for change. Similarly, Schnarch (1991, 1997, 2003) has advocated a clinical stance that he likens to "playing hard ball". This therapeutic stance reveals a respect for patients and their strengths, while refusing to "dumb down" to or placate them. Rather than speak to the part of the patient that is frightened, for example, we speak to what is best in them—to their desire to tackle their difficulties head on.

Handling anxiety

Schnarch (personal communication) reminds us that the self grows when challenged. Davanloo has always advocated an approach that is geared to the patient's highest level of capacity. Rather than backing off in the face of anxiety and seeking to create "safety", the therapist first tests out the patient's ability to tolerate the anxiety necessary to face difficult feelings and truths and then proceeds accordingly. Anxiety does not get reduced before feelings are experienced, only afterwards. In fact, anxiety often rises as "forbidden" thoughts and feelings become aroused. If the therapist intervenes to reduce anxiety, she will simultaneously de-pressurize the feelings generating that anxiety and delay achieving therapeutic goals.

In ISTDP, patient and therapist form an alliance based on an agreement to face the truth, no matter how difficult or distressing that might be. The patient's life is precious, and time is of the essence. Delay tactics and half measures are discouraged, while the patient is encouraged to face and express directly previously avoided thoughts, feelings, and memories. Following this experience, anxiety is reduced and the patient's sense of mastery and competence is enhanced. This is the process through which the ego's adaptive capacity is strengthened. As patients become increasingly capable of experiencing intense, mixed feelings without undue anxiety or without resorting to defensive manoeuvres or symptoms, their functioning improves, often markedly. This is not simply a matter of learning new behaviours, but of stimulating personal growth and revising one's view of self.

Mid-treatment

Increasing ego strength and resilience: the head-on collision

This process of building ego strength is illustrated in the following session. The patient entered the session with meaningful material and initiated the work, revealing the changes that had already taken place. He began by reporting a pattern of procrastination at work, noting the various ways that he had been sabotaging himself. The therapeutic focus now needs to shift from symptoms to his characterological difficulties, which will require a more challenging stance on the part of the therapist.

> Th: So to procrastinate, avoid, and put off what needs doing at work has disastrous effects.
> Pt: But sometimes I don't deal with my anxiety that way—I focus and get more intense.

The patient revealed that he has the capacity to harness his anxiety and use it as fuel to accomplish a goal. This was a communication to the therapist that she should not settle for anything less from him in their work together and was a manifestation of the unconscious therapeutic alliance.

> Th: If we look at the parallel here, you've set yourself a goal and there is a job to be done—to get to the bottom of your emotional difficulties so you can fulfil your potential, both at work and in your relationships with people.
> Pt: Yes.
> Th: And if you look at it, it seems to me there is a similar pattern—that you get anxious as you approach the work, and the way you deal with the anxiety is to jump around, keep your emotional distance, to be cool and aloof: you avoid my eyes, your voice is a monotone, and you shut off your feelings. You don't let me close to your most intimate thoughts and feeling.

Pt: (*Laugh*) Oh my God, I tell you everything.

Th: You *tell* me things, but . . .

Pt: I tell you about my feelings.

Th: You don't withhold your thoughts about your feelings, but when it comes to *experiencing* your feelings, you cut off. Isn't this one of the major problems you came for help with—that you keep a distance from your own feelings and keep an emotional distance from others?

Pt: But I don't see it.

Th: You mean, here with us?

Pt: Yeah . . . um . . . yes and no.

Th: Perfect. Always on the fence. Never to declare—such ambivalence.

Pt: I am aware of consciously telling you everything. I am not withholding anything. Unconsciously, I'm aware—or you've pointed out—that I'm holding back.

Th: But what are you aware of that you are holding back?

Pt: Nothing?

Th: What about avoiding my eyes?

Pt: Well, yes, but not consciously.

This kind of response is often used as yet another stalling technique. Once the patient has acknowledged a conscious awareness of the pattern, he can no longer use a lack of awareness as an excuse. The ways in which he was trying to fool both himself and the therapist had to be addressed head on.

Th: But is it or not?

Pt: Yes.

Th: You're saying that to make me happy, or you see it's a way of keeping a distance?

It is essential to determine whether the patient is really in agreement with the therapist or is just complying to avoid authentic involvement in the process.

Pt: I believe that what I'm doing is something that people like me do.

Th: Oh, my goodness.

Pt: You know, and probably ten other psychologists would know, that if I avoid your eyes, I'm trying to keep an emotional distance.

Th: But even now you are talking in a distant, hypothetical way. The verbiage is part of the barrier here. Rather than being direct and making contact, it gets in the way of us seeing what is really going on. Are you aware you avoid my eyes?

Pt: Yes.

Th: Is that a way you keep an emotional distance from me?

Pt: Yes, and I don't believe my answer.

Th: So, why is that? Do you see?

Pt: Yes, OK. I will accept it.

Th: You accept it, but I'm not sure.

Pt: But I'm not sure I'm doing it in order to . . .

Th: Not *why*, but *that* by avoiding eye contact, you keep a distance. And, also, by constantly ambivalating—maybe, maybe not, could be— this intellectual rumination is another way that you maintain your emotional distance. Now that you look at it, do you see that? Because a part of you is trying to communicate, but going on and on in an intellectual way with every "if, but, and wherefore" creates emotional distance.

Pt: I see it, but I have trouble feeling it.

The patient communicated very important information here. He was getting the point intellectually, but remaining emotionally detached. The therapist must persist with pressure on these defences until a genuine feeling emerges.

Th: We're talking about these mechanisms you use to keep detached. It creates a barrier between you and me. You come here physically and bring your intellect, but the emotional part of you is sealed away under layers and layers of concrete.

Pt: Alright (*smiles*).

Th: So we're not dealing with the full deck.

Pt: Granted.

Now that the patient sees the wall and the detachment, and how it is interfering with the therapeutic process, pressure is placed on the patient to do something about it.

Th: So what are we going to do about this cement—your aloof and emotionally detached stance?

Pt: Yes, I agree with you. If we could break through that, we could really accomplish something.

Th: So you see you've been keeping your distance, which will cripple this process.

Pt: Which is unconscious.

Th: But now you're conscious of it. Yet you hold onto this withdrawn, detached stance, hmm?

Pt: Yes.

Th: It's an impediment between you and me. As long as this continues, how will we reach your goal?

Pt: We won't.

Th: So the question is what you're going to do about it. Is there a desire to change?

Pt: Very definitely a desire to change.

Th: So you don't want to continue to live as the observer?

Pt: No.

Th: So what are we going to do about it?

Pt: Break through the concrete. I have to. What do I do about it?

Th: You're asking me? Now you go to helplessness. You are the architect and the builder. What are you going to do about this lack of emotional involvement?

Pt: But I don't know how.

Th: Now you ruminate.

Pt: I'm going to break through.

Th: So what is the feeling underneath?

Pt: I don't know. I have no feeling.

Crystallization of the resistance in the transference

The phase of pressure and challenge can be an arduous one. This man has been detached all his life—nearly 60 years—and will not stop without a struggle. The therapist must be willing to take the resistance head on and maintain the focus, targeting one layer of defence after the other, until they are all exhausted. Often, there is a signal from the unconscious that comes in the form of some kind of nonverbal communication, suggesting that feelings and impulses are ready to break through the defensive barrier. Patients might make a fist, kick their leg, or raise their voice as feelings of anger grow within them. Then, and only then, does the therapist switch the focus from defence and resistance to the underlying feeling and impulse, which are being expressed nonverbally.

Th: So you are still detached.

Pt: Yes.

Th: So what's going to happen to our time together?

Pt: Be non-productive.

Th: Was there some feeling in your voice right now?

Pt: Yes, anger.

Th: So how do you experience that anger inside?

Pt: A tenseness within me—almost wanting to become steely.

Th: That's not anger.

Pt: I want to jump out of my chair and yell.

Th: So there is some impulse to lash out. If that came out, in your imagination, how would that be?

Pt: Jump out of my chair, stand up and look down at you, tell you you're wrong.

Th: Do you see your hands?

Here the therapist is making use of an unconscious communication from the patient signalling that the impulse is ready to break through into consciousness.

Pt: Yes.

Th: What's the feeling in your hands?

Pt: No, nothing physical—just to yell and let off steam.

Th: But the anger is towards me. So if that came out, no holds barred?

Pt: I would stand up, yell, tell you you're wrong.

Th: But telling me I'm wrong is not a feeling.

Pt: I want to say it's a feeling like I have towards my mother, like I don't want to have anything to do with you.

The persistent pressure has resulted in tremendous progress—the patient spontaneously makes the link with the past, where, of course, all the trouble arose. Yet the therapist must not be deceived into taking this up, for the defence of avoidance is still very much present and must be challenged.

Th: That's not a feeling—it's a way to flee from the feeling.

Pt: To yell at you.

Th: That's not the experience of the feeling but a way to get away from it.

Pt: What is anger?

Th: Let's not go to a hypothetical discussion. If you were to declare this anger directly, what would that look like? (*Pause*) You deflate now.

Pt: Because . . .

Th: If we don't go to because and you weren't holding it in. . . . Again, you sigh. You let the anger deflate.

Pt: I 'm afraid. I'm afraid I could hurt you.

Finally, the patient's core conflict emerged in the transference. As we got through the defence and resistances to his underlying feelings and impulses, a great deal of anxiety got aroused. The patient got in touch with the fear of his own destructive impulses—unconsciously forecast in the very first interview, with his remark about doing "bodily damage" to a car.

The anxiety and guilt over these impulses has led to self-punishment, which must be made conscious.

Th: But who gets hurt? You detach from this impulse to hurt me and you hurt yourself, with anxiety, depression, and self-defeat.

By the end of this session, the patient was able to see how turning his anger inward resulted in procrastination and passivity, while depriving him of liveliness and the ability to assert himself. The goal of these interventions included turning his ego against these self-defeating defences and liberating his personality from the strictures of these oppressive forces. Changes were reported immediately following this session.

Freedom to feel and express emotion directly

There was a breakthrough away from the session, which was repeated in the session:

Pt: I have been aware of feeling anger towards you.

Th: OK. What was that like? What were you feeling inside?

In order for a patient to be considered "in touch with their feelings", all three elements of that feeling must be present: (1) the identification of the feeling; (2) physiological arousal associated with that feeling; and (3) mobilization of the accompanying impulses. If any one of these elements is missing, there are defensive processes in operation that must be removed. This particular man has tended to detach from the physiological sensations of his anger, remaining emotionally detached and paralysed in his functioning. While he could talk about anger and describe in some detail what he would like to do to the person he is angry with, he blocked the visceral sensations of that anger in his body. Before proceeding with a portrait of the impulse, the therapist needed to make sure the patient was actually in touch with the somatic experience of the anger he was declaring.

Pt: Yeah. I was feeling, uh, feeling of hot, kind of thing. I could feel flushed or something. I, I was saying things to myself that I would have said to you, had you been there. I was doing things to you that I wouldn't have done, had you been there.

Since it was clear the patient was actually experiencing the physiological sensations congruent with anger, we could proceed to the fantasy of expressing it, in this case, towards the therapist.

Breakthrough of rage in the transference

Th: But there was the fantasy—facing the impulses that went along with this anger.

Pt: Yeah. I felt I had worked it out.

Th: So do you want to let me see?

Pt: Yeah. I was angry at you because of what you said, that it might not work out, which really hit me. It was like somebody punching me in the gut. I thought that was something really mean and cruel to say to me. There's no reason to say something like that. That's thoughtless for you to say that.

Th: So there was anger towards me.

Pt: Yeah, and I realized there was an anger towards you and I wanted to grab you and shake you. I even reached the point where I wanted to throw you on the desk and rape you and when it was all over, wipe myself off on your skirt and walk out, the hell with it, and leave you like that.

Th: So, then, how would that go—you would pick me up . . .

Pt: Yeah, I would pick you up, shake you, grab you by the shoulders, I would throw you over, throw you on the desk, half rip your clothes off—uh, and not care if you enjoyed it or not, which I'm sure you wouldn't because it would be a vicious—something vicious and mean and nasty to you like you were nasty to me.

Th: Penetrating and assaulting.

Pt: Yes, I'd be going inside of you, just as you've been going inside of me, and afterwards . . .

Th: So how am I, lying there?

Pt: Yeah, uh, you look dishevelled. Your clothes are half torn. You were just laying there in a state of shock. Your face was really totally blank.

Th: Was there any struggle?

Pt: Uh, I don't remember. I just so overpowered—it was so quick.

Th: So you are bigger and stronger and just overpowered me, push me down, tear off my clothes, and rape me—and I'm stunned and what else? How do I look—am I beat up or bleeding?

Pt: No, no. It may sound contradictory that I'm assaulting you, yet I'm not assaulting you. I'm assaulting you but I'm not going to black-and-blue you.

Th: But it's a major assault.

Pt: I'm hitting you more in your mind than physically.

Even at this point in the process, the patient tried to back away from his own aggression (and guilt about it) by minimizing. The therapist must not collude with such manoeuvres but remain determined to face these primitive impulses unflinchingly.

Th: Oh, but you're attacking me physically too. What am I feeling, lying there, then?

Pt: I think you're feeling hurt and frightened of me . . . confused . . . and I think you just want me to get out.

Th: And your feeling, as you look at me, lying there?

Pt: It's a good kind of feeling.

Th: And the feeling towards me?

Pt: It's total indifference.

The issue of concern and compassion

While it is tempting to think that all defences will fall away once the impulses start to emerge, it doesn't always happen that way. I have found that there can be layers of defence against each new layer of feeling that emerges. In other words, it is possible to break through defences against rage, only to confront a layer of defence against the guilt and grief concerning the harm done to the other. The question of whether this patient's lack of guilt and remorse following the expression of aggression towards the therapist was due to conflict or deficit had to be put to the test. He had been diagnosed with a narcissistic personality disorder on the MMPI, and my experience with him certainly confirmed that clinical picture. One of the hallmarks of that disorder is an icy detachment from and contempt for the feelings of others. In order for the patient to recover, he needed to be able to experience guilt and concern for the other, as well as his rage and pain over loss and disappointment.

Carveth (2001) has suggested that the turning point in the treatment of narcissistic characters occurs "at the point of becoming ashamed of one's narcissism and incapacity to experience guilt". I believe that that is exactly what happened in this case and was, in fact, a turning point in his treatment and his life. This man's tendency to cut himself off from sad and tender feelings was as least as big a problem for him as his tendency to go limp in the face of his own anger. The therapist needed to work tenaciously in order to help him experience all of his intense and conflictual feelings towards others without resorting to defensiveness of any kind.

Th: So, if I had been raped and attacked and lying there dishevelled and torn apart, you would have no feeling.

Pt: No, no. What am I supposed to do, feel, feel . . . ?

Th: It's not about what you're supposed to do.

Pt: No, I have proven myself and I'm leaving now and the hell with you.

Th: What?

Pt: Look at my hands—they are shaking.

Th: Yes, and you take a big sigh. So, you say there is no feeling, but I'm not sure.

Pt: You mean feeling towards you as a result of that? Yeah, there's a feeling within me right now, I feel released. It is out of me. It's not internal. It's also . . . I have said things to you that, in the past I couldn't have said to you, because I would have been afraid you'd get angry at me or wouldn't like me or something, but now I can be honest and straightforward with you, even though it's not pleasant.

This last communication was extremely important. Even though it was very difficult, the patient was letting the therapist know how grateful he felt for the opportunity to speak honestly about "unpleasant" things. Weiss and his colleagues (1986) have done a great deal of process research that supports the idea that patients test the therapist constantly to see what she can handle, and they only venture forward if the therapist passes the test. In our current example, the patient was letting the therapist know that she passed the test.

Th: Uh huh, but again you take a deep sigh. What is the feeling?

Pt: Yes, because when I'm talking I'm not breathing and . . .

Th: It suggests there's some tension you're trying to get rid of.

Pt: No, no, not at all—other than I feel hot right now, I feel very relaxed. I get this out of me and it's almost, like, non-stop, without breathing. Now I can stop and breathe.

Th: OK, so there is this massive anger towards me and an assault in which there's kind of a merging of sexual and aggressive impulses.

Pt: Yeah, it's a way of hurting you—just like you hurt me.

Th: Yeah, and then you leave me there, and what happens then?

Pt: I don't know. It's the end.

Th: But what happens then?

Pt: What would have happened? *I would have had a great deal of regret afterwards* that I would do something that violent towards you. I realize that, if you were hurting me, I don't think you were hurting me intentionally. But I hurt you intentionally.

The defence of projection finally drops away. Prior to this session, when the patient felt anger that was not being fully faced, he projected his aggression onto the therapist, viewing her as mean and spiteful. It is useless to try to talk a patient out of this perception. However, facilitating the direct experience of anger will render these defences inoperable. In other words, experiencing the feeling directly and defending against it via projection are incompatible. Once the feeling is experienced, the defence of projection, along with the anxiety that had propelled its use, drops away naturally. After experiencing the rage fully, the patient's perception of the therapist was clarified. Once he faced his aggression without defensive justification, regret and sorrow followed.

It is essential to stick with the feelings and images involved in the portrait until all the layers of emotion are exposed and integrated. This drives home a point often misunderstood by those who are first introduced to this kind of work. Our goal is not simply to get patients in touch with their anger, but to face *all* the intense, mixed feelings they have defended against.

Th: So there is some feeling of regret.

Pt: Oh yeah. I have no right to physically assault you—to physically assault anyone. To do that is wrong.

Th: So there is some feeling towards me, about having hurt me.

Pt: Yeah, about having done wrong.

Th: Just about having done wrong—being a bad boy, or . . .

Pt: Well, that I've hurt you—that I've wronged you.

Th: So there are some positive feelings towards me, too?

Guilt and remorse are not negative emotions to be avoided. Feelings do not cause problems, defences against them do. Remorse is, in fact, a manifestation of love and reflects a capacity to care for and about another. It is the lack of such feelings (or lack of tolerance for them) in narcissistic and psychopathic patients that renders them pathological. In this man's case, facilitating the conscious experience of guilt and remorse was absolutely crucial to his well-being (as well as to those in close contact with him!). In the past, he defended against the experience of both his own feelings and the feelings of others. Only by facing his own aggression and hostility, and the feelings of guilt about them, could he get in touch with and acknowledge how much he cares about the other. This led to a significant softening of the edge in this man's demeanour.

Pt: Yeah, as I look back at it, I, I was more overwhelmed with regret over what I had done to you more than anything else, because I can't erase that from you. I can't take it back and say, OK, let's run this in reverse.

Th: No. So what would happen?

Pt: You can't. You can't back up time.

Th: Right. So you regret . . .

Pt: I regret what I have done.

Th: Yeah, because what effect would that have?

Pt: It would kill the professional relationship, that's for sure. I think also it would have the effect of making me feel that I had done something horribly wrong, because to physically hurt someone is wrong unless you're defending yourself—unless they are physically hurting you. All I'm doing is proving I may be stronger than you, but might doesn't make right.

Often there is a spontaneous link between the transference pattern of behaviour and the past, which emerges following a breakthrough of previously repressed emotion. If this does not take place automatically, the therapist can ask if anyone else comes to mind (especially when time is running out in the session!). In this case, I heard a covert link to the past, which I asked the patient about.

Th: Can you listen to what you're saying right now? Who are you talking to?

Pt: I don't know if I'm talking to you or myself.

Th: That "might doesn't make right"—that just because one is bigger and stronger doesn't give them the right to physically assault.

Pt: It also relates to my mother and me.

Th: Absolutely. In that case, she did actually physically assault you. And you're saying, that in that case there's an impulse to want to fight back. Have you ever had these kinds of feelings and impulses towards your mother?

Pt: To sexually assault her, no.

Th: But there is anger and a desire to lash out.

Th: Oh yes, but there was nothing sexual about it. I want to smash her body and leave her in the sewer to die alone.

We spent many subsequent sessions working on this reservoir of rage towards his mother [predicted in Hypothesis by both DM and JM]. He recalled how angry he felt when his mother would come visit him at camp. He had an impulse to throw her back in the bus and stomp on her until she was dead. He wanted her to die alone, as retribution for leaving him alone all those years. Of note, as he allowed himself to freely experience this rage towards his mother, more and more tender, loving feelings came to the surface, though not specifically towards her. It was as if his desires for closeness got liberated in the process of coming to terms with his feelings from the past. Previously, his desires for closeness were buried beneath this repressed rage. He was terrified to let anyone close to him, especially someone he cared about, like his wife, because that could trigger this murderous rage. He could "let go" only in anonymous sexual situations with strangers he didn't care about. Now he was able to tolerate and integrate all of these mixed feelings, so that he could have intimate relationships with others.

Emergence of compassion in his outside life

In the following session, he reported the experiences he had while visiting his extended family for the funeral of his brother-in-law, Abe. It should be noted that he not only reported feeling very different, but looked different too. By this time (40 sessions of therapy), he had lost 30 pounds and looked considerably younger and more attractive than he did when he started therapy (see chapter 11 for some objective evidence on this). These are the kinds of changes that often occur in ISTDP. While such changes are difficult to quantify or adequately describe on paper, they are of the utmost importance. Patients' entire look and demeanour can change drastically as their internal world gets reorganized. The loosening and dropping of defences often has a physical component. Patients become more relaxed and fluid and, frequently, more attractive. Certainly, that phenomenon occurred in this case (as it did in the case of the Woman with Dissociation).

Pt: I feel like a human being. I'm experiencing all kinds of feelings.

Th: So you really felt sad when you heard about Abe's death.

Pt: Yes. I was able to function, and yet, there was a sense of loss—a feeling of sadness.

Th: Yet with that, you didn't have to seal yourself off and go cold (*as he had with his parents' deaths*). You could be there with the others and with the kids.

Pt: There were a lot of people over at the house—friends of Lizzie's (*his wife*), and I didn't feel comfortable with them, so I was an observant bystander, but in terms of the family, I felt very close. Even with their grandchildren, who are both around 12, they felt very close to me and I felt very close to them, too.

Th: That must have meant a lot to you.

Pt: It did. It gave me an extended or expanded family. Now, I don't feel that way towards some other cousin's children, but I did with these children and their parents. I felt very close to Lizzie's sister-in-law, who was married to Abe's brother. She's a widow, and I felt very close to her. She's a dietician by training, and she took care of all the food preparation. Like, at 8 in the morning, she was, when everyone was still asleep, in the kitchen, preparing everything. You know, before I left, I went and hugged her and I called her a good soul.

There is a Yiddish term for it, "Gute neshome". I told her that, and I could feel my eyes misting over and my heart fill up. It felt good. Yeah, I find even just talking about things can move me to the point of tears. Like, we were talking about great experiences on television, and I remembered two that really moved. When I think about them today, it makes me want to cry as I'm relating it, which seems pretty stupid . . . but during the McCarthy hearings, the comments made by Joseph Welsh, one of the attorneys—how he spontaneously tore into McCarthy but did it in a very dignified and gentlemanly way.

Th: Uh-huh.

Pt: And then another time, I remember watching John Kennedy on television talking about the missile crisis in Cuba, and they were just riveting—they really touched me. When I look back at it, I realize they touch me more today than they did back then.

Th: Could you describe the emotion?

Pt: I want to burst out crying. . . . but I find I'm feeling that way now about a lot of things.

This is an enormous change. Early in the treatment, this man revealed he had not cried since childhood. Once he was sent away to "health camp", he shut down all his emotions and behaved in a cold, detached fashion. Now that his defences had "melted", he was becoming more truly human.

Th: Do you have any ideas—about this dignified man who won't let this man get away with this?

Pt: Have you even seen TV clips of it?

Th: Yes.

Pt: When McCarthy attacks one of Welsh's young lawyers and he claims he had been affiliated with some Communist front when he was in college, I remember Welsh saying, "Senator, have you no . . . have you no compassion . . . have you no dignity?" He was pleading quietly but very forcefully, and when it was all over you could see he had broken McCarthy. It was almost like a mountain crumbling in front of your eyes.

Th: So he put this man in his place, but without stooping to his level— there is something about that that touches you on a very personal level. Do you have any idea what that is for you?

Pt: No, I could come up with all kinds of theories. Do you?

Th: I have an idea.

Pt: What's your idea?

Th: OK, and you'll tell me if it sounds right. It's not to say that many people wouldn't find this very moving, but it's very personal for you too. Here is this man accusing people right and left with no evidence, and, for a long time, nobody would stand up to him or put him in his place, which sounds very much like your situation growing up. McCarthy is a stand-in for your mother, who would accuse you, calling you a Nazi and every other thing. And where was your father, or some other strong figure to come in and put her in her place?

[*This issue was predicted by JM, and hinted at by DM in terms of his father's ineffectiveness.*]

Pt: OK, so Welsh was my advocate. Now, how do we explain Kennedy's speech?

Th: Well, let's just stay with the first one for a minute (*both chuckle*). I think this is what you longed for and never had, and so to see—my God—people actually do that, stand up in the face of these bullies and, again, without being lowered to their level. There was never anyone to protect you.

Pt: Yeah, either that or, how it was said was so eloquent. I think sometimes, the Gettysburg address, there is an eloquence. Something else that has always moved me . . . have you seen the film, *To Kill a Mockingbird*?

Th: Uh-huh.

Pt: In the final scene there, one of the black ladies up in the balcony says to the little girl, "Stand up, your father's passin'". (*Choking up with tears*) Every time I see that, it's incredibly touching.

Unearthed beneath the anger, guilt, and grief he had avoided all these years came the yearnings for closeness—the poignant desire to have someone in his life to protect him and provide him with a healthy model of identification. During this session, the emotion in the room was quite charged and the interchange was very moving. There was a quality to his style of communication, and the nature of the interaction between us was completely new. It was a truly intimate interchange in which a free sharing of feelings and ideas flowed easily. This ushered in the consolidation phase of the therapy, in which the patient is helped to understand, as well as experience, his feelings and put it all in perspective.

Integrating sexual and loving feelings

A few sessions after the one just detailed, the patient made a comment about the therapist's appearance on the way out the door, saying she looked "sexy". The feelings behind this comment were pursued in the following session.

Th: So what were the feelings that generated that comment?

Pt: Well, I didn't see any need to bring it up.

Th: But these are no different from any other feelings.

Pt: Um, no, because most of my feelings towards you have not been sexual. They have been feelings of warmth, closeness, tenderness, and sharing. I would say that those feelings are completely separate from that entity called sexual feelings.

Th: Well, you try to keep them that way, that's something we know about you. (*The patient smiles*)

The patient's desire to keep his sexual feelings towards the therapist separate from his warm, loving feelings was a reflection of an internal split within him that has wreaked havoc over the years, as he had not been able to integrate sexual and loving feelings towards his wife.

Th: Actually, that's not the case here. It's not as if these feelings just popped up out of nowhere. It sounds like there's both warm, close feelings and a sexual attraction—it's not divorced from the way you feel about me.

Pt: Right.

Th: Are you just agreeing with me or do you see what I'm saying?

Pt: I see it. . . . No, because I'm clear about the ground rules, that there could be no physical contact between us, I mean, that would be the end of it. I think because of that, maybe I have taken it and suppressed.

Th: Even the feelings, you mean. But it's like with any other feeling. Just because you're mad at me, doesn't mean you're going to bop me over the head. So the important thing is that we honestly discuss and face all the feelings and fantasies, because it sounds like you considered this off base.

Pt: Yes, because I felt that if I had sexual fantasies about you it would cause this to fall apart. I don't know.

Th: How do you imagine that?

Pt: I don't know, because sex involves contact.

Th: But we're talking about feelings and fantasies. You're afraid that if you even let yourself feel it . . . I mean, it's like with anger, we're not talking about you acting on it. If you told me that you had sexual feelings and fantasies, then that would ruin it somehow.

Pt: I don't know if it's telling you, or even just having them would ruin it.

Th: How would that happen?

Pt: I don't know. I think it would destroy something. Maybe I idealize you and, in so doing, take the sexual aspect and throw it out or try to deny it or suppress it or whatever. Now I'm sitting here thinking, what if you were my therapist and you were 77 years old—would I have those feelings?

Th: But it is what it is and you do have feelings towards me, so could we look at those?

Pt: I feel like I want to be close to you.

Th: And in your imagination, how do you want to express those feelings?

Pt: I want to put my arms around you. I would like for you to hold my hands. I'd like for us to be away from here.

Th: Tell me how you see this, then, this fantasy. Last session you commented on my physical appearance, and it's associated with these warm feelings towards me, with a desire to be close physically. So how does that go?

Pt: How do I see the closeness?

Th: You would just approach me, or . . . ?

Pt: We're not here, I know that. The feeling of closeness that I have to you is . . . I, I would like to be standing next to you and put my arms around you and just hold you close to me. We'd walk out of here holding hands, not saying anything.

Th: No words.

Pt: Just sharing the warm feelings. Obviously, you're responding to me and so you're feeling what I'm feeling, which is warmth, tenderness, closeness, and we go out of here. We get in my car and we drive somewhere, maybe to a restaurant, where we have dinner. There's candle light, and we talk about books, movies, politics, music . . . we're not talking about me, and in a sense we're talking about you, because I'm learning what you like, what you don't like, that kind of warm, comfortable sharing. Afterward we go someplace, I don't know where. The next thing I see, it's the next morning. I wake up and you're next to me and I have my arm around you.

Link between transference pattern of behaviour and that with his wife (T–C link)

Th: So you block out what happens between dinner and waking up in the morning. Isn't this the same thing that's happening with your wife? You've been able to develop a really warm, close relationship with her. You enjoy all kinds of things together. It's a rich relation-

ship except for sex, which you've been skipping over. So there's
something getting in the way of having those warm, close feelings
along with intimate sexual feelings.

Pt: 'Cause sex has never been an intimate, close thing for me.

This was a new awareness for the patient, who had always objected to
such suggestions from the therapist. Now he was very aware of the
ways he has kept sex and intimacy apart.

Th: But now those feelings emerge as a spontaneous outgrowth of
warm, tender feelings.

Pt: So how do I visualize that? I visualize that as my not thinking that
"Hey, I'm going to screw her" but that my being with you—just the
warmth and closeness of our undressing each other, and maybe not
even having sexual feelings at that point but just feeling even closer
without clothes than with clothes. . . .

  I think the closeness and the warmth and the love between us
starts to develop a sexual arousal where I don't think it's about
fucking you but a matter of feeling even closer to you. Without
clothes it's closer, and in bed and being in you is even closer, too. I
don't want to . . . I don't even think of anyone else, it's just a matter
of thinking about you, being with you and being happy to not have
any third person there.

Th: That's a first, huh?

Pt: Uh-huh. And . . . just . . . and ultimately, when it's all over and we're
both lying there exhausted, it's not a matter of wanting to get
dressed and up and leave, but it's a matter of being with you even
more. And, I feel incredibly happy, and I don't have the feeling of
"another one . . . just another woman that I fucked". I don't have
those thoughts and feelings.

Th: What is the feeling?

Pt: It's a feeling of incredible happiness. I have shared all of me, honestly, with you, and whatever I feel is a mirror image of what you
feel.

Th: You feel accepted, and responded to in kind?

Pt: Yeah, I'm not working at it, I'm not . . . I remember saying to my
wife recently, when I fucked other women it was almost like I was
physically in the bed but mentally I was like a ghost standing on the
side of the bed watching everything very dispassionately.

If you recall, the patient adamantly denied that he was detached in these
sexual encounters when we began to investigate them in the first session. Now he spontaneously reports his own awareness of the split
within him. This awareness underscores the change in him. In the past, a

detached, numbed state seemed normal for him. He knew nothing else, so it didn't stand out. Now the detachment strikes him as odd, revealing how dystonic those old defences had become. The fact that he shared this awareness with his wife was also significant and spoke to his expanded capacity for intimacy and closeness.

Th: Very detached.

Pt: Yeah, I don't feel that way now.

Th: So you are able to integrate all these feelings and share them freely, rather than detaching and splitting and depersonalizing the whole thing.

De-repression of memories from the past

In the next session, the following material emerged spontaneously.

Pt: After our last session, driving home, I thought back to my adolescence and how I would put girls and women I liked and admired on a pedestal. I had no sexual feelings towards them—I idealized them.

Th: And are you saying that's how you were regarding me too?

Pt: Yes. It's like you were too good for ordinary fucking. I separated the two.

Th: Yes, separating fucking and making love and between Madonna and whore. But, in the last session you imagined, and I think felt, what it would be like to be sexual with someone you care about.

Pt: Did you see the show, *LA Law*, last week? There was a scene between Arnie and a therapist. The therapist said, "You use sex to avoid intimacy". I thought, "Bingo. That's what I did". As I think about it, after that experience last week, I began to realize how much that was true. Last week I experienced sex in an affectionate, loving way rather than merely a physical activity. I guess, because of how I approached it with my partners, there was no intimacy involved.

Th: To keep them separate is a way to deal with an internal conflict.

Pt: You said something last week about the relationship I have with my wife now—it's so close and I enjoy giving, but I haven't been feeling sexual attraction towards her.

Th: And we could see that, initially, that's how you described the fantasy of a relationship with me—that we had this lovely dinner and then you skipped to the next morning. What you blanked out was the sexual feelings. Now, is this a problem for you? Do you want to be able to feel sexual attraction and desire for your wife, whom you also love?

Pt: Yes I do. I realize I keep myself from intimacy. That is a hard-hitting truth.

Th: So we need to understand and get to the bottom of this need to keep these feelings separate.

Pt: The question I've wondered about is why I've been so driven to have all these sexual partners. *I think that I was driven by anger towards women because of all the anger towards my mother . . .*

[*Predicted in the Hypothesis by DM in terms of "an immense reservoir of anger . . . possibly directed against women in general".*]

Also seeking out the closeness and affection I craved but never got from her. I think they're both involved.

Th: I think you're right. Somehow the sexual and aggressive feelings have gotten closely tied. There's a terrific need and desire for closeness, and incredible anger because those needs were thwarted. So it was no real surprise when your anger towards me was initially expressed as a rape. That also makes sense of why it's been so hard to feel intensely sexual with a woman you love, because sexual feelings have been so suffused with anger and aggression. So you idealize the woman you love and siphoned off the aggression with these other women. My sense is that the hunger in you to be loved and cared for is so great, you'll take it wherever you can get it. One way that you can feel responded to is by attracting women. I think you have sexualized that need to be noticed, loved, and responded to.

Pt: Yeah, I think it's a desperate need for caring. I guess I grew up in an environment where sexuality was hidden—affection, too, for that matter. It's sort of like, when a woman would be open sexually, it really felt like she was giving to me. I remember many, many times, when they would just touch my face, it was electrifying.

Th: It sounds like that's what you were so hungry for—that touch, to be cared for, and some concrete proof of their caring for you. You channelled this sexually, but I'm not sure it filled the need, and so it wasn't satisfied in that way. You would need another one and another one. You also threatened your primary relationship and could have lost the woman you love.

Pt: I remember that night we stayed up all night talking, once it all came out about my affairs. It was then that I realized I have something amazing here, and things began to change in our relationship. I began to realize she's a remarkable person. She never became hysterical—we really talked and got much closer.

Th: But still, somehow, you keep a distance and don't allow yourself to be sexually open with her.

Pt: I'm aware that I've taken sexuality and split it off from closeness and sharing. It was a mechanical process for me. I have a feeling it's a combination of all these reasons. And I think that . . . it's because I'm just learning how to feel towards other people and in response to other people too. I wasn't capable of it. The feelings I have towards my wife and children are much more intense now and I enjoy them a great deal, even though it could develop even further.

This is another phase of consolidation, resulting in a deepening understanding of his own development. There is a pattern of intense work at experiencing previously warded-off feelings, followed by cognitive understanding in light of these feelings. While the experience of the feelings is an essential prerequisite to this kind of insight, Pennebaker (1991, 1997) has found that it is this new understanding of themselves that patients find most helpful in the end.

Towards termination: the severity of his former depression

Pt: What I'm going to get into today is very difficult. What started it all was, after our session last week, I saw on the TV news that a local teenager had just committed suicide. Apparently, his best friend had committed suicide about six weeks earlier. The report said that suicide is considered a form of punishment for those left behind. Then, I woke up at 3 in the morning and I started to think—things came to me in waves. When I came to you originally, it had been the third or fourth major bout with depression that I've had. Have you ever been really depressed over a period of time, like I did?

Th: I don't think I've ever had a clinical depression. I've certainly had low mood but not the sleep or appetite disturbance.

Pt: I had the sleep problem, anxiety, feelings of helplessness, sadness. I had a great deal of pain. It was a physical pain and also it was mental pain, and I got to thinking, when I was driving over here, that I've never really experienced the loss of someone I cared for deeply, because I'd never been able to care for anyone deeply before. But thinking about people who experience loss like that, you look at their face and you can see it's almost distorted with pain. It's not a physical pain, but you see it.

This is a remarkable statement. He realizes how incapable he was of caring for others. He now sees pain in others and has empathy and compassion for them. Previously, he expressed contempt for anyone who had feelings, as if they were weak and pathetic. This reveals the extent of character change that has occurred during this year-long treatment.

Th: That pained look.

Pt: When I first came to you, I had already sold our house downtown and had made arrangements to move to the townhouse. The townhouse had one advantage the house in the city didn't have—it had a garage. Between the time I was referred to you and when I came to see you, I had made myself a bargain: I would give myself six months—a year at the most—and if it didn't help, I was going to go into the garage, turn on the car and commit suicide. The pain, to me, was something that I just couldn't bear. It was . . . it's tough to describe it. If you would try to explain to me the pain of giving birth to a child, I couldn't really feel it.

Th: Well, you could try. Could you try to describe the pain you felt?

Pt: It was a pain where I . . . I couldn't open my eyes. It seemed like everything was overwhelming. Every movement hurt. It was like a physical pain . . . to move, to turn the page of a book, to talk with people, to do anything—even go shopping—it hurt. And there was such a feeling of lassitude to it that even picking up a knife, a fork, or a spoon was such an effort. It was such an effort I wanted to give up or cry out. I didn't know what to say or who to cry out to, but it was a physical and mental pain. It just—doing anything—hurt. You know, I'm feeling some of it right now, as I talk with you about it. I had been through this at least three times, maybe four. I had decided I'd work with you for six months to a year and if it wasn't any better, that was it. It wasn't something that happened periodically, it was there 100% of the time when I started with you. Naturally I was down, and it got worse because of how you were at the time. I think if you had been a man it would have affected me differently. Because you were a woman, it was like my mother yelling at me or finding fault with me and it was like, Oh no, I'm back there again. You seemed antagonistic but I needed and wanted someone to . . . to help me and I really felt that I wasn't getting it. It's like if someone falls and breaks a leg and someone says, God damn it, get up and walk anyway. It doesn't make someone feel better. I ended up feeling worse initially, and I didn't think I could feel worse. We moved into the house, and every time we pulled into the garage, especially if I was by myself, I used to think I could do it. It was too much for me to cope with. I don't know what happened or why. I never said, "OK, now" and I never said, "Don't do it". Maybe I couldn't make a decision, but then . . . I don't know exactly when . . . but things started to change between us. I started to change and I think you changed too. That overwhelming thought and the overwhelming pain wasn't there, and things started changing for me.

Today I'm a lot different as a person. I thought about it on Sunday night when I went out to dinner with my wife. We sat down, and she saw her hairdresser. We went over to say hello, and her mother was there with her too. I feel so comfortable with people now that I said, "Hey, why don't you come over and we'll all have dinner together." In the past, I never would have done that. I enjoyed being with people, talking with the mother and daughter, and I realized, this isn't the old me. (*Big smile*) Yeah, I'm very happy with how I'm turning out. I don't think I'm finished—I'm still evolving. Last Thursday or Friday morning, this all came back to me.

Th: After hearing this piece on the news?

Pt: The despair. When it was coming back to me, it wasn't just recalling it, I could feel waves of tears welling up within me. I came close to crying. I didn't, but it felt as if I was.

Th: Can I stop you for a minute? I don't know how much is showing, but I feel very moved. I feel almost overwhelmed by what you're telling me. This wave of emotion—close to tears—is getting communicated, like an emotional resonance. The full impact didn't hit until you began to tell me about the experience in the restaurant. I think it's the contrast—to see that enormous change in you, compared to how desperate you were and how the . . . the word I kept thinking of was heavy . . . it felt so heavy—not acute pain but every movement is difficult and like you were really weighted down. The trust you put in me . . . I feel honoured and blessed that we could do this together—to have an impact on your life.

Pt: (*Quiet, nodding, and attentive*) I thank you for saying that. How I feel about you, towards you . . . because of what I'm like now, compared to then, it's, for me, incredibly beautiful. Now I see people around and I notice their pain and depression—the furrowed brow. You can't just take an aspirin for it. It's difficult to express how much I feel about how much you've helped me, and what we've gone through together. . . . I felt at times, in the beginning, that you were like my mother.

Th: Let's go back and look at that. When you talk about the beginning of the treatment and your sense that you got worse, rather than better, my thought is, that's not uncommon. It goes that way a good deal of the time because the despair that was there has a kind of numbing quality—so it's turning the chronic pain into something acute. So, I agree that there are ways to focus and get down to work without being abrasive, and there may have been a quality to my early work with you that may have seemed that way, but I remember you saying it was mixed. If it was just negative, you wouldn't have come back. I remember you saying you didn't like it but you felt some kind of confidence that we were going to get somewhere. You said (*at the end of the trial therapy*) you were glad you had come.

Pt: I wasn't used to the interaction. I was used to "Ah-huh", "and tell me more". I found myself frightened of you, as I was frightened of my mother.

Th: Or frightened of the feelings towards her and me?

Pt: I never had the feeling that it was getting worse by doing this—it was painful. If a doctor has to treat you with something painful in order to make you better, that's what you have to do. That's what it was like. But, you're right, I had the feeling you knew what you were doing.

Th: And given the experience you've had with your mother, there was no way around it. You were going to have angry feelings towards me, and they had to get faced. As we faced them towards me, it got linked to your mother and was drained over time. There were also real ways in which we changed over time in regard to your changing needs. . . . I never knew it was as bad as you're telling me today. You never told me about the depths of your despair or feeling suicidal. Are you aware of that?

Pt: It was, first and foremost, very difficult for me to be forthright with anyone about what I was feeling. I was always "Joe Cool".

Th: To know now that this was your last hope.

Pt: Well I had been through two or three extended therapies before and they hadn't helped, so I thought, if you don't help, that's it. I lucked out—I really lucked out. I had no idea, when I went to the clinic, that they would refer me. You just triggered a thought . . . you indicated before that you've felt down before and everybody has those and . . . I don't know what that's called, but the clinical depression, where you're in it a long time and can't get out of it, is despair. To say I was in despair is more accurate.

Th: You said it was going to be hard, even today, to tell me about it.

Pt: Recalling it and reliving it. This is what came to mind, and I'm sure this will have all kinds of implications, but it's like burning your hand. If you burned your hand a year ago and then you go back to describe it, the pain will come back. But now, when I talk about it, it comes out of me and it's a relief.

This is more evidence of the change within him. He can no longer detach and just tell me a story. When he talks about the pain he's experienced, he feels it. Then there is connection and relief. The reference to the burned hand is highly significant. He always remembered that incident with his mother but had numbed himself to the feelings and created a cold, calculating façade in his interactions with others. As much as he feared these feelings initially, and as painful as it was to face them, the effects of having done so are obvious.

Th: I'm really glad you told me. I had no idea your despair was of that magnitude.

Pt: Like what Churchill called, "The Black Dog". I saw the book by Styron (*about the experience of clinical depression*) just a week ago, but I thought, I don't need to read that—I've been there and I've come out the other side.

The therapy came to a natural close as all his feelings became accessible and he found ways to be open and loving with others. His work was going well; so well, in fact, that he had more business and higher revenues than ever before. All his symptoms had been removed and every defence replaced with a healthy alternative.

During our final session, the patient gave me a gift—a copy of Harper Lee's *To Kill a Mockingbird.* The inscription directed me to the page on which the family's housekeeper, Calpurnia, says to Scout (the young girl who serves as the narrator), "Stand up, your father's passin'". He told me that this was the way he felt about me. He no longer idealized or devalued me, but respected me as a person whom he held in both esteem and affection. I was deeply moved by this and shared that with him. There was a celebratory feel to this final session, as is often the case in ISTDP. Both parties have worked hard at a desired goal and feel a tremendous sense of accomplishment and camaraderie as treatment comes to an end.

A week or so later, I received a call from the patient's wife, asking if she could come to see me. She assured me that she had spoken to her husband, who was in favour of the idea. She came to express her gratitude for the help I had provided her husband and went on to provide additional data concerning the dramatic changes in him. Her report underscored the impact this individual work can have on those intimately connected with the patient. Just as the patient's symptoms and defences can have such a damaging effect on others, their internal changes often have a healing effect on relationships. This man, who had been a cool, detached father, was now the first one on the floor with the grandchildren.

Follow-up

The follow-up took place 18 months after termination. The Criteria were formulated by DM and JM, both of whom were blind to therapy after the first two interviews.

Criteria

[1] DM: Anxiety and depression to be replaced by enjoyment and effectiveness.
JM: To get a more positive feeling of self-worth. Lifting of depression. Increased self-acceptance and confidence.

> Pt: "There's a real change in me. It's a deep change, though it's hard to describe."
>
> "I'm a different person and I'm much happier. I've come to the realization that I'm human. There are times when I get anxious or down about things, but I feel it and it passes. I feel more in control of my life. I'm doing a lot more business and that's helped my confidence. I feel differently—I'm more involved in life."
>
> "I have more confidence in myself as a person. I've got a retirement date set for next year. I've done substantially more business in these last few years, which is why I'm able to retire early and still be financially secure. We've decided to move so as to be closer to the family. And I'm looking forward to doing some work I really love,

something with music (*his eyes widen and his face glows*). No more pressure, just pleasure.

His weight: This was not included in the Criteria, but it needs to be mentioned:

> Pt: "I've kept the weight off, and I exercise regularly. I lift weights and feel strong. I'm proud of myself."

[2] DM: Emotional closeness and commitment to his wife.
JM: Increased closeness to wife and family.

[3] DM: Improvement in sexual performance and enjoyment, with loss of the need for extramarital relations.
JM: Improved sexual functioning.

> Pt: "My wife and I get along very well. I feel very close to her. We've been taking full advantage of the Albany area before we leave—going to New York City, concerts, museums, restaurants, and so on.
> "I'm not so angry any more, especially with my wife. I'm understanding. I no longer need to have affairs. I don't need to prove myself. Sexually, I'm able to function very well—not just mechanically. I'm there and involved. Even if I'm not sure about my erections, it doesn't matter. We can talk about it. At times, I'm so happy with the closeness we have, I don't care so much if it's not wild sex."

The therapist wrote that at this point in the interview, she needed to "find out if there's any way in which he's toning down the intensity of sex and settling for less than he can have":

> Th: Maybe it's not wild, but is it satisfying?
> Pt: It's certainly very pleasurable. It's a great experience when we get going. It's not as often as it used to be, but it's open, and close, and satisfying. We talk a lot more now, and I find that quite stimulating, too. I make love to her in lots of ways. Even when we're sitting in a concert hall and listening to music, when I take her hand and hold it, it's a great experience and a good feeling. There is physical and emotional closeness.

[4] DM: Ability to replace his inappropriate potential violence with realistic anger in appropriate situations, and the ability to assert himself constructively:
JM: Ability to express anger appropriately.

For this Criterion, there is little direct evidence. He described above how he was "not so angry any more", whereas at the initial interview he had said he was angry all the time. Also, he must be able to assert himself, or he would not have been able to do so well at work.

[5]   DM: Increased effectiveness and enjoyment at work.
JM: Resolution of anxieties about work and going to work. Loss of physical symptoms.

> Pt: "I feel calm and confident. I don't need to prove myself, even at work. Things are going really well there. I've done so well that I can plan for retirement now. That feels great."

[6]   DM: Much greater closeness with his children and grandchildren.
JM: Increased closeness to wife and family. Ability to feel and express emotional warmth appropriately.

> Pt: "I recently went out to visit my girls (*he has four grown daughters*) and to meet my new granddaughter. I feel close to them and can show them affection. We had a marvellous time—I so enjoyed them and even got down on the floor to play with the baby, so very different from the time I went to see them when I first came to you."

General criterion

DM: To lose his defences; to develop the ability to feel appropriate emotions and to act on them constructively, leading to a benign circle of *getting* and *giving* satisfaction and fulfilment. This should apply especially to softer feelings such as love, grief, tenderness, compassion, and joy.

It shines through the whole interview that he has lost his defences against feeling. He has clearly been able to feel and express love and tenderness with his wife and to set up a benign circle with her. He has also set up a benign circle at work.

He was able to express gratitude, empathy, and compassion towards the therapist:

> Th: How did this change (*in his relationship to his wife*) occur?
> Pt: It was the work we did. Really, you did the work and I benefited.
> Th: But you did a great deal of work yourself . . . You also helped me to help you. You communicate in a rich way. I have found you compelling to work with.
> Pt: Wow, that's really nice to hear. I'm taking that in and just glowing . . . But chemistry was there too. I had several other therapies, and they might have helped a little, but nothing like what happened here between us. . . . I was a little worried when you called because you sounded tentative somehow It almost seemed like you were

embarrassed to call and ask me to come in for the follow-up. It reminded me of how I used to feel when I was "cold calling". . . . In the past I couldn't really be bothered with people. Now I really enjoy people.

There is no direct evidence from this interview concerning grief and compassion, but the whole atmosphere suggests that he would be able to experience these feelings in appropriate circumstances, and we know from therapy that he is capable of both compassion and tenderness.

SUMMING UP

There is overwhelming evidence that this man, who suffered from a "narcissistic personality", has been converted into a normal, sensitive, loving, sympathetic, self-confident, and effective human being. No trace of the original narcissism could be detected.

Level 3 evidence (the "level of authenticity")

The following features fulfil the criterion of "authenticity":

1. From being hardly able to get himself to work, or to function when he got there, he has done so well that he is now able to retire early, with financial security. This evidence is objective.
2. His description of holding his wife's hand at a concert.
3. His description of getting down on the floor to play with the baby— which would have been unthinkable as he was when he first came.

Final judgement

This can only be: "total resolution".

Additional note

A disadvantage of this method of assessing outcome, without any knowledge of what happened in therapy, is that there may be evidence in the therapy itself with great relevance to follow-up. With this patient, the following parts of the therapy are highly relevant to both of two aspects of the General Criterion—namely, Level 3 evidence of his ability to feel both *grief* and *compassion*.

In the session following the "breakthrough" session in which in fantasy he assaulted the therapist, he spoke of a relative whom he had met at a family funeral, saying that he had gone and hugged her and, "I could feel my eyes misting over and my heart fill up. . . . I find even just talking about things can move me to the point of tears." To confirm this with objective evidence: later in the same session he spoke about the passage from *To Kill a Mockingbird*, and at this point his tears were so intense that he became choked with them. Moreover, he gave her a copy of this book in the final session.

In a late session he described the pain of his depression, and he went on to speak of people who had experienced loss: "you look at their face and you can see it's almost distorted with pain." His depression had involved almost overwhelming physical lethargy and explicitly formulated suicidal plans. This has now been converted into obvious happiness and self-confidence.

CHAPTER 6

The Good Girl with Ulcerative Colitis

Initial interview—trial therapy

We enter the trial therapy of the Good Girl with Ulcerative Colitis (single, age 34) blind to the patient's difficulties and begin by asking about the problems that lead her to seek treatment.

Th: Tell me what brings you.
Pt: What brings me is a discontentment with my life, in the sense that it's not all I want it to be. In particular, my relationships with men— that's in the forefront, though it's not simply due to that. In the realm of work, given my professional goals, I'm not fully actualizing them, but I wouldn't have come here simply on account of that. I also know enough about therapy to know that what I think is the problem may really be a mask, but what I'm conscious of is a dissatisfaction with my personal life. I'm often in a good mood. Today I'm in a good mood, but it seems that what will bring me down and cause sadness in me is my recent inability—by recent, I mean the last few years—to develop a relationship with a man that is full blown and sustained.
Th: You made an interesting comment—that today you're in a good mood but that you frequently get sad. I noticed—and wondered if you were aware of it—that as you talked about the dissatisfaction with your life, you had a smile on your face.
Pt: That kind of incongruity—yes.

Th: So, what's the smile then?

Pt: The smile is probably just my discomfort with really facing up to the true anguish and true pain it causes me, and I know I tend to put the best face on everything, including, quite literally, my face.

Th: So you have some awareness that you tend to cover up these deep, painful feelings.

Pt: That's right, I think that's right.

Th: And the smile is part of that.

Pt: Yes. And on different levels, I think my training as a woman in my family, the way I was brought up . . . that there is/was a discomfort with deep, painful feelings and really evincing them in their true form. I've noticed that at times. It's hard to say how, but I notice the contours of my face, even.

Th: You have this training . . . you're aware that, in your family . . .

Pt: It's not wholly denial, but I get this feeling that I'm not supposed to be "down".

Th: So are you saying that you're a good girl—you go along with that. You're out of the house now, I assume, but you tend to automatically put on the happy face.

Pt: This is interesting. I've never worked with a woman therapist before. I think it comes out more immediately with you. It's hard to know. With men, I think a truer range of my feelings can come out. I tie it to my Mum and wanting to please and a sense that I need to conform, whereas with men—even though it's trouble with men that compels me in here—I feel more comfortable on some basic level, with me being up when I'm up and down when I'm down— just crying and getting angry—the whole range. It's not to say everything comes out with them, but it's a fuller range.

Th: You have some awareness that you're more comfortable with men and more likely to smile, put on the happy face, be pleasing and conforming with women.

Pt: More of a sense of being what you said—the good girl—doing everything right . . . whereas with men I feel more latitude.

Th: So what was it like coming here, knowing you'd be seeing a woman today?

Pt: You know, you inspired confidence on the phone somehow. I feel frightened, but I'd feel frightened even with a man. Therapy elicits a full range of feelings in me, from the excitement of discovery to the fear of what I'm going to find out. I'm aware of some of the pain in me, but I know the process of therapy can reveal to me things about myself that I just don't know. So the feelings about coming today weren't tied into gender but were just about therapy. And that does, in me, elicit fear.

Th: So you were aware of some fear. Tell me how you experience that inside.

Pt: You know, I say I feel fear, but at this moment, and when I woke up, I was feeling good today. Something I think is important for you to know is that I have a chronic intestinal condition called ulcerative colitis. I don't know if you know anything about it.

The patient begins by articulating her presenting complaint, which involves an inability to create and sustain a loving relationship with a man. She is articulate and psychologically minded, revealing a capacity to observe herself and reflect on feedback given by the therapist. These are strengths and reveal the presence of an unconscious therapeutic alliance. However, the examination of her experience of anxiety revealed a serious medical condition (ulcerative colitis). This condition is a warning to the therapist that anxiety is poorly tolerated and channelled into the gut. The use of a graded approach will be required to protect against any exacerbation of symptoms.

Further examination of her symptoms revealed several important facts. Her father died 20 years ago, when she was 14 years old, and her first bout of ulcerative colitis was precipitated by the ending of a romantic relationship—a pattern of loss often noted in patients with this disorder (Lindemann, 1944). Her condition was so severe that she had to be hospitalized on several occasions and was being maintained on potent steroids to manage her symptoms. At the time of the initial evaluation, she was off steroids but still complained of urgency, frequency, pain, diarrhoea, and bleeding. The treating physician dismissed her concerns about emotional triggers and told her she was "over-psychologizing" her illness. Despite this, she initiated therapy on her own.

Examination of the Triangle of Conflict

Th: We can see that there was some anger with the doctor for being dismissive—and you have a tendency not just to be nice, to be the good girl and compliant, but you have a difficult time with your own angry feelings—so it's driven, as it were, by the tendency to avoid the experience of the anger and wanting to please the other person.

Pt: What would be the motivation for me to avoid that? I'm aware I'm hesitant to reveal the anger and to upset the apple-cart.

Th: You don't want to get the other person upset?

Pt: It would be the end.

Th: Oh.

Pt: But you said it was driven on two counts—one, by my not wanting to jeopardize the relationship, but the other would be not to experience it myself. Why would I do that?

Th: It looks like there are defences, if you want to use a technical term, that you employ to avoid your own anger, as well as defending against letting anyone else know about it, which is more of what we've been talking about so far—you covering it up with a smile and being pleasing and so forth. Still, you have your own reasons for wanting to avoid facing your own anger.

Pt: What I'm aware of is being blank, in terms of avoiding it myself. I'm afraid it will jeopardize my relationships, I know that, but I'm blank as to why I'd want to avoid it.

Th: We don't know. At this point, rather than speculate about it intellectually, what's important is that we go for the experience of the anger and then we'll see what's there. What you're most aware of is being afraid it will lead to loss. As I say that, a sad look comes across your face.

Pt: No, I'm not aware of it. I'm only conscious of feeling . . .

Th: What?

Pt: My father comes to my mind.

Th: So there's something about jeopardizing a relationship that connects with your father?

Pt: I don't know if it's because of this anniversary or what. This is probably just intellectual, I don't know if it's just the temporal juxtaposition or what . . . but I just really miss my father.

Th: What does it feel like inside?

Pt: Really sad. I feel it in my head. I just feel so sad, really sad (*crying*).

While grief over loss is very real, this vignette reveals the patient's tendency to replace anger with anxiety and sadness, rendering her vulnerable to depression.

Examination of transference pattern of behaviour

Later in the interview the therapist suggested a five-minute break, after which the patient spoke as follows:

Pt: I feel drained. I feel sobered. I'm also aware of how I feel about you and our interactive style. It's a complicated double feeling. On the one hand, I'm finding it useful; on the other hand, I'm feeling irritated. I'm resenting that you're the one . . . I'm saying it's necessary and I'm feeling the necessity of it, but I'm also conscious of the resentment.

Th: So there's some irritation towards me. How do you experience this irritation inside?

Pt: Why can't I say what I feel towards you? You're not telling me about *your* life. It doesn't matter that rationally I know you're not here to tell me about you, and frankly I don't care, but I have this resentment that it's *my* pain that's being unearthed and it's me and my complexity, ME that's being commented on—feeling like an object in some way. You're drawing attention to certain things I do that I might not be conscious of—I recognize that rationally. I'm just telling you, viscerally . . .

Th: But you don't like it.

Pt: I don't like it. I mean, you don't tell me about your life and I don't really want to know. It doesn't matter, but it's the same discomfort I have being called a patient—any position of powerlessness makes me uncomfortable. Then I ask myself why.

Th: Well, let's not go to why yet, because you have a tendency to go to your thoughts. I asked you how you experienced your irritation, and you tell me about your thoughts—not the feeling.

Pt: Why is that not the feeling?

Th: Those are thoughts.

Pt: How would I experience the feeling? Maybe I don't experience the feeling! To me, that thought is the feeling.

In this vignette, the patient gets in touch with the extent of her own defences against the visceral experience of her feelings—specifically, how she has mistaken thoughts for feelings. The tendency to mistake the defence (intellectualization) with the feeling itself is characteristic of patients who require restructuring. As long as symptoms and defences are mistaken for the feeling itself, any pressure to feel will result in an increase in symptoms, defence, and resistance. The first therapeutic task involves making the distinction between the actual experience of emotion and the ways the patient avoids that very thing. In the previous vignette, the patient began to realize, for the first time, that she has mistaken thoughts for feelings. This opens the door for an exploration of the feelings she has been avoiding.

This work is aimed at consolidating the insight into the ways in which her internalization of anger has resulted in anxiety, depression, and intestinal symptoms. The goal here is to expand her capacity to experience anger towards others without internalizing it and becoming symptomatic. In addition to these internal changes, the patient wanted to replace her people-pleasing manner of interacting with others with honesty and self-assertion, so that she would be able to develop and sustain intimate relationships. Her ability to observe her own defences and to begin to turn on them, along with her strong will to get well, were signs of capacity and allies in the treatment process. So, despite the serious nature of her physical illness, I decided to take her on. Remember, it is the patient's response to intervention, more than history or factual information, that determines suitability for treatment.

Summary of the trial therapy

As already noted, the patient complained of anxiety with intestinal symptoms, a tendency towards depression, conflicts in the area of intimacy and closeness, and some sense that she was not functioning as well as she could in her professional and creative life. After getting an advanced degree from an Ivy League college, she worked in New York City at a very prestigious firm. She was ambitious and hard working, hoping to climb the corporate ladder quickly. However, her illness became so debilitating that she gave up life on the fast lane and came to Albany, where she could practise her profession in a more relaxed fashion. She had written both prose (first published at the age of 12) and music as a young woman, but she had been creatively blocked for over a decade. In these ways, she felt she was not living up to her true potential.

The patient suggested that grief regarding her father's death was unresolved. In a certain way she had been trying to recapture a feeling of paternal warmth and security in another man's arms. She made a clear connection between a former fiancé and her father. When her fiancé broke their engagement, she became severely depressed, saying she felt as if she had died.

Strong mixed feelings towards the therapist were expressed and connected to those same conflicted emotions towards her parents. She said she felt helped and encouraged by the therapist's active and focused approach, but also angry about being put on the spot and being exposed. Her ability to work in the transference and make meaningful connections between the therapist and significant others in her life boded well for this kind of therapy. She left the trial therapy feeling that a good deal had been accomplished.

Additional information

The relation with her father

The following composite extracts from the transcript will give a clear impression of the extraordinary degree to which the patient had mixed feelings about both of her parents.

> Pt: The problem with my father was that he was absent even before he died. He wasn't interested in my life at school and such, like my mother was. What I did have with him, though, is a babying. I have problems about my father dying, but the problems preceded that. I was 14 when he died, but I lost him before that. I miss him, though, and I want to hug him (*crying*). I wanted him to see me grow up (*crying harder*). I loved hugging my father. He used to stroke my hair and I loved it. I miss him.

The relation with her mother

> Th: I don't get a sense of what kind of mother she was.
>
> Pt: I was afraid of her. She inspired fear without yelling. I was motivated not so much to do well as not to get into trouble. I did not have a physical relationship with her like I did with my father. More recently she's tried to become more physically demonstrative and to show more unconditional love. I told her I didn't feel loved by her, and I see her trying. I said to her, "You never fully loved me". She never loved me for *me*. Now there are times when we have fun together, and it is almost like we are in love with each other.

FORMULATION

The hypotheses given by the two judges were essentially the same. We choose that given by JM.

Hypothesis by JM

1. She suffers from mixed feelings of love, grief, and anger in relation to both parents, which she finds difficulty in facing and experiencing.
   a. Her father provided physical and emotional comfort, and she still suffers from unresolved grief about his death. However, she felt she lost him before he died—he was no longer interested in what she was doing, and she felt he did not really care about her.

b. Her mother provided interest and encouragement, but she was also demanding and difficult to please. The patient was afraid of getting into trouble with her and "had to be delightful" in order to please her. In addition the patient "never felt truly loved by her".

All these feelings have been internalized and have led to depression and anxiety and have possibly exacerbated her ulcerative colitis.

2. She is afraid to express anger because of (a) her fear that it will jeopardize relationships, and possibly (b) because of the degree and extent of it. She is driven by the need to be acceptable and please the other person, which still permeates her present relationships. In particular she needs to be compliant with women.

3. Her experience of the loss of her previous boyfriend echoed that of her father.

ISSUES TO BE DEALT WITH IN THERAPY

Both judges were entirely blind to events subsequent to the initial interview.

The two judges emphasized the need to help the patient express her feelings of grief and anger in relation to both her father and her mother. Only JM added the same feelings about her previous boyfriend, who could not commit himself to her and then left her and married someone else. JM wrote of the need to explore the dynamics of her relation with her siblings. DM predicted that it was anger with her *father* that would be most likely to lead to therapeutic effects.

CRITERIA

Criteria are covered in the follow-up section.

Therapy

The therapy for The Good Girl with Ulcerative Colitis consisted of 68 sessions.

INTRODUCTION: MODIFIED TECHNIQUE WITH A POTENTIALLY FRAGILE PATIENT

Patients with severe functional disorders such as ulcerative colitis must be treated with special care. At the time of this initial assessment, I was in the early phases of training in this method of ISTDP. Davanloo, who was supervising me, advised me to proceed slowly and cautiously, to address grief before rage, and to restructure the ego so that she would be able to tolerate the experience of her feelings without undue anxiety or conversion into somatic symptoms. He emphasized the importance of tracking the somatic pathways of anxiety, in order to make sure it was not getting channelled into her gut, which could exacerbate her condition. Given this, I went much more slowly with her than I might have otherwise.

I began the treatment by *pointing out* defences rather than *challenging* them or pressing for the underlying feeling. My goal was to restructure her ego and to strip the anxiety away from the feelings so they could be experienced without symptomatic flare-ups. I also wanted her to get a very clear sense of how she turned her feelings and impulses towards others inward, with self-attack. Helping patients to make a connection between their presenting symptoms and the defences they use to ward off their true feelings bolsters the therapeutic alliance and increases motivation. Linking the suppressed sadistic impulses with symptoms is a key element in restructuring. Her capacity to do the work needed to be assessed, as it is with all patients, by exposing her to the active ingredients of the therapy and evaluating her response to each intervention.

The fact that this patient experienced relief during the first session after expressing her irritation with me seemed a positive indication of her ability to benefit from this approach. So, there were both positive signs and indications of fragility. The cautious and graded approach required in this case took longer than the traditional treatment model, but was required to minimize risk. The 68 sessions that her treatment totalled is longer than most courses of ISTDP but is relatively brief given the severity of her condition and the magnitude of change achieved. I know of no other treatment method that could have approached these results within that, or any other, time frame.

I have chosen pivotal sessions to elaborate upon and give the reader a real sense of the work as it progressed. This approach is in alignment with research previously cited (chapter 3), suggesting that positive outcome is highly related to the incidence of "significant" sessions.

SESSION 2

The patient came in reporting that, since the initial evaluation, she had been experiencing waves of grief and sadness about the death of her father [predicted by both DM and JM]. She recalled how she felt when her mother walked into the room to tell her of his death. The patient knew this was unresolved and began to link this to guilt over the fact that she did *not* feel sad at the time of his death. She remembered resenting the fact that she had to visit her father in the hospital when she was wanting to be out shopping or having fun. She was an adolescent who was more concerned about her own fun and appearance than visiting her dying father. In fact, she snuck out of the hospital room and went out to buy a mini-skirt.

At the cemetery, she recalled looking down at her brown patent-leather shoes and focusing on how she looked. She had wondered if she should wear make-up to the funeral, and she took all this to mean that she was insensitive and self-absorbed. I pointed out that these were mechanisms she used to avoid experiencing her true feelings about her father's death; this had never occurred to her.

Following this comment, she recalled being allowed to sleep in her mother's bed during this period of time. Such closeness was typically forbidden, so there were many guilty pleasures involved with his death. In fact, on the rare occasions when her father was away on business trips, she would be allowed in her mother's bed. The patient became increasingly aware that a part of her was glad to be rid of her father, so she could be close to her mother. She realized the truth of this, adding that, if her mother had died, she couldn't imagine feeling happy and going out shopping. She feels she would have been full of grief and there would be no fun. As the truth of all this sank in, she began to report feeling disgusted with herself for behaving as she did at the time of her father's death. The therapist pointed out that, in the past, she had punished herself rather than feeling the guilt. This is a very important point and one worth repeating: *the self-punitive behaviour is used as a means of avoiding the conscious experience of guilt,* while exacting a psychic toll. The patient must be helped to experience the guilt consciously in order to give up the self-punishment. The guilt is connected to love. If she didn't care about her father, she wouldn't feel guilty about being glad he was dead.

The patient was then able to acknowledge that the depression she experienced the year after his death had less to do with the loss of her father than her anger about the consequences. Because her father was a "ne'er do well", who did not leave his family with any financial means, they incurred many losses subsequent to his death. The family had to move out of their home, her mother had to go to work outside the home, and the patient received less attention all around. Her mother was "grim" during this time and "steeled herself" in order to fulfil all her family responsibilities—so she lost a positive connection with her mother as well. Clearly the entire family was struggling during this time. One of her younger sisters became severely anorexic. She had to be hospitalized and, even there, refused nourishment. The family was summoned to conduct a mock funeral in an attempt to make them all face the reality that she was killing herself. In contrast, the patient tried to win affection and praise by being "good" and helpful and repressing all her own feelings and needs.

Session 3

The patient reported that the last session really hit her, like a eureka moment, in realizing how much more depressed she would have been if her mother had died than she actually felt when her father died.

Th: Can we look at the feelings you are experiencing?
Pt: It's hard to remember, because I was just thinking about it.
Th: Isn't this a way to avoid feeling?
Pt: I have felt very sad during this last week. Sad, but also grounded.

(This is a therapeutic effect from experiencing hitherto avoided grief.)

Resistance against emotional closeness in the transference

Th: Do you notice that, as you tell me about the sadness, you look down and avoid my eyes?

It is very important to assess where the primary defences lie—whether they are primarily aimed at avoiding the experience of anxiety-provoking feelings or are erected against meaningful emotional contact with the therapist. In this session, the therapist was aware of the ways in which the patient was maintaining an emotional distance from her and felt that needed to be addressed. *If defences against emotional closeness are present, then a focus on defences against impulses and feelings is misplaced and is unlikely to yield much therapeutic benefit.*

Pt: You start to seem like a stranger. I feel self-conscious. Your scrutiny is so intense.
Th: So what is the feeling towards me?
Pt: I start to feel angry at you. Then I feel fear—almost alarm. I don't want you to see this shit—what is dirty and messy.
Th: Let's look at this. You feel angry towards me but get anxious, and then what happens to the anger?
Pt: I incorporate it.

This is an intervention aimed at restructuring her defences—showing her the relationship between her feelings, the anxiety they generate, and the defences she employs against them. The aim of these interventions is to turn her ego against these defences, while simultaneously strengthening the therapeutic alliance so that feelings can be faced directly. Finally, this intervention is also being employed in order *to remove barriers to closeness and to prevent the development of a transference neurosis.* In ISTDP, the transference pattern of behaviour is monitored from the very first interactions with the patient. Rather than allowing the transference to develop, it is actively worked on in order to facilitate the direct experience of feelings and to remove defences in operation.

Pt: But, you know, there are other feelings too. I had a dream about you. It's hazy, but we were talking about something deep and then we got interrupted. Someone was in the other room. You explained to me that there were others you had to attend to and I had to understand.

Th: And, again, the feeling?

Pt: I don't understand! These feelings are primal. I feel possessive. I know this is about my mother—wanting her to myself and resenting the others.

(This is a spontaneous T–P link in the triangle of person—see chapter 10.)

The patient then recalled specific memories of competitive feelings towards her siblings, especially her younger sisters. She had been the centre of attention for the first three and a half years of her life, as the only girl in the family. This was lost when her baby sister entered the picture. Then, a few years later, another one came along. She began to face her hostility towards them, her desire to be rid of them, and her guilt about those impulses.

We recapped what we had learned in the session, emphasizing the guilt over her aggression, and the self-punitive mechanisms at work. She seemed increasingly motivated to stop punishing herself. This was the focus of the first block of therapy, lasting about 15 sessions. As her defences got restructured, she assumed a more active role in the treatment and brought in affect-laden material.

Session 16

Hostility towards a man connected with work

Pt: I wanted to talk about feelings about my brother, who I saw last week, but then feelings really got stirred up at work, which really made me aware of this problem I have with my anger.

Th: Tell me about it.

Pt: Several months ago I dealt with someone at work on the phone who was very angry and difficult. I was filled with self-doubt. Yesterday, I had an experience with an attorney on the phone in which I knew I was in the right, but he started attacking me. I was so overwhelmed by it that I short-circuited. I get so . . . I get depressed. I was depressed all day. Now I understand the problem, but I am blocked.

Th: It sounds like you don't let yourself experience the anger towards him, even once you're off the phone. You internalize it and become depressed.

Pt: I felt it in my stomach—my intestines get clenched, and then I have to go to the bathroom more often.

This gives clear evidence of a psychosomatic mechanism affecting her ulcerative colitis.

Th: So do you want to focus on the anger instead of making yourself sick?

Pt: Yeah, well, when I was talking to my friend she said, "why don't you just imagine what you want to do to him", so I imagined, like, really pounding this guy—not just pounding him, but visualizing him up against the wall (*arms moving to demonstrate*).

Th: Where?

Pt: Hitting him in *his* stomach!

This is evidence of an aggressive impulse formerly self-directed.

> That's interesting. I see him pushed against the wall, and then I stab him with a baseball bat—pushing it into him. But this is combined with fear of my own making—could I really do it? Am I strong enough?

This last statement revealed her awareness of the specific link between the impulses she represses and the symptoms she was experiencing. She felt pain in her gut after the phone call. During the session, she became aware of the impulse to hit this man in his stomach and could put the two together—seeing how she had been doing to herself what she wanted to do to him.

Th: But the impulse is?

Pt: The impulse is to kill him, but . . .

Th: You qualify it immediately.

Pt: But I think that's significant. Part of what holds me back in confronting someone is the fear that they'll get me first.

Th: We have to look, because no one else is here, but still you back off. My sense is that, at least part of the fear is of your own anger and the viciousness of it. It's hard to face—that inside you is a murderous rage.

Pt: Now tears are coming, and this is what happened all day yesterday.

Th: That's the way you avoid the experience of the anger.

Pt: That's what I tell myself.

It is clear that the patient has a good cognitive understanding of her own inner workings but is still defending against the *experience* of her anger. We continue to focus on the defences in order to liberate the buried feeling and relieve her of her symptoms.

Th: This man means nothing to you.

Pt: You're right.

Th: So, if we stick to the experience of your anger towards him . . .

Pt: Yeah, that's it—not just with a baseball bat but pounding him with my arms. And then, actually, I feel it in my gut, but not as pain . . . I'm energized (*sitting forward and moving arms in a chopping manner*). I do feel like pounding him on his shoulders. Then I would feel like punching him in the face—and you're right, I do feel like being rid of him completely, because then I won't have to deal with him any more.

Th: How do you get rid of him?

Pt: Punch him in the face. Then, if he's not dead, shoot him. I want rid of him.

Th: So how do you see this?

Pt: I pound him on his shoulders, then his face. Actually, I want to squash his face. This actually makes me feel good—yeah, he's on the floor and I squash his face.

Th: And you're smiling—so are you still being nice?

Pt: Because it feels good. I feel better. I'm not being gracious, but I smile because I realize I feel better.

This is the flip side of the realization that repression of her feelings results in symptoms—*facing them leads to a feeling of freedom, energy, and well-being.*

Pt: So then he's on the floor, and I stomp him. I stomp him and step on his face.

Th: What happens?

Pt: I killed him.

Th: So, what's the scene?

Pt: He's dead.

Th: Can you describe what he looks like?

Spontaneous link to hostility towards her brother

Pt: I'm not sure if his eyes are open or closed. Actually, his head is tilted to one side and his eyes are closed. He's just gone. This must have something to do with my family because, you're right, I don't care about this guy, but I start to think about a member of my family, like my brother, being gone. It reminds me . . .

Following the full experience of her sadistic impulses towards the man on the phone, she made a *spontaneous link to a genetic figure from her past*. This is one of the hallmarks of what Davanloo calls "a breakthrough into the unconscious".

Th: We have to wonder whether you have had these very feelings and impulses towards him.

[*Predicted by JM in terms of the need to explore the dynamics of her relation with her siblings.*]

Pt: Yeah, there probably were.

Th: Let's go to an instance with him.

Pt: I ended up feeling like a failure with him. He wanted me to be something I wasn't. I wasn't an athlete, and he would tease me.

Th: Like what?

Pt: He's always ready to laugh at me, to tease me, and he *did* laugh at me and make fun of me.

Th: So, your feeling towards him?

Pt: That's what I realize, see. I just go to feeling bad.

Again, she has a cognitive understanding of the mechanisms she is using to deflect her anger, but it is, in fact, still in operation.

Th: Inside you feel bad, but the feeling towards him—that's what you don't face.

Pt: That's the hard part. I know it's anger, but I don't feel it. I must be honest with you.

Th: So what happens inside?

Pt: I feel like crying.

Th: When you think of him laughing at you?

Pt: Yeah, I feel like crying.

Th: But the feeling towards him, who humiliates you . . .

Pt: That's what gets left out.

Th: We now know that the man on the floor represents him. It's important to face that directly.

Pt: And I want to say, can't we just do it to him, that guy I don't care about.

Th: It was when he was on the floor, dead, that the image of your brother came—so it's him.

Pt: I see him turned away and helpless.

Th: It almost sounds like someone sleeping, but it has been a brutal attack, with you stomping on his face.

Pt: I leave that part out. His face is not bruised but looks angelic.

Th: Would that, in fact, be the case?

Pt: No, it's denial.

Th: We have to look at it.

Pt: It would come out indirectly, with snide remarks and intellectual barbs.

Th: We can see that's the way you avoid looking at the impulse to make direct jabs.

Pt: I can feel myself not wanting to face that.

Th: Even though it's so . . .

Pt: Yeah, it was so pervasive. Between my mother and my brother, so much of my personality is built up of these strategies—these brilliant strategies to keep these people . . .

Th: But it's not just to keep them happy or to keep them at bay . . .

Pt: To keep them alive? I realize how angry I am with my mother, but I can't let myself feel it.

This transcript highlights the strength of the resistance when it comes to facing feelings towards those who are ambivalently held. The good news is that she comes in recognizing that she has a problem feeling her anger, and she begins with a recent example. She allowed herself to experience the rage and imagine letting this co-worker have it, rather than internalizing the impulse and punishing herself. In fact, she let herself feel good and strong and powerful instead of sick, depressed, and weak. When the link was made with her brother, however, the forces of defence and resistance return. She understood what she was doing on an intellectual level, but could not seem to access the feelings towards him. We continued in this gradual, step-by-step approach until she was able to experience intense feelings without the need to resort to regressive defences.

Session 20: The beginning of therapeutic effects

The material in this session provides evidence of therapeutic change. As a result of the work done on liberating her anger towards a man she was working with, changes occur immediately.

Pt: I realize all the problems I have at work all happen when it comes to my rage. I've mentioned my boss, Alice, with whom I've felt angry in the past. On Thursday we had an interaction that I felt very angry about. I was very busy and got interrupted by a colleague who came to me, really wanting to talk. She was very upset because of a problem with her husband. He had a major disappointment in his own life and she was dealing with that. Suddenly this woman, Alice, came barging in, demanding a response to a question she had regarding some of her own work. When I told her I didn't know, that I was in the middle of dealing with something else, she got very angry with me. Well, she berated me in front of this other colleague and was very rude. I was enraged but couldn't even feel it. The fact is, I don't know everything, and I can go to feeling horrible rather than feel my anger at her. But then, the next morning—this is progress for me—I would have apologized and been conciliatory. Now I'm aware of rage. This is no way to talk to me—it's not a way to talk to anyone. If we were friends, I would have confronted her, but we work together and she's my superior, so I need to be politic. Even there, in the past, I would have stopped my own work and grovelled. This time, I finished my own work, and, when I had time the next day, I got her the answer she needed and presented it to her, but without all the apologies and such. Interestingly enough, she apologized to me, saying she was out of line. I accepted it and respected her for acknowledging it. But this was very different for me. I feel good about that, but I'm left with feelings towards her. I know that she reminds me of my mother. She's extremely competent. Not only is she great at work, but she's a great cook, great gardener. I can be intimidated by her. I ended up telling my mother about it. She told me, "You are so hard on yourself. I'm glad you said that to her. I'm glad she apologized to you." She's changed too. In the past, she was hard on me. She's so full of self-hatred and hard on herself, she did that to me too. Now I want to break out of this. I won't walk on eggshells any more, and I won't accept this kind of treatment. I was more capable of feeling it, even though I didn't tell her. I feel like killing her but have to be more composed when I deal with her.

There is a great deal of information contained in that rather long rendition of recent events. The important thing is that she allowed herself to experience her anger and use it to stand her ground. Furthermore, she realized her boss was rude and that she does not deserve to be treated that way. The changes in her were clearly communicated to her boss, who apologized and gained a new level of respect for the patient. Further evidence of change is revealed when she makes a spontaneous link with her mother, along with the desire to pursue the issue. She is not content to leave it as is, but wants to go further with the process.

Th: These are two different things. You want to be free to feel all your feelings. How you're going to express it involves judgement. You used the anger to hold onto yourself. You didn't go to grovelling and passivity and compliance. You did the work when it suited you, and then she ended up respecting you and apologized for her own rage.

Pt: Yeah, but I'm so sick of her. I still feel like killing her.

Th: How?

Pt: I feel like wringing her neck. I am bigger than she. I see it in my office: I grab her around the throat and squeeze. I could kill her. Now I know, if she really died I would feel bad, but I feel really angry. I also feel like kicking her. The other thing I've felt this week is the desire to get strong. I've been exercising and getting more upper-body strength.

Pt: I feel like smashing her face in—taking my foot and grinding it in her face. She was hitting below the belt, and I feel like getting her back, right in the face.

Th: What else?

Spontaneous link from her boss to her mother

Pt: It's very focused on her face. I see it black and blue. I see myself stamping and grinding. I'm sick of her and sick of my putting up with it. I want to destroy her. Now I feel tearful and think about my mother.

Th: When did your mother come?

Pt: When I saw her dead. She always mocked other people, kicking people when they were down. I would advocate for the underdog. It was a way of advocating for myself. I grew up being excessively sympathetic because she was so critical. I feel very angry because I'm so afraid of trying things, because I'm not perfect and am afraid of being laughed at. This is progress, isn't it? I was polite but I told her, "I'll get back to you". So I could do it there, but I notice as soon as I go to my mother, I feel it in my stomach.

(This is more evidence about the psychosomatic mechanism.)

It's easier with Alice than with my mother.

Th: You were feeling it freely until you got to your mother.

Pt: You're right, I did.

Once again, we see a freeing up of feelings and impulses towards those outside the family. Her boss clearly has more meaning and significance than the man discussed previously, but not nearly as much as her mother. She gets closer each time, but anxiety and defence are still aroused when anger comes up towards a loved one. [*Anger with her mother was predicted by both judges.*]

Session 21:   Anger with her mother;
the patient's idea about the link with her main symptom

The patient comes in talking about her anger towards her mother and her difficulty in facing it.

> Th: You get terrified of your anger and internalize it. Then the attack is on you. You spare the other and punish yourself.

> Pt: I read how antibodies . . . ulcerative colitis is an auto-immune disease. Here I am attacking my own cells. For some reason my body reads my colon cells as foreign, but they are me and I'm rejecting them. This field of immunology is nascent but, with my background . . .

> Th: It's not just your background, but the way you dealt with it, along with some organic vulnerability . . .

> *(It is so important not to assume that everything is entirely psychodynamic!)*

> . . . clearly there's a convergence of factors, but this thing that seems foreign—that you can't seem to bear—is your anger, your rage.

> Pt: Uh-huh.

> Th: You go weak in the face of it, attack yourself, get sick, and then there's some secondary gain. (*Patient nods her head*) Then you can be reunited with your mother (*the patient goes home to be cared for when she gets sick*).

> Pt: Intellectually it's fascinating—the economy of my own psyche, but in reality, this is terrible. Yet I persist. I still choose to kill myself and take it out on myself rather than face it towards her.

The patient is beginning to turn against her own defences. She says it is "terrible" what she does to herself. That comment suggests that the healthy part of her is beginning to stand up against the self-punitive part of her personality.

Session 28:   Crucial issue of withholding in
the transference leads to fantasy of violence
against the therapist

The patient came into this session saying she received a bill for a missed session (which is my policy). She began to argue about the policy. Rather than engage in a debate, this issue was used as an opportunity to access her feeling towards the therapist. She claimed to be irritated but avoided the experience of this by intellectualizing. When that was challenged, she went to a helpless, victimized position, defending herself. She avoided my eyes. As I challenged these defences, an underlying withholding and defiance emerged. We could see that she was subtly expressing her anger towards me by withholding the direct experience of it. This pattern is often unearthed in patients with a history of compliance. Becoming defiant when challenged is just the flip side of the coin to the compliance. In neither case is the patient in touch with genuine feeling. Both aspects of this defensive stance must be addressed.

As her stubborn defiance was identified and challenged, the experience of the anger towards me emerged. She had the impulse to lash out, beat my shoulders, and punch my face. She imagined me on the ground, with my face a mush—broken and bloody. She then felt a wave of grief and guilt.

SESSION 29:   Anger in transference linked to her mother; therapeutic effects

The patient came in reporting that the last session was a pivotal one for her. She got in touch with her own defiance and withholding in a deep and visceral way. She was able to see that her withholding was a disguised expression of anger. Her mother was demanding, so she could express her anger indirectly by withholding what her mother wanted. Her mother was very ambitious and wanted her children to achieve at the very highest level. She insisted that the patient take an entrance exam for a prestigious high school. The patient did not want to go to this school but took the exam at her mother's insistence. She remembers being sick to her stomach on the day of the exam, which she now understands as anxiety over her anger towards her mother. Despite the fact that she made herself sick, she passed the exam and was forced to attend the school.

The biggest change that emerged from this session was that the patient started writing a novel. She had come up with the title for this novel a decade ago but had not been able to sit down and start writing. She realized, after the last session, that she was blocking herself from creating this novel in order to get back at her mother. The self-defeating nature of this strategy was quite obvious to her, and she commenced with writing immediately. She went on to write on a daily basis for three months and completed the novel. Later on, she actually invited her mother to read the book and serve as editor, suggesting that her withholding in the face of anger was replaced with cooperation. This change also suggested to me that her healthy ego was getting stronger than the self-defeating part of her.

Session 35: Violent anger with a previous boyfriend

The patient begins the session by bringing up rage towards an old boyfriend who invited her to a hotel, started making love to her, and then stopped abruptly. She felt "hurt" and remembers going home in a cab feeling devastated. Now she realizes how enraged she has been towards him and wants to face it directly.

> Th: You know the things you do to avoid the experience of your anger, so what are you going to do about this sweet, nice little girl who doesn't feel her anger?

The reader will note a change in the nature of the therapist's interventions, from simply pointing out her defensive avoidance to challenging these defences head-on. We had done a good deal of restructuring, and I sensed that she was strong enough to experience these feelings and impulses directly. However, only her responses to this intervention could confirm that clinical hunch. This is where art and science merge.

> Pt: It's the murderous impulse towards him that gets internalized. I almost had a flash of being able to hurt him. I feel like kicking him in the balls—that wouldn't kill him, but I really want to hurt him—really focusing on the picture of myself hurting him and then leaving.
>
> Th: So you want to do what?
>
> Pt: I picture kicking him in the balls while he's standing there naked. Instead of waiting until morning—why did I stay there? I was angry. I was furious. But I was so attracted to him. I just felt rage—rage at being yanked around. I wasn't imagining things—he invited me.
>
> Th: He was teasing you. You're focused on his genitals.
>
> Pt: I kick him, and I feel that I would kill him. Then I think of his neck. I feel I could have killed him, I was so angry (*clenching hands*). I actually pulled his hair. He said I was hurting him, so I stopped. But I wanted to hurt him—I still do. I feel like hitting his face. I would pound on his face—and actually his face was weak to begin with because he was in a car accident and they had to put it back together—so I really could have hurt him. It's all coming back to him. I feel like pounding him. I actually feel like destroying him. I would have killed him. I would pound on his head. Then kick the shit out of him. I could have destroyed him, but I do it to me. Now I want to go for his balls because I really wanted him inside of me. That would get him on the floor. Then I see him unconscious, but I guess he would cry out in pain.

Th: You want to destroy him—limb from limb—and kick the shit out of him so his insides are oozing out.

Pt: In the bed I pulled his hair. He said stop, but I wouldn't. I would really tear it out . . . When I used to get angry with my brother, I used to scratch him. Here I would have started with his head and his neck. I feel like going to his neck and cutting it, then pounding on his head. In bed, what I'm faced with is his face. My next impulse is to go to his genitals, but my next impulse is to kiss his penis and go down on him. For a moment, when I imagined standing up and I looked at his penis, I still wanted to make love to him.

Th: You beat him into submission.

Pt: That's the image that popped into my head. Then I felt sadness because he was withholding himself when he was conscious, but now, if I go down on him . . . but I really wanted him inside me.

Th: First was to stimulate him orally.

Pt: And he gets erect. Then I see him ejaculating in my mouth.

Th: But you say you wanted him inside you.

Pt: I like him in my mouth, too. I want to bend him to my will, because I still love him.

Th: Is that about love or about sex and aggression?

Pt: Well, you cut right through, yeah.

These interactions provide a good example of what happens in the process of ISTDP. All the intense, mixed feelings towards the other emerge in an undisguised way. I never would have predicted the kinds of impulses and images that were emerging here. The therapist must be flexible and follow the material as it is revealed, yet remain ever vigilant for the re-emergence of defences. In this case, it was essential to follow the sexual imagery, but not to buy that this was simply a manifestation of love and desire. Men are not the only ones who use sex to express hostility. As soon as I pointed this out to her, she acknowledged it.

Th: You are enraged about his withholding of sex and love, which gives rise to the aggression.

Pt: I still feel rage, and it was years ago. I still feel rage.

Th: And you want revenge.

Pt: And for a moment I felt tenderness, but I still feel like killing him, I really do. If I can't have him, I don't want anyone else to have him. I heard through the grapevine that he got married this year, and I was furious.

Th: You wanted to wipe him out.

Pt: Yes, I do and I don't want him to be happy. I guess with him I go to hand-to-hand combat—no gun. I see pounding him to . . . it gets artificial . . . when I imagine pounding him, I don't imagine his face getting purple. Also I don't see him fighting back. He was kind of weak. He used to lose his voice. In bed, his voice would go.

Th: He would go limp.

Pt: Not limp.

Th: But he would come immediately.

Pt: Right.

Th: Still uncomfortable facing this anger in you?

Pt: I feel I could kill him.

Th: But we don't see the murder scene.

Pt: If I go to his neck. I still have a hard time, but to truly see him dead. I would slash his neck.

Th: Slash his neck.

Pt: And now I go to my own neck.

Th: Which you thought of doing (*fantasy of suicide by slashing her own neck following a break-up years ago*).

Pt: I repress the scream, too. I feel like *I* lose my voice when I get to anger. Like I lost my voice when I wanted . . .

Th: The choking. You choke yourself, but you wanted to choke him—to choke the life right out of him.

Pt: I'm really sorry I didn't. I'm angry I can't kill him and all the men in my life who . . .

Th: But it's there, so we can face that.

Pt: I kill him, but I don't know . . .

Th: But you keep going like this with your arm and you say "slash".

Pt: I avoid it. I hark back to when I thought of suicide and imagined slashing my neck.

Th: And you didn't face that's what you wanted to do to him!

Pt: No. Now, as we speak, I have a hard time seeing myself with a knife in my hand. On one hand, I can't get him dead with my fists, but when I think of a knife and really slicing his neck, I have a hard time, because I know what that looks like. I've seen it. I've worked on murder cases where I see pictures of necks slashed.

Th: A murder case?

Pt: Yes, and I'm smiling. I worked with a private investigator and wanted to write a book.

This material is completely fresh and is another hallmark of this work. Supporting data emerge spontaneously and help to shed light on the core conflicts involved.

Th: So you know.

Pt: In one case, a man arranged to have his wife's neck slashed for $5,000. So I know what it looks like, with the mouth open . . . and neck slashed . . . big slash. You know, as I speak, I could have done that. I want him out—wanted him dead—no happiness for him. He yanked me around. This isn't something I made up.

Th: So there's an intense desire for revenge.

Pt: Yeah. I have a vivid picture of him—to slash his neck. I imagine putting it right down to his solar plexus—right where I feel such hollowness. When I think of leaving that hotel and driving off alone, I can actually imagine going straight down into his centre.

Th: Then what?

Pt: He's dead—real dead—and I feel happy. At the first moment, I feel glad. I don't go right away to feeling horrible and guilty. I feel happy. It's one big . . . actually, with him, I could have done it. I was furious, and in that moment, that first moment, I feel happy. It still makes me happy to see him dead. If I were to take a huge carving knife, and into the centre of him—carving and carving.

Th: You can see it and feel it?

Pt: As you mention it, I can see slicing him, but that's . . . to really imagine it. I see the blood. I see myself as a crazed woman. Crazed with rage. Even now, I feel happy. This is why I don't want to face it.

Th: There is pleasure in it.

Pt: Yeah. Then I can leave the hotel.

Th: What happens?

Pt: I leave him alone there, dead in bed. When I see myself getting into the taxi now, it's very different (*laughs with delight*). I walk with a spring in my step. This is awful, but I'm not really facing the consequences. I feel ebullient—I got something done.

The patient has not only succeeded in facing her rage towards this man—which had originally been internalized with depression and suicidal ideation—but she has faced her own sadism—the part of her that feels happy and delighted to seek her revenge.

While difficult to face, once she does, it is liberating. She feels powerful, happy, and fully alive—rather than feeling "dead" or wanting to kill herself, as would happen in the past when love was lost. This is what we aim to see—a real change in the patient's emotional state. Her guilt and self-punishment are lifting and being replaced with life energy.

The patient reported feeling much better after this session. Several more sessions were spent focusing on this pattern. Now, instead of feeling anxious, sick, and depressed when anger gets evoked, she feels energized, happy, and alive.

SESSION 40

Anger in the transference once more

The patient began this session by bringing her anger and sadistic rage into the transference. This clearly indicates that major restructuring has occurred. Now she initiates these interactions herself and is anxious to express her feelings directly, even in the transference, which is typically the most anxiety-provoking of all communications.

> Pt: But, you know, I was feeling anger this morning about you. I was waiting out there and wondering what would happen if I had an accident. You've said I tend to focus on my hurt rather than my anger when I'm rejected. I think you're right. So, let's say I had an accident and you *did* reject me. I would feel really bad, but also angry.
>
> Th: Did you imagine that, actually?

Spontaneous link to her mother, once more

> Pt: Yeah, well, it's my mother actually. I don't want to have to perform any more. I don't want to bend to your desires. I don't want to work at it any more. I just don't want to . . . (*very animated, with voice loud and clear and arms swinging*). My writing block is over, my work is flowing. I'm on schedule and I'm doing it.

The therapist brings her back to the transference, leading to a fantasy of a fight with the therapist

It has been fairly common for this woman to make links from her current experiences to those in the past. Here she is quick to link her feelings towards the therapist with those of her mother. While, in all likelihood, there is just such a link in place, it is preferable not to go directly to the past, but to stay in the present and then see what materializes. Feelings in the transference are often as anxiety-provoking for the therapist as the patient, and it can be tempting to collude with avoiding it. However, much will be lost. Here was an opportunity to face her complex, mixed feelings in the transference, so that was where we began.

> Th: But here, in this relationship, you resent having to work.
>
> Pt: Yeah. It's mixed. On one hand I feel gratitude and love, but on the other hand I see you as this woman—this woman who makes me

face this stuff and get . . . Actually I do feel anger and resentment, but, you know, when ever I think of you rejecting me, it always comes down to my shit. If I had an accident here, you would be revolted.

Th: So how do you imagine this? You have an accident and . . .

Pt: I don't make it to the bathroom. Actually I'm doing quite well (*knocks on wood*), but let's say I lose control and have diarrhoea and it's smelly. It's not pretty. It's not the way you look. It's not the way I look. It goes all over me.

Th: So how do you . . .

Pt: I imagine you going . . . actually, as I look at your face, I have a very different reaction than if I just imagine it. If I imagine it, it would be "YUCK—Get out of here!" I imagine you pushing me away and saying "Get out of here!"—being really revolted and disgusted— that I'm awful and putrid and hideous and, you know, this office is so perfect.

Th: So you . . .

Pt: "Get out!", so you can clean it up. You'd want me out. I'm the locus of it. You see me as so disgusting. Because your reaction is so instinctive, you couldn't control it, which is like my mother—it was so instinctive.

Pt: What do I do with this anger? Actually, I can answer my own question because I find I'm being much more honest and tell people how I feel. I don't do it blithely, but when I feel the person can tolerate it, I'm opening up and allowing for greater closeness.

Th: And even in those cases where you decide not to share it, you can free yourself to experience it without putting it into your gut and getting sick.

Pt: Yes, but sometimes when I get angry I eat, if I can't express it.

Th: Again, let's deal with it as it's occurring here with me. You still tend to diversify—to hit on it but then go off. You feel anger towards me and imagine my reaction to your accident with disgust—and that I would reject you.

Pt: Uncontrollable rage.

Th: That *I* would experience uncontrollable rage?

Pt: That I deserve to die. As you speak, though, I don't feel like dying. I feel angry and I feel like striking back. I'm more in touch with it. I would fight you back. This is progress. I don't feel like crying. I would fight back.

Th: How?

Pt: I would push you back.

Th: How do you see it, because . . .

Pt: We're going to get into it and have a fight. I don't think it's by any means clear who would win if you're in a rage and I'm in a rage. I push you, and you push me back. When I look at you now I know reason would prevail, and I see sympathy in your eyes, but in my mind, in this fantasy . . .

Th: So this is where I become . . .

Spontaneous link to her mother, this time not defensive, leading to a fantasy of extreme violence

Now that there is genuine emotional activation, along with a link to the past, the therapist follows the lead of the patient. Earlier, it seemed intellectual. Now she is fully in touch with feelings of rage.

Pt: It's my mother. She's fierce. I just feel like hitting her back.

Th: How?

Pt: Her face. Pushing her away.

Th: Where do you see this?

Pt: You know, I go back to the potty scene. It's in that long, narrow kitchen. I don't picture myself a three-year-old, cowering. I picture myself as an adult, pushing her away. How would she react? I think she'd hit me back. She'd hit me back. My mother is tough.

Th: She wouldn't crumble.

Pt: No way. She'd come back at me with redoubled force. That actually happened once. I lashed out, and she restrained my hands. Now I feel like, as an adult, I could kill my mother.

Th: This is hypothetical, or you are facing that that is there?

Pt: Now I feel like pushing her away and knocking her down.

Th: On the kitchen floor?

Pt: I still feel angry.

Th: That's not enough.

Pt: I feel myself tearing up too.

Th: What do you say?

Pt: It's probably a defence, but I still feel really angry and, on that level, I really want my mother dead. I want to get her dead. I still feel angry about it.

Th: How? The impulse is what?

Pt: It *is* hand-to- hand combat. It's not a gun or the knife. I want to strangle my mother. I want to kill my mother. This "Control Your-self!"—I can't stand it!

Th: Do you want to let her know this?

Pt: No, I don't want to talk. I feel angry and I don't feel like explaining myself. I still feel I'm controlling myself (*puts hands around her throat*). I don't feel like explaining. I'm sick and tired of her being the only one who's entitled to feelings. I want her OUT! I actually want her out.

Th: She's on the floor, and you go for her neck?

Pt: I just squeeze the life right out of her. I feel so strong lately. I had to shovel snow, and I felt strong. I am squeezing her neck. I'm in a blind rage and I want her out—just squeezing the life right out of her. She's tough, but bird-like. You could do it, you know, you could do it. I think I'm detaching though—like serial killers do. I'm objectifying her and not really facing that it's my mother. I'm not stepping back. I want to be me!

Th: So you imagine choking her, or you break her neck?

Pt: I choke the life out of her. I feel that same insensible feeling I felt with that boyfriend. I feel very cold-blooded. I just see her eyes and I would know. I would go for her neck, but I must be repressing, because I feel it in *my* neck. I'm repressing something.

Th: What does it feel like?

Pt: UGH! I would scream. It would be "UGH!" It would be murderous, it would be animalistic—everything she hates. Everything she hates, it would be. I feel so much better now. It's that same animalistic pleasure I had with my boyfriend. You're right, I'm not just sweetness and light. After it's done, I don't start crying right away. That's actually the most painful revelation of this process—it's not that I go to tears, but that this is what I want. Mission accomplished! I feel proud of myself. That feeling of "This had to be done" . . . so, I must be detached.

Th: But you're saying you feel strong and capable.

Pt: I still feel angry, and I don't know why. It's like killing her isn't enough. I still feel angry. I still feel in a murderous rage.

The goal is to drain all the rage out of the body, so you proceed until every ounce has been expressed.

Th: Is there more you want to do with her and her body?

Pt: I feel like screaming. I still feel angry.

Th: Towards her?

Pt: Yes. Maybe I have to tell her, *I can't stand your demands.* Ugh, it's too much! You're crazy! She was tyrannical—like her father. That same authoritarian, tyrannical side.

Th: *So*, like her father . . .

Pt: Her father used her. She was like Hitler. He was like Hitler.

Th: So there's a desire to crush her psychologically as well?

Pt: Yes, it's just these rules and regulations!

Th: To kill her isn't enough.

Pt: It's to exorcize these rules.

Th: Like with your boyfriend, it's not enough to kill him, but then you wanted to have sex with his dead body—all those rules you want to break.

Pt: To decapitate her. It's real. If I'm in a blind rage, I'd slice her neck. I want her out. I think I'd actually incinerate her. I'd want to get her out. What do they do to chop things up—I want her ground up. I want her gone. Even when I picture her gone, I feel this rage. It's still not enough.

And then the love

Pt: Something is still buried because I still feel like screaming. Maybe it's that I want to tell her (*becoming tearful*) . . . *I still long for my mother.* I want my mother. I don't know, because I also love my mother. I don't . . . maybe what it is, but I don't want to have to kill my mother in order to live! (*Crying heavily now*) That's not what I want. I want my mother to love me.

Th: Tell her.

Pt: I want you to love me. I don't want to have to kill you, but I'm sick of all these hoops—always—always!!

Th: There is pain . . .

Pt: Always, just always. Never good enough, never. Such . . .

Th: So much in the way. You want get rid of that part of her and to gain access to her—to be loved by her and to feel close.

Pt: I still feel so choked up.

Th: There's a lot of emotion.

Pt: She's great, but (*she speaks as if her mother were there*), "Why do you feel so bad about yourself?"

Th: You want to put her self-loathing aside?

Pt: That's what got in the way. I mean, Patricia, my mother is *extra-ordinary*. And, when I think of the shit that she went through (*weeping*). Sometimes I see her smile and she looks like she's capable of happiness.

Th: So, stay with this.

Pt: You're so beautiful, and you have so much. I wish you could have been happy because when you smile like that I see the little girl and

I see the life you could have had. My mother, I wish, I wish you could have been happy. I wish you weren't treated so badly (*weeping*). Those stories . . . I just feel so bad you had to go through all that.

In this session, the patient began with anger in the transference, which was linked with her mother. As she got in touch with her sadistic rage, it did not seem enough to just kill her. As is often seen in more complex and difficult cases, the rage is torturous. Once the full extent of the rage is experienced, it is followed by deep feelings of pain, grief, and finally love and compassion for her mother. The patient shows she is capable of experiencing and containing all these intense mixed feelings without resorting to defensive avoidance or self-punishment. This also under-scores the point *that we are not simply interested in releasing anger, but in helping patients experience all mixed feelings towards others.*

Session 41:
Immediate therapeutic effects

The patient reported feeling calmer, stronger, and more grounded since the previous session. She also reported feeling closer to the man she has started dating, and she realized that her freedom to enjoy this relation-ship was related to facing her anger towards her mother. She recalled early physical closeness with her father, which her mother did not like. She remembered being with her father at bedtime and saying "Stay with me, Daddy". Then her mother would come in and says, "Let go, you're going to spoil her. That's enough now!"

A mix of feeling emerged. At first she felt anger towards her mother for interfering, but then she recalled that her mother had been sexually abused by *her* father. She could understand that her mother would be anxious about too much closeness between fathers and daughters.

She also commented on her increased sense of comfort with the therapist and reported that her perception of her has changed from someone she viewed as cold, aloof, and authoritarian to someone with whom she feels closeness and warmth. Her perception of her mother has changed too. She realized that her mother did love her and was not disgusted by her, but that she has defended against her own pain and anguish by keeping a certain distance. Just as she has freed herself from self-induced suffering, she no longer needs to punish her mother for the disappointment and anger she has felt over the years. Compassion and genuine understanding began to predominate, and this was reflected in the development of a close, mutual relationship with her mother. This change in perception of self and other is another frequently noted result of the work on liberating feelings.

THE ISSUE OF TERMINATION

As the patient resolved her difficulties and began to live life fully, the issue of ending therapy arose. Her feelings about leaving therapy brought up feelings about the loss of her father. Then she realized that he had not left her in a wilful way—it was not a rejection—he died. She imagined that he would want her to live—fully and freely. As she imagined this, her mood "perks up". She began to imagine maintaining a connection with him that is life-giving, instead of self-destructive.

Session 68: Entirely positive

In the final session, the patient reported feelings of gratitude and love towards the therapist, as well as pride in herself for working hard and facing very difficult things. She was feeling excited about life. She commented on how different the actual feelings are about ending therapy from those she would have anticipated. She expected to be sad and upset but found that her way of dealing with loss had changed profoundly. She felt healed in this way, as if the holes inside her had been filled. She has the memory of her father inside her and feels she has internalized me too. She said she would miss me but has no regrets. So, while there is sadness, there is no guilt in leaving. The goodbye was not experienced as traumatic, which was a first for her. She had never ended a relationship on good terms before. It felt good, like graduating.

All of her symptoms were gone, and defences had been replaced with healthy alternatives.

She was no longer prone to anxiety and depression. The symptoms of ulcerative colitis were reduced and nearly eliminated. She was able to feel her feelings and use them to create and maintain healthy relationships. The only goal not yet realized was that of creating a relationship with a man that is "full blown and sustained". Only time would tell if our work would result in such an outcome.

Follow-up

Follow-up for The Good Girl with Ulcerative Colitis took place 2, 8, and 10 years after termination.

TWO-YEAR FOLLOW-UP

All gains were maintained. She was actively dating but had still not found someone she would want to marry. Coincidently, she had her yearly colonoscopy the month before our meeting and could report that there was no evidence of any active disease in her colon. There was scar tissue evident, but no inflammation whatsoever. Her doctor was amazed and she was delighted (as was I).

EIGHT-YEAR FOLLOW-UP

Traumatic event

This follow-up session was coloured by the sudden, tragic death of Rebecca, her younger sister, which had occurred some months before our meeting. When I phoned the patient to set up our follow-up interview, she told me about her sister's sudden death and her dramatic response to it: when she heard the news she collapsed to the floor and emitted a "piercing, blood-curdling scream". (Of interest, her mother had the same reaction, though they were not together at the time.) She reported feeling grief-stricken and determined not to allow herself any happiness. In particular, she mentioned denying herself sexual pleasure with her fiancé. She said she felt as if a part of her had died with her sister. I said something like, "Grief is natural and inevitable, but guilt and self-punishment are optional. You are denying yourself pleasure out of a sense of guilt over her death." She responded immediately and said she felt much better after talking on the phone and would come in shortly for the interview.

Much of the early part of the follow-up interview was taken up with therapeutic work on her highly ambivalent relationship with Rebecca. She said that her guilt was about not being a good-enough sister. I reminded her that she *wanted* Rebecca dead, and the patient admitted that she had hated Rebecca from when she was born—"I made no bones about it". She was quite conscious of wanting to get rid of her. It emerged that the hatred was due to jealousy in three triangular relations—namely, those involving her sister and (1) her mother, (2) her father, and (3) her elder brother.

However, into her early thirties she consciously worked on her relationship with Rebecca and achieved a degree of closeness with her. She apologized to Rebecca for her former behaviour, which the latter accepted. She emphasized in the interview that they came to trust each other and were able to confide in each other about highly intimate things.

The patient said that when she heard of Rebecca's death she felt that she was not allowed to have sex, and the therapist asked why not:

Pt: Because I killed Rebecca when I wanted my brother.

Th: Sexual possession.

Pt: Of my brother and my father.

She said that her feeling was that she had to punish herself, or even kill herself. In fact, she overcame this feeling without much difficulty, and shortly afterwards she was able to have a very intense sexual experience.

It was only this single session that was needed to clear up her feelings about Rebecca.

RELATION BETWEEN CRITERIA AND OUTCOME

[1]   DM: Recovery from depression. If further losses occur, then we would wish her to react with appropriate mourning, followed by recovery, without continuing depression.

JM: For her to have fully experienced her grief and anger relating to her father's death and for the depression to have disappeared.

One of the first things that the patient said in the follow-up interview was, "I'm very happy". Later she spoke of "coming back to life" and being "very lively". There is no doubt whatsoever that depression has been replaced by pleasure in life.

With reference to *reaction to loss*, the death of someone with whom she had such a close and intensely ambivalent relation is as severe a test of a patient's mental health as can be imagined. It is clear that though she was extremely shocked by Rebecca's death, she did not become *depressed*.

Relationship to men

[2]   DM: Ability to sustain a mutually fulfilling long-term relationship with a man.

JM: For her to develop a meaningful, close relationship with a man who is willing to commit to her.

Before she came to treatment, she reported a history of involvement with men that would end because of their inability to commit to marriage. Her main close relationship had been with a man who suffered from a serious inhibition against marrying her. It is important to say, however, that she was clearly in love with this man, wanted desperately to marry him, and had no obvious inhibitions in her relationship with him, including the sexual relation.

She has now found a new man, Don. She described the gradual development of a relationship between two people who fell in love with each other almost at first sight. There could hardly be anything more "normal" than her description—Level 3 evidence *par excellence*. She experienced an intense physical attraction for him from the beginning. He had to visit her home to make some measurements (or so he said!), and before he arrived she got a "powerful sexual urge, together with an image of him". When they slept together, although he was impotent the first time, "I just loved being in his arms. In addition to loving sex, he's a very warm person, I just loved being near him. Some couples can be almost chemically in love." She said that sexually she can do anything with him, and she can talk about anything. She said several times, "I'm crazy about him".

There are many other aspects of his personality that attract her. Although they come from different cultures and he is not formally educated in the same way as she is, it is clear that they share intellectual ideas. Also, she greatly enjoys travelling with him and introducing him to things he had never known before—"it was such fun seeing his delight". "His charm feels like an antitoxin to me." He stood by her after Rebecca's death, when she described being as "ugly" as she could be. She said that the year that they have been together has been one of "a total expression of emotion, but he hasn't backed away".

So far everything would seem to be perfect. However, she discovered that he had a drinking problem, and on one occasion he missed a date with her because of his drinking. He has had a typical history of someone dependent on alcohol who has struggled to give it up; in the past, he has actually succeeded for as long as a year but has relapsed. On this recent occasion, she confronted him with it and he gave up temporarily, but he then relapsed again and did not tell her. She handled this very forcefully, as described below under "self-assertion". She said that she wants to marry him as long as his drinking can be overcome.

Sex

Issues of sexuality were implied, but not specifically mentioned, in the criteria formulated by both judges.

It is clear that she is extremely passionate sexually. She said, "I love sex so much and it makes me so happy". After Don recovered from his impotence, she said, "It was a wonderful, deep experience. I was very raw and wild. . . . Sex is very exciting, but I also have warmth."

Anger and self-assertion

[3]   DM: Ability to feel anger and express it when appropriate, and to assert herself constructively, without the fear of jeopardizing a relationship.

JM: To be able to express her angry feelings more openly, and to learn that this need not jeopardize relationships. To be less concerned and less sensitive about the perceptions of other people with regard to her and to be able to "be herself" rather than a false, compliant person.

She has behaved in an extremely forthright way over Don's recent bout of drinking: "I was very angry and very disappointed, and also angry that he hadn't told me." She reported her words: "I'm not living a life like this. You know I love you very much, but you have a choice here. It's not negotiable."

She also described an incident concerning an indiscreet remark on her mother's part: "I really lit into her."

Her mother

[4] DM: In recent years there has been a considerable improvement in the spontaneity and intimacy of the relationship with her mother. We hope that this may continue and that she can lose her fear of her mother's disapproval and become completely able to "be herself" with her.

JM: To have an improved relationship with her mother and siblings.

The patient made a remark implying that before Rebecca's death she had been withdrawn and unforthcoming with her mother; however, after Rebecca's death she spoke as follows: "That night I really started crying. My mother just held me. I was allowing her to be a mother."

This is Level 3 evidence of a moment of great closeness.

Work and creativity

[5] DM: Ability to fulfil her potential in work.

JM: To obtain advancement at work.

As far as creativity is concerned, the position is as follows. Before she came to therapy she had thought of the title for a novel but had not actually written a word. After the session in which the therapist brought out that she was withholding her feelings as an act of defiance, which was linked with her mother, she started writing the novel and finished it within a few months. Her writing continues, with a second novel in the works.

She has developed speaking skills and is reportedly "the darling of the office". In fact, she had just returned from an especially successful seminar when she received the phone call about her sister's sudden death.

Feelings in general

[6]   DM: The ability to face and express appropriately all her true feelings, in such a way as to prevent them lingering on and having adverse effects.

JM: To be able to face and experience feelings more fully, especially in relation to loss and anger.

There is no doubt that this criterion is completely fulfilled. She has been able to express the following feelings freely: happiness, love, warmth, and sexuality, all with the greatest intensity, anger (with both Don and her mother), and all her mixed feelings about Rebecca, which include shock, grief, closeness, death wishes, envy, jealousy, and guilt.

Her description of her agonized reaction to learning about Rebecca's death shows the degree to which she was able to express her true feelings openly, rather than channelling them into her gut. This presumably accounts for the fact that she did not suffer a relapse of her ulcerative colitis.

Ulcerative colitis

[7]   DM: It seems impossible to require her to recover from this illness. We can only hope that she may at least improve, without suffering from exacerbations in response to adverse circumstances.

JM: For the symptoms of ulcerative colitis to diminish and for the patient to feel well and unthreatened by it. For the ulcerative colitis no longer to affect her life socially and professionally.

Colonoscopy reveals scarring but no active disease whatsoever. She experiences no pain or urgency and has not been on medication or had a flare-up in the 8 years since treatment ended.

She spoke as follows:

> Pt: I radiate good health, my stomach's been terrific, unbelievable. I've been enjoying great health for four years. I just feel terrific. I wouldn't know I had the disease.

Regarding the criterion that she should not suffer "from exacerbations in response to adverse circumstances": as described above under "Traumatic event", the death of Rebecca is as severe a stress as could be imagined, and she has not relapsed. This was confirmed at the 10-year follow-up.

All this is Level 3 evidence—she has far exceeded the criteria.

TEN-YEAR FOLLOW-UP

The patient phoned the therapist for an appointment, wanting to report on her present life.

Because this interview revealed that all the original criteria were exceeded, we propose to add a list of criteria as if we had allowed our imagination to run wild, making some use of hindsight, and expecting the patient to achieve an "unrealistic" and "idealized" state of "total positive mental health". These criteria are put in italics.

Depression and reaction to loss

After the 8-year follow-up, we did not formulate an additional criterion specifically concerning her later reactions to her sister's death. If we had, it would have read as follows:

• *We would like to see that she has recovered from the severe distur-bance caused by her sister's death, so that her life is no longer adversely affected by it, and in particular that she no longer suffers from irrational guilt about it.*

With greater insight we can now add:

• *She should have worked through to a state in which she can both accept her complex mixed feelings for her sister and can feel comfortable with the memory of her.*

She made clear that the single session she had had with the therapist after Rebecca's death had enabled her to resolve her feelings.

The follow-up interview opened as follows:

Pt: It's so nice to come here and see you when I feel happy. I'm really happy. The last time I came I was happy in some ways, but my sister had just died and I was having a hard time.

Th: Yes, indeed. So perhaps that's where we should start, because we could see that you responded to her death with a great deal of guilt and self-punishment.

Pt: Yes, but that's not a problem any more. I have a real sense of peace about it. No matter how it comes up, I always end up with a feeling of peace. I also realize that even though she is dead, my relationship with her goes on. I can have all kinds of feelings about her. I can love her, hate her—but it's a very rich relationship. I can get competitive and say, "she got the good legs", but it's OK to feel it—I don't feel guilty. I actually feel that those who have died look after me now. In fact, when I feel pure joy I can feel her presence. It's her spirit with me. I feel she looks after me and wants me to be happy.

Her reaction to other losses

Since the previous follow-up, her stepfather and her father-in-law have died, both of whom she said she adored. She was able to mourn these losses without suffering from depression.

We can now add the following more stringent general criterion:

• *"Depression should be replaced by joy and pleasure in life."*

This criterion has already been partly covered in her opening statement quoted above, but will be covered further under the next headings.

Relationship to men

The original criteria can now be greatly expanded:

• *We would like to see her fall passionately in love with a suitable man whom she likes as well as loves, and who returns her feelings. This should lead to a permanent relationship, which gives her a sense of security and extreme happiness and which includes great closeness, mutual respect, common interests, and the ability to share deep feelings. There should be intense physical attraction on both sides, leading to an utterly free sexual relation. Differences should be resolved by open discussion, with as much self-assertion on her side as the situation requires. This should be constructive, highly effective, and carried out both with determination and with warmth and sympathy. It should lead in the end to greater closeness between them.*

She has been married for a year now. She reports one major crisis that erupted shortly after the wedding. Somehow, it was revealed to her that her husband had indulged in a single episode of drinking just before the wedding, which—just as at the 8-year follow-up—he had kept secret from her. She handled it even more forcefully than before:

Pt: (*With voice raised*) I let him know it. I was outraged and very angry, and I even left the house. I came back after doing some soul-searching and told him, "This is a betrayal". I made it crystal clear to him where I stand. I told him that I love him but this is not what I want from my life. I told him he had a choice, but these are my terms and conditions. I'd do whatever I could to support him once he made the decision, but I wasn't going to do it for him. He didn't drink again.

It is clear that in the long run this episode has not spoiled their relationship in any way:

Pt: It's a slow thing, to re-establish that trust, but I let him know where I stood, and he responded. So, as difficult as this was, it's been good too. We've been through it together and we're stronger. It's almost a feeling of mastery. He knows he can't drink at all, and he knows it's self-destructive. In some way, it'll always be there, but as far as our daily life is concerned it's not an issue.

Th: The important thing is that you have the closeness now.

Pt: Oh yes, every single day, because, you know, people say to me, "Oh, you're just newlyweds", but still, every day I feel so happy. If I wake in the middle of the night, it just feels so wonderful. And I come into the office saying, "I'm so happy". They get sick of hearing about it. I treasure him and feel treasured, so I feel that, in spite of the problems, I am so happy (*sitting forward*). My life has changed. I love him and I feel loved . . . When we have conflicts, he may distance himself initially, but it's so intolerable to have any barrier between us that in fairly short order we sit down and talk about it.

Much important information about further details of their relationship has already been given in the previous follow-up.

Ulcerative colitis

We can now expand the original criteria:

• *We would like to see the process of ulcerative colitis completely halted endoscopically, leaving only scarring. She should be entirely symptom-free, even under severe stress, and the former symptoms should have been replaced by good health and a general sense of well-being. If possible she should have become aware of the connection between her emotions and variations in the severity of her former illness.*

She mentioned that nowadays she deals with her feelings very differently from before:

Pt: And, you know, this is very important for your research, that when I get nervous, *I don't feel it in my gut*. Symptomatically, I FEEL FABULOUS. It doesn't go to my stomach any more. I feel great and I'm energetic. I don't know where that anxiety goes any more—well it doesn't go somatically, *I guess I just let it out*. I feel in my heart that the changes I've made in myself and in my behaviour have collaborated to shut this disease off. And I'm also not feeling shame and humiliation about the incontinence. And that is HUGE.

Th: So there's no urgency, or frequency, or incontinence.

Pt: No, none. There is simply no evidence of it.

Th: No more pain, weakness, and depletion.

Pt: I just savour feeling good—it's like an animal pleasure. Not killing myself any more.

Her mother

We can now add:

•   *We hope that, while recognizing and tolerating some negative feelings about her mother, she will be able to feel really close to her; and that she will be able to take reasonable responsibility for looking after her in her old age, without unnecessary self-sacrifice leading to resentment.*

The therapist mentioned that after the dramatic session in which she got in touch with her sadistic and murderous feelings towards her mother, she had said, "I don't want to have to kill myself to keep her alive":

Pt: I don't feel that way any more. Now when I talk to my mother, who is alone and ageing, I don't approach it that way. I love her and feel loved by her. At times she can be irritating, but I tend to let it roll off my back. She's a great Mum. I'm an adult and I have my own life. I want to be there for her—she's suffered the greatest loss anyone could—but I don't enslave myself. I used to do too much, because I'm the only one who lives close by, and then I would resent it. Now it's a more equal, give-and-take relationship.

Work and creativity

We can now add:

•   *We would also like her creativity to be freed and fulfilled to the maximum of her potential.*

She spoke of her job as something that supports her and allows her to do the other things that she wants to do. Her energy has been liberated because she is happy. She also is greatly valued at work. They gave her a huge party to celebrate her marriage, like no party she had ever experienced before.

Her creativity is separate from her professional life. Now she is writing another novel and, in addition, is composing music.

Pt: I had to come to terms with the fact that I'm not a musical genius. I could not be a performer, but I can write and create music. . . . It's very possible that eventually creation will take centre stage. Ideally I could take early retirement in four or five years and switch to creating full time.

Her step-daughter

In this connection the following criterion becomes highly relevant:

- *As with all good dynamic psychotherapy, we would like to see the patient able to use self-analysis in her life, so that she can resolve situations that are potentially destructive and cope with them realistically.*

The therapist emphasized that the patient had had difficulty over competition with women for male attention. This issue emerged in relation to her step-daughter. What had happened was that her step-daughter (an eighth-grader—i.e. aged about 14) had behaved in a surly manner towards her and had conveyed an impression of not liking her. The patient found herself reacting to this as if she herself were an eighth-grader—presumably being unforthcoming and covertly hostile—which threatened to set up a vicious circle:

Pt: So, right before she came up for the holidays, I took myself aside and confronted myself that this was not right. I don't feel the marriage can be a success if we're not happy as a family. Before she got here, I said to myself in a deep way,, she's an adolescent and she will have good days and bad days and my job is to make this a safe, happy home for her. . . . The odd thing was, I just decided this in such a deep way, that it was communicated somehow, because from the moment she came into the house it was different. It was extraordinary. I made her a special dinner for her birthday, and she really appreciated it. She got the message that I cared a lot. It was quite adorable. She came up again for the weekend, and it was great. It's hard work, but I tell you, there are unexpected joys. She just came in and plopped on the bed and talked to me. I feel enriched by her, and this is something I never could have expected.

Additional information: the question of having children

She made clear that she had never wanted children and does not regret her decision not to have any.

FURTHER FOLLOW-UP

Taking into account subsequent phone conversations and finally a chance encounter, we now know that by 13 years 9 months follow-up she has remained entirely symptom-free. She is still married to the same man, and they are deeply in love with each other. He has not resumed drinking, which is a tribute to her capacity for effective self-assertion.

COMMENT

As the reader will see, every one of these supposedly "unrealistic" criteria is fulfilled. Almost all the evidence is on Level 3.

CHAPTER 7

The Woman with Dissociation

Initial interview—trial therapy

The Woman with Dissociation (married, age 42) shows to an extraordinary degree the power of inner strength to rise above the most appalling trauma—so much so that events showed her to be not merely a good candidate, but an outstanding candidate, for ISTDP.

INITIAL INTERVIEW

The patient entered the trial therapy telling me she was referred by her doctor, who has seen her frequently over the years for a host of physical ailments including severe headaches, stomach distress, and backache.

Th: What brings you?
Pt: I always have anxiety—it's a constant thing from the minute I wake up until I go to bed at night.
Th: OK, let's start with that, because that's part of why you're here— you say you've suffered from chronic anxiety. Tell me how you experience the anxiety.
Pt: Constant turmoil—turmoil in my stomach—but that's not what scares me, because it's so much a part of my life . . .
Th: As long as you can remember you've had that?

Pt: As long as I can remember—as long as, since I was a child. But now I feel it coming up into my chest, like heartburn but without the burning sensation—just pressure. This is the stage of it now. It's always been down here (*motions to abdomen*), but now it's coming up. There's a burning sensation and pressure. Sometimes I can't even breathe.

Th: Pressure and constriction in your chest muscles.

Pt: Yes, it has to be that, because I can actually feel it coming up.

Th: You can feel it—and what else do you feel with the anxiety other than this pressure in your chest?

Pt: Insecurity—and that's getting worse.

Th: Let's stay with physical sensations for now. Anything else with the anxiety?

Pt: Becoming disassociated with myself. That's happening more and more. I'll be talking with someone and I just go off.

Th: Can you give me an example of when that happened recently?

Pt: Oh yeah, on Sunday.

Th: What happened?

Pt: I just left (*motions with hand*).

Th: What was happening that lead up to it? Where were you and what was going on?

Pt: It was Sunday night. I went into a rage—it was triggered.

Th: By?

Pt: My husband. I'm feeling very insecure with my husband—wondering what he's doing—is he screwing around on me? These are the kinds of things that are going through my mind (*smiles*).

Th: When did this start?

Pt: Over the summer it started (*this interview took place in early December*) and got more and more, or I was aware of it and it got worse.

Th: Worried that he is unfaithful to you?

Pt: Yeah, because that happened.

Th: It has happened?

Pt: Oh yes, when my middle daughter was a baby we had a bad time in our marriage. I should backtrack.

This opening segment reveals both current ego strength and a clear history of ego weakness. The patient makes excellent contact with the therapist: looking her straight in the eye, sitting forward, and giving detailed information about her presenting problems. All this bodes well for her ability to engage in, and benefit from, therapy. However, she reveals a history of dissociation going back to childhood, which indicates a need for caution and careful assessment. The patient began to dissociate around the age of 8 or 9 years (both ages are given by the patient in therapy) in response to severe trauma—beatings by both of her parents, being raped and sodomized by her father, and observing the beating and torture of her siblings. Her tendency to dissociate continues in the present and seems to occur without provocation at this time

Examination of her pattern of dissociation

Th: So this is something you've always known and remembered about the abuse, but you've had dissociative experiences too. You go into trances, you say. How long has this been going on?

Pt: I've been able to do that for a very, very long time. I remember doing that in the acts, when my father . . . I would go to a nice warm, safe spot under a tree—somewhere where I didn't have to be there. I could remember that feeling of being in a nice safe spot under a tree, and I've done it all my life because I like that feeling. I still do it, and it's so embarrassing because someone will be talking to me and I go away. It's not that I'm not interested in them but I can actually feel myself starting to go away. I can feel myself leaving—going out the window—and I can see myself sitting there but I'm outside and going somewhere safe. That's why I'm having a hard time in school, because I did that all the time in school.

Th: As a kid you mean.

Pt: As a kid and as an adult. And then I wasn't there and I couldn't learn. Now when I go to class, I'm not there, and that's happening more now.

Th: This is very important, so I want to make sure I'm straight on your experience. It sounds like you're saying it's almost a capacity you developed.

Pt: Sure.

Th: Which has been a terrific . . .

Pt: It's my defence.

Th: But it was very adaptive at the time. It was remarkable, in a sense, that you could develop a capacity to preserve yourself in the worst possible circumstances.

Pt: Right, because it wasn't me he was doing this to.

Th: So you could divorce yourself from it—distance yourself and calm yourself. So, in that situation, it was the best you could do . . . but now the problem is, it is no longer something you're doing consciously and wilfully but it seems to happen automatically and even when you don't want it to happen. So then it ends up depriving you. You want to be in the classroom and you want to learn but you can't take in the good stuff because you're off somewhere else.

Pt: Yeah, that's right. I'm not there. I can't take anything in and can't retain anything. People tell me something but I'm not really listening—I'm not really there.

Origin of the pattern of dissociation—
and catching it as it happens

Pt: I can't remember anything before the age of 9. I remember the first incident with my father and most of the encounters after that.

Th: So what age?

Pt: Nine. I remember that first time, naturally, most people would, but I blocked out other things. But you know, I'm more upset with my mother even than my father. She allowed it to happen. She pulled him off me twice and knew it was going on, but I was told there was no other alternative because she had nine other kids to take care of.

Th: You're one of ten? Where are you in the order?

Pt: I'm the oldest and then a year, year and a half apart at the most. And she was always in the hospital. I hated that. I hated that the most. I knew she'd come home with a new baby—another one I had to take care of, and then I had to take care of my father. I hated it when she went to the hospital. I really did.

Th: When you say you hated it, are you aware of the feelings?

Pt: Sick to my stomach because I knew he'd be coming into my room.

Th: Which you say started at age 9, and for some reason you block out these early years of your mother's constant absence—leaving over and over again, going away and coming home with a new baby. But this was happening from the earliest time.

Pt: Yeah.

Th: Because the next sibling from you is . . . ?

Pt: A boy, a year younger.

Th: Then, within a couple of years (*I can see her drifting off*) . . . What's happening? Are you going away?

Pt: (*Staring off into space*) OK, I'm back.

Th: Let's look at what happened there.

Pt: I was thinking about my brother. She never liked him and used to beat him up terrible (*starting to cry*). I think that's why he's slow, mentally slow. He would get mad when he was younger and get into so much trouble with my mother. She hated that boy, she just hated him. She busted his lip and did terrible things. I always felt so bad because I couldn't do anything for him (*weeping*). He's no better today.

This segment illustrates how the patient's responses can be used as a guide in intervention, as well as a diagnostic tool. Given her horrendous childhood and severe and debilitating symptoms, it would be easy to fall into the trap of assuming she would not be able to do such demanding work and would require long-term therapy. However, her response to my interventions reveals a remarkable flexibility and resilience within the system. As soon as I noticed her drifting off and mentioned it to her, she brought herself back. Furthermore, the feelings immediately came to the fore that she had been avoiding by dissociating. With the aid of the therapist, the patient began to face and experience all the pain, terror, and rage she had been avoiding all her life. This suggests tremendous will and courage. The alliance is so high, and her willingness to abandon defences so strong, that the therapy can proceed without delay.

De-repression of murderous wishes towards her mother

Th: Was there any positive figure at all? (*I'm wondering where she got her strength and resilience.*)

Pt: Yes. There was a woman across the street who I used to call Mum. She used to take a special interest in me and would make me a special dinner or buy me a dress. She was kind. There were people interested in me and knew what was going on. They didn't intervene. Why didn't someone stop it? I don't know. I wonder who I would have been if this hadn't happened. I often wonder. If they knew, why didn't they do something. If someone had cared . . .

Th: You're saying there were people who cared. Another one of your strengths is getting people interested in you and taking what they have to offer and using it for all it's worth. That's a terrific strength, but there's also pain and anger that no one had the strength or courage to intervene.

Pt: Yeah, especially my mother.

Th: Who's not just passively standing by and watching but is also an active perpetrator.

Pt: But if someone else did that to my children, I'm not embarrassed to say I'd kill them.

Th: So, isn't that what's already happened? You watched that as a child, as your mother—this maniac—threw your brother out the door. So are you aware that you had those murderous feelings towards her?

Pt: Yes. That's what I'm afraid of—that rage. What if I hurt someone.

Th: Let's look. Have you ever?

Pt: Once. When my oldest was two years old I spanked her. She was dressed and ready for bed. She was in her rocking-chair but she was too young and always fell out. I got angry, and all I saw was red. I was so horrified when I saw her red bottom that I never touched another one again. Oh my God.

Th: So who was that beating for?

Pt: I don't know.

Th: Part of you doesn't want to look at it, but you're saying there's a murderous rage towards your mother that leaked out towards your daughter. It really is for your mother.

Pt: Yes.

Th: You say you face it now. Do you remember thinking or feeling that you wanted to be rid of her—dead and gone?

Pt: I don't think so. There was no stopping her. How do you get her to stop? I don't know if someone came.

Th: But no one did.

Pt: If someone ever went near my kids . . .

Th: But these *were* your kids.

Pt: You're right. They were. I felt so bad. I was the only one that loved them.

Th: And here was this woman . . .

Pt: This monster. She smashed him. I thought he was going to die. Blood was pouring out. That poor little baby. At that moment I hated her.

Th: So you hated her and wanted her dead and gone.

Pt: Sure.

Th: A part of you was also fiercely protective, and no one else was going to do it.

Pt: I think you're right. I felt bad about leaving when I was 16. We had a terrible fight, she and I. She called me a tramp. After all that, what I went through. She started to hit me. I never hit her back. I wanted to, but I didn't. I pushed her back and left.

Th: Sounds like you were afraid to get started. There was such pent-up rage, you could kill her.

Pt: Yes.

In this segment we can observe the entire Triangle of Conflict in operation. Feelings of murderous rage towards her mother are mobilized, which evokes anxiety and is defended against with displacement and initial denial. She has all the pieces but does not want to put them together. As long as this is the case, she stays fragmented. Very rapidly, however, as the therapist persisted in having the patient examine her own words, the patient was able to acknowledge her wish to kill her mother and protect herself and her siblings. Again, we see that her defences are easily relinquished in favour of the direct experience of previously unbearable affect.

Examination of feelings in the therapeutic relationship

Th: As you're going through this, I find myself filled with admiration for you—you are so brave to face this so rapidly, here with me. What's it like to hear from me that I admire your courage?

Pt: Uncomfortable. I never take compliments too well.

Th: What else?

Pt: I don't want to believe it.

Th: So you want to push it away by saying, I must be making it up. You don't know me very well, but do you think I'd make it up?

Pt: No. I find it hard to believe. I don't absorb it.

Th: What would happen if you did take it in?

Pt: I don't know. It makes me uncomfortable. I don't know if it's be-cause I don't believe it or because there's some object to it. For any good thing anyone ever told me, there's an object to it. There's always an objective—something they want.

Th: Oh, you mean a string attached or something? So you get a bit suspicious. What would that be with me?

Pt: I don't know.

Th: On the other hand, you're not used to it. You didn't get much positive attention in your life.

Pt: Right.

Th: Some of the ache has to be about that.

Pt: I'm sure you're right.

Th: But there's also a part of you that's a little suspicious, which I'm sure you've had a good reason to be. People closest to you in your life have been the biggest threat to you. So, you pull away and have developed a guard there. But how did this work in particular, this getting something positive you would pay for?

Pt: Oh, well . . . "If I buy this toy for you . . . if I buy this toy for you (*long pause, looking as if she's far away*) . . . If I buy this toy for you, you can't tell your mother what I did to you last night." (*Suddenly seems to snap out of it*) I don't want the toy.

Th: So nothing is given freely.

Pt: There was never unconditional love.

The patient's ability to make links between the past and the present—her reluctance to accept compliments, for example—reveals more strength. The results of this initial evaluation clearly suggest that, despite severe and long-standing symptoms, this patient is motivated and capable of doing the work.

A DISCUSSION OF TRAUMA AND DISSOCIATION

Like a cub abandoned to the wolves, she was grossly neglected by her mother and was defenceless in warding off the sexual attacks of her father. As Peter Levine, co-author of *Waking the Tiger: Healing Traumas* (Levine & Frederick, 1997), reminds us, humans (like all primates), when faced with imminent and inescapable harm, instinctively enter a state of consciousness that is akin to freezing. This frozen and detached state is a last-ditch survival effort and creates an altered state of consciousness in which no pain is experienced. However, what is adaptive in promoting survival at the moment of threat becomes maladaptive once the threat has been removed. In fact, to zone out and dissociate can render the trauma victim vulnerable to repeated episodes of victimization, as well as hindering the healing process.

It has been suggested (Levine & Frederick, 1997) that there is a psychic healing mechanism available to all of us that is as real and powerful as the healing capacity of our physical bodies. If we get cut, we will heal, as long as our immune system is in good working order. Long-lasting symptoms prevail only when something interferes with this natural healing process. This is just as true in the realm of emotional well-being as it is on a physical plane. It seems as if the mechanisms that kick in to protect the child from the overwhelming terror and retaliatory rage precipitated by abuse prevent the experiencing and processing of the emotions triggered by the trauma. The traumatized person becomes so frightened by the intense and disruptive effects of his emotional reactions that he learns to avoid them permanently, preventing the natural process of healing from occurring.

It is our job, as therapists, to help each patient remove the defensive barriers against the experience of all the feelings locked within them. Research suggests that physical sensing and somatic experiencing of these emotions is essential in the healing process (Levine & Frederick, 1997; Pennebaker, 1997). In other words, just talking *about* traumatic events without the visceral experience of the feelings involved proves to be of little, if any, therapeutic benefit. However, it is also important to note that catharsis alone provides only temporary relief, but little lasting change. What seems to be required is the combination of a deep visceral experience of feeling, followed by reflection and integration (Greenberg & Paivio, 1997; Pennebaker, 1997). This is just the approach taken with this patient.

It should also be noted that an assessment of the patient's strengths is essential before embarking on this task. This patient, who had been grossly neglected and viciously abused throughout childhood, entered treatment reporting a lifelong history of massive symptoms, including dissociation. Taken alone, these facts create a dire, but incomplete and inaccurate, clinical picture. In order to assess suitability for treatment, the patient's strengths must also be assessed. In this case, there were many. She was highly motivated and determined not just to survive, but to live a healthy, happy life and provide her family with all the love and stability she never had. She was able to establish rapport with the therapist immediately and erected very few defences against emotional closeness, allowing a strong therapeutic alliance to develop. In addition, her history showed immense strength (see below).

In ISTDP we assess both the strength of the resistance and that of the therapeutic alliance. We seek to ally ourselves with the healthy part of the patient's ego in order to join forces to overcome the resistance and, in so doing, to face the feelings and impulses that were previously experienced as unbearable. This allows the natural healing process, which had been derailed, to take place.

THE THERAPEUTIC VALUE
OF THE INITIAL EVALUATION

In ISTDP, the patient's response to intervention is used as both a diagnostic tool and a guide to further intervention. Rather than take a history, as is typically done in the initial session of most psychotherapy, the ISTDP therapist begins by enquiring into the nature of the patient's current difficulties, getting specific details about recent examples of these difficulties, and moving right into the examination of feelings (along with the anxiety and defences that accompany them). This process of dynamic evaluation is therapeutic in and of itself. The patient is given an immediate experience of how the therapy works. Patients often comment that they have accomplished more during our first 2-hour session than they had achieved in years of previous psychotherapy. This clearly has an immediate and marked impact on the therapeutic alliance and on eventual outcome.

Recent research findings (Klein et al., 2003), designed to tease out the relationship between therapeutic alliance, clinical improvement, and outcome, showed that the rapid development of a therapeutic alliance predicted subsequent change in depressive symptoms, even after controlling for chronicity, co-morbid anxiety, personality disorders, the highest level of social functioning in the last 5 years, and a history of abuse and neglect in childhood. While there is ample support for the contention that the therapeutic alliance has a "modest, but consistent, relationship to outcome" (Horvath & Luborsky, 1993; Martin, Garske, & Davis, 2000), "few exclude the possibility that this association is accounted for by 3rd variables, such as prior improvement and prognostically relevant patient characteristics" (Klein et al., p. 997). This rather large study (N = 367 chronically depressed patients) demonstrated unambiguous findings in this regard. The early development of an alliance paved the way for successful intervention, which boded well for outcome (Martin, Garske, & Davis, 2000). These two factors—alliance and symptomatic improvement—may well have mutual and reciprocal effects (Barber, Connolly, Crits-Christoph, Gladis, & Sinqueland, 2000), suggesting that attending to both would produce superior results to a treatment model that only fostered one or the other factor. These findings confirm those of J. Weinberger (1995) whose meta-analysis of "common factors" suggested that interventions designed to confront the patient with feelings and thoughts that he tends to want to avoid accounts for most of the variance in outcome (approximately 50%), while the alliance seems to account for somewhere between 11% and 20% of the variance. We suggest—and believe our data demonstrate—that a therapy, like ISTDP, that combines techniques both to confront defences and strengthen the alliance produces robust results.

While the way in which psychotherapy works remains "a crucial question in need of empirical investigation" (Pos, Greenberg, Goldman, & Korman, 2003, p. 1007), more and more research data demonstrate that techniques designed to enhance and improve emotional processing are consistently related to positive outcome (Greenberg & Paivio, 1997; Hendricks, 2002). This is exactly the approach taken by the ISTDP therapist. Both phenomena—active work from the start on improving emotional processing, with subsequent enhancement of the therapeutic alliance—are demonstrated in the following therapy.

FORMULATION

The following is an amalgamation of the formulations made by the two judges.

Hypothesis

The main features of her childhood were:

1. Physical abuse by both her father and her mother of the patient and her siblings.
2. Sexual abuse by her father, which her mother did little to prevent.
3. Having had little mothering herself, she had to take the responsibility for caring for her siblings.
4. She herself finally abandoned her siblings by leaving home at the age of 16.

The result has been a mass of unresolved feelings, together with defences against them.

Her main defence has been dissociation, originally quite conscious but now automatic and beyond her control. Another defence is somatization.

Above all, the feeling against which she is defending is (1) *murderous rage* against both her father and her mother. In addition she is defending against (2) the *distress* arising out of all these experiences; (3) *guilt* about her intense anger; and (4) both *guilt* and the *pain of helplessness* resulting from her inability to protect her siblings.

Criteria

The *Essential Criterion* is that she should be able to face and express all "normal" feelings, and use them positively in her life, without resorting to her defence of dissociation—while retaining all her admirable qualities such as courage, determination, and emotional honesty. Specifically:

[1] *Aggression and self-assertion:* Great mitigation of her murderous feelings, to the point at which she is able to express anger appropriately without the fear that it will get out of control. This should lead to the ability to assert herself constructively, and not to be swayed unrealistically by other people's opinions.

[2] *Her husband, or other man:* We hope that she may be able to resolve the situation with her husband and continue with him on a more rewarding basis. If this is not possible, then we would hope that she would be able to mourn him and eventually—perhaps—form a mutually satisfactory relation with another man.

[3] *Sex:* Further improvement in her ability to enjoy sex.

[4] *Children:* We hope that she may be able to retain her good relationship with her children and handle difficulties with them as best she can.

[5] *Studies:* We hope that she will be able to focus on developing goals for herself, especially in her studies, to enable her to have something for herself and enhance her self-esteem.

[6] *Self-worth:* Improved self-esteem, feeling more respected and more powerful, learning to "like herself".

[7] *Attitude to past events, irrational guilt:* She should be able to regard past events as something extremely distressing that happened, but which no longer affect her life. She should no longer feel irrationally guilty and responsible for her part in them.

[8] *Symptoms:* Loss of all symptoms (in addition to dissociation): constant anxiety; inner turmoil; physical symptoms of headaches, gastrointestinal distress, backache; depression.

SESSION 2

The therapist regarded this session as the second part of the trial therapy.

The patient began by saying that she was anxious about coming today. What emerged was that she had received reassurance and approval from the therapist but was angry that she was only getting it *now*. She then linked this with the love that she gave to her daughters: "I get angry and resentful that they have it better than I did and don't seem to appreciate it." She said that the therapist reminded her of one of her daughters, who "is solid like a brick", and she feels jealous of this.

The therapist said that these feelings were quite understandable, but that they interfered with her feeling good about what she had given her daughters. "We need to face this anger head on—otherwise you won't get to the positive."

This led to anger with the patient's mother. She said that it was like her anger with her husband—"I could kill her".

Thus this patient has been able (1) to speak openly about the transference; (2) to bear her mixed feelings both about the therapist and her daughters; (3) to begin to face long-buried feelings about the past; and (4) to make spontaneous links between past and present. All this suggests that she will be able to make good use of ISTDP.

Therapy and follow-up

The therapy for the Woman with Dissociation consisted of 14 sessions, and follow-up took place 7 years after termination.

THERAPY

SESSION 3

The patient came in reporting anxiety, which had started the previous day as she began to think about coming to her session. The process of facing feelings, especially anger and her own violent, destructive impulses, was very upsetting for her. She was feeling so anxious and shaky inside that she wanted someone to drive her to the session. Despite this, she could not bring herself to ask for help, and she managed to get to the session on her own.

She revealed a fantasy she had while waiting in the waiting-room—that I wouldn't be available to see her. She was aware of intense mixed feelings towards me, including a fear of being hurt or abandoned. Then she remembered that her father used to threaten to kill her if she told anyone about what happened. As she reported this memory, she became very anxious and then shut down, reporting that she felt numb. She began to berate herself for not doing better at accessing feelings, even though she was trying hard to do so. This was, in a sense, a re-enactment of what would happen in those childhood situations. In an

217

attempt to help her understand what she was experiencing, I explained to her the effects of repeated childhood trauma on the central nervous system (CNS).

SESSION 4

The patient came in reporting that she feels "better than I have in ages", which she attributed to what happened in the last session. She said that hearing me talk about the effects of trauma on the CNS was enormously helpful. She felt the need to understand things—not just what happened but how it affected her—and no one ever supplied this information to her. In addition to being chaotic and terrifying, much of her childhood experience was incomprehensible to her. This settled, she raised the issue of anger with her eldest daughter. We used this current example to do some restructuring, getting through anxiety and defence to the experience of her anger. She was able to experience the visceral anger towards her daughter and then made a spontaneous link to her mother. When she realized that she had been viewing her daughter (and reacting to her) as a stand-in for her mother, she immediately differentiated one from the other. Her mother was totally inaccessible and irrational. Her daughter was not. She imagined telling her daughter directly what she was upset about, and she had the sense it would go well. She decided to speak to her in person, as soon as possible, in order to clear up the current tension between them. So, here we see *character change*—from withdrawal and passivity in her interactions with others to constructive self-assertion.

SESSION 6

The patient entered this session with a very high level of anxiety. She had cancelled the previous session due to a snow storm, which kept her from getting to the office. She reported having trouble breathing and feeling highly agitated, as if she might explode. She had been crying all day and could not focus or function at work. When asked what precipitated these feelings, she reported having discovered more evidence that her husband was, in fact, having an affair. She found a gift and card from her husband to the woman in question. She confronted her husband, who made light of her concerns and laughed at her.

Anger and anxiety in relation to her husband

Th: Let's look at how you're feeling towards your husband.
Pt: I feel this terrible pain in my gut.

Th: That's anxiety in you—it's not the feeling towards him. In fact, you avoid the feeling towards him and turn it on you, which is torturous.

Pt: I know it's anger, but I'm afraid of it—it's like a monster. I'm afraid I could explode and be violent like my parents, and I don't want that.

Th: Obviously you don't want to act on those feelings, but that doesn't mean you don't have them. If they aren't faced, the attack is on you.

Pt: But I'm afraid I could lose control and do something horrendous.

Th: Has that ever happened?

Pt: No. Well, just that once when I lost it with my daughter and spanked her, but never again.

Th: So what you fear now is the experience of this intense, monstrous rage. What does it feel like inside?

Pt: Like a volcano erupting.

We spent the rest of the session focusing on the experience of anger, as distinguished from anxiety and self-torture. The impulse was to lash out at him and beat him on his face and chest—then to go for his genitals. After imagining attacking her husband (not herself), she felt deep waves of grief about all that has been lost between them. Then she began to feel calm. She was amazed to discover that the calm came after the storm of her violent impulses.

Session 7: Breakthrough session

The patient reported being in touch with deep, painful longings, along with a searing sense of deprivation of her most basic needs for love, comfort, and reassurance. This current betrayal by her husband, along with her decision to leave the marriage, brought all the pain around deprivation very close to the surface. She began to cry, "Where was my mother?" She reported memories of two distinct times in which her mother found her father attacking her sexually. We began to explore these memories in order to facilitate the experience of all the feelings associated with them.

Feelings towards her mother
regarding her father's sexual abuse

Pt: Even when she pulled him off me, she didn't do anything about it. When I cried out, she said, "Oh, he's not hurting you. I can't call the police, I have nine other kids to take care of."

Th: Could we look specifically at these incidents in which your father was assaulting you and your mother knew it—even pulling him off you—but did nothing?

Pt: It was late at night. I was in bed sleeping. I woke up, and there was this heavy, heavy feeling on me. I woke up, and he was there on top of me. I don't know if he was inside of me, I just know he was on top of me and he was drunk. He was always drunk.

Th: So you have that heavy feeling, like when he was on top of you.

Pt: He was on top of me.

Th: Can you tell me what you see? Do you have a picture?

Pt: I can see the bedroom, how I was looking all around the bedroom. It's small. I think it's pink. So anyway, I just remember waking up in that room and focusing on him on top me and saying, "No, I don't want to do anything. Leave me alone, leave me alone." And I was scared and confused, and I don't even know how old I was. (Pause) I'm trying to remember how old I was. I don't remember how old I was.

Th: What comes to your mind?

Pt: Eight or nine. Eight. She came in and she pulled him off, and I said, "I didn't do anything wrong" (voice has a pleading tone). She didn't say anything. She just pulled him off, and they had a terrible fight. I just remember feeling very sad and feeling like I did something wrong but I couldn't quite understand what was going on. I didn't know what to do.

Th: You remember her coming in and pulling him off.

Pt: Pulling him off (making the movements of pulling him off her). Pulling him off.

Murderous fantasy against her father

Pt: (Weeping) I'm so angry

Th: And what do you feel you want to do now, when you go back to that?

Pt: I want to stick a knife in his heart.

Th: You actually get an image of that and can feel that?

Pt: It was disgusting

Th: Are you in touch with the anger right now?

Pt: No.

Th: What happened to it?

Pt: I just accepted it.

Th: Do you see that, now, this is a way you avoid the anger and the impulse to lash out at him? Right? Your mother wasn't going to rescue you. The only way to be rid of him was to kill him.

Pt: That's how I felt.

Th: You wanted to kill him, and the impulse is to drive a knife into his heart.

Pt: Yes.

Th: Do you see it—what kind of knife?

Pt: I don't know what kind.

Th: What's the picture?

Pt: Just doing what I was told to do and not questioning.

The patient moved back and forth between acknowledging her own sadistic rage and defending against it by retreating to helplessness. Going to the helpless position now, as an adult, rendered her vulnerable to being repeatedly used and abused. This defence must be undone for her to get well. The therapist must work vigilantly to remove the regressive defence and face the underlying impulses.

Th: That's what you actually did in that situation. But now, what you are aware of feeling is that you want to stab him—in the heart.

Pt: Yes.

Th: And you get an image of that and it's in the chest?

Pt: No, I feel that now.

Th: So you're not aware that you felt it then but you do now?

Pt: I just remember then doing what I was told to do and not questioning it. No, no, I couldn't question it, I couldn't. I would say, "No, I don't want to do this". "Just lay down. Daddy loves you. Let me do this." I just remember lying there and doing what I was supposed to do. I was on automatic pilot.

Th: Sure. So it's really now that you're feeling this outrage and have this image of, like, just sneaking up on him when he's in bed—or it's back at that bed where you . . .—because you said specifically that you see him lying in bed . . .

Pt: I think I see him lying in bed but it's in, like, a hospital bed, and I could just go in and take the knife and stab him and go in there and cut his penis off and shove it in his mouth.

Th: How does that feel?

Pt: It feels OK . . . not earth-shattering, but OK.

Murderous fantasy against her mother

Pt: And then I'd like to do that to her, too, and then, when they both die I'd like to . . . I read this story about a survivor who danced on her parent's grave, and I thought . . . how wonderful to do the jig right there on their grave. Then I'd pull my pants down and pee all over them and say, "There! It's over."

Th: So you want to piss on them.

Pt: That's right. I think that would give me the greatest pleasure.

In this last vignette we see that her self-abdication and self-torture have been eliminated. She is no longer horrified by her own feelings and impulses but can actually acknowledge experiencing sadistic pleasure in seeking revenge. This must be felt, not acted upon. We are not advocating getting back at anyone, but resurrecting one's sense of self, so that this kind of abuse could never happen again.

[*Both DM and JM predicted the essence of this session. DM wrote: "The overwhelming feelings are (1) murderous rage against both parents, and (2) unassimilated distress." JM left out the distress, but wrote: "She needs to experience murderous rage against her parents."*]

Session 8

The patient came into the next session reporting on her progress. She felt much better and internally stronger. She had been able to declare her needs at home and at work and found they were getting met. For example, instead of just doing, doing, doing for her daughters, while building up resentment about how easy they've got it, she decided to sit down with them and tell them how she was feeling. They ended up devising a plan in which they could all pitch in with household duties. She was delighted with the outcome.

She contrasted the responses she got from her daughters with that from her husband. While she felt frightened about the divorce and all the changes it would entail, she reminded herself, "You've survived much worse than this". Her husband had an affair earlier in their marriage. She had been willing to stick it out and work through it at the time but told him, in no uncertain terms, that if it happened again, the marriage would be over. She was sticking to her guns, standing her ground, and refusing to let him off the hook.

Changes in symptoms and functioning

Th: Since you've reoriented some, focusing on your own feelings and needs and speaking up about them, you're feeling better and stronger.

Pt: Good, yeah, I feel good.

Th: Less anxious and fearful and like you're going to fall apart. Also, you are more directed and focused.

Pt: Yeah. You remember that last time I came in here and I was such a wreck. I don't honestly think I've had a day like that since then. *I don't have any more anxiety attacks*, I've discovered that. *I don't have any more migraine headaches*—did I tell you that? I haven't had a headache since that first day I came to see you, and I know because I chart them. And that's amazing to me.

Th: That's really something.

Pt: It's amazing! Because I've had migraine headaches since I was 8 years old.

Th: Wow! I don't think you mentioned that, but obviously it corresponded with . . .

Pt: I keep forgetting to tell you about it, but it's wonderful! It's wonderful and it's a way of confirming, Yes, this happened, Yes, you do have these feelings and you were burying them, and Yes, this is the way you were handling them. Yes, it's sort of like another, what's the word . . . another clue as to this big picture or proof—it's like proof.

Th: Well, there were many things that you've always remembered—you didn't need proof of that—but what was buried were all the feelings and reactions to what happened. You went numb; you went into a trance; you weren't really there, in a sense. But since you've been coming here and allowing yourself to feel what you felt and put the feelings and the memories together, you've had no need to put it into a headache.

Pt: It's dissipated, it's gone.

These changes speak for themselves. Since facing her feelings of fear, rage, and grief, all her symptoms have disappeared. [*Essentially predicted by DM.*] Furthermore, there was evidence that healthy alternatives were taking their place.

In addition to the task of freeing patients emotionally, we must aid them in piecing together a coherent life narrative (Neborsky, 2001). Human beings have a need to understand, explain, and make sense of what has happened to them (Frankl, 1959). When confronted with overwhelming and inexplicable experiences, an abused child will often construct a life narrative in which reality is grossly distorted. This is particularly true when the abuser is a parent, upon whom the child is dependent for his or her life and survival (Bowlby, 1980). In the case being presented here, the patient survived being assaulted by her father by dissociating and telling herself, "This isn't happening". She dealt with the overwhelming feelings of helplessness and guilt evoked by watching her mother abuse her younger siblings by blaming herself and assuming responsibility for actions totally beyond her control. These beliefs served to distort not only her history, but her very sense of self. Through the therapeutic process, all these beliefs and perceptions are reconsidered and reconstructed following the experience of all the feelings involved in what actually happened. This kind of cognitive re-analysis of the process facilitates integration and coherence within the self, so necessary for a sense of continuity and well-being.

Session 9

This was a session focused on consolidating gains. The patient reported that she continued to feel better every day. She felt angry about some unfairness at work and was assertive with her employer about the issue at hand. There was no anxiety about her feelings or behaviour. In fact, she felt good about herself for acting in her own best interest. Not only did she achieve a boost in self-esteem, but she achieved the desired results from her boss and found that other employees were starting to look up to her, viewing her as a leader among them.

She mentioned that memory flashes of being assaulted by her father were still coming back to her after that pivotal session. In one vivid memory, she reported seeing her father outside her room, naked and jerking off, with an awful, leering look in his eye. She could feel rage rise within her, along with an impulse to jump on him, pin him down, and punch his face until it's squashed. "Now he can't look at me like that anymore." She could really feel the desire for revenge—wanting him to pay for what he did to her as a child. These feelings and impulses were accompanied by a sense of personal power, strength, and forti-tude. Following the breakthrough of sadistic rage towards her father, she reported feeling liberated. She came to realize that the real libera-tion was from her own anxiety and constriction in the face of these feelings, which she could now embrace and use for her own empower-ment.

Session 10

Pt: It's amazing, because now I feel like the incest was in the past. It happened, I know how I felt about it and how I dealt with it, but now it's in the past. That heaviness and pain is gone, and I'm putting my energy into things I want for myself now.

This amazing statement was accompanied by a request to see the tapes and go over the process of how she had got here. All this progress made her think there could be an end in sight.

It is worth comparing this statement with the wording of Criterion [7]:"She should be able to regard past events as something extremely distressing that happened, but which no longer affect her life. She should no longer feel irrationally guilty and responsible for her part in them."]

SESSION 11

The patient entered this session feeling very agitated and upset. When asked about it, she understood that some of it had to do with issues around the separation from her husband, as well as some remaining tendency to "feel crazy" when he denies the reality of what has happened. I wondered if it might also be a reaction to her bringing up the issue of termination, which she acknowledged. Most of the session was spent on the issue of her having surrendered her own sense of knowing what she knew by complying with the view of the other. Now she is not swayed by her husband's lies and his attempts to put the focus back on her, as if she is crazy and making things up. She knows what she knows and is becoming her own authority.

SESSION 12. She resolves the emotional situation with her husband

The patient began by recounting a heart-to-heart talk with her husband, who finally acknowledged the affair. They were able to cry together and grieve for a long marriage with many happy times and three wonderful children. This was very healing.

SESSION 13. She resolves the practical situation with her husband and suggests termination

Now she is opening up to her husband—not just angry and blaming. After crying together, she opened up and told him she just could not forget this second betrayal. She was willing to face being alone rather than stay in a relationship where there was deception and ill-treatment involved. She recognized that it was not just the affair, but the way he dealt with it, that was so damaging. He was willing to play on her insecurities and tendency to blame herself to get himself off the hook, and she recognized this as cruel. She was not willing to subject herself to that kind of treatment any longer. Furthermore, she felt she deserved to be loved and supported in a relationship. She was no longer so afraid to be alone, and she declared her intention of getting a good lawyer . This stand was a manifestation of her solid sense of self, and was not coming from the mouth of a victim. She was saying, "I deserve better", not, "Look what you did to me, you rotten bastard". It is very important that the therapist be able to distinguish genuine self-assertion from the tyranny and manipulation of the weak.

Her decision to explore going back to school was yet another example of her new-found sense of self-worth. During the second half of her life, she wanted something better for herself. She was thinking about where she could make the best use her talents as well as have an impact on others. With this, she suggested that she was ready to end therapy.

Again, it is worth comparing this with Criterion [5], which was formulated by JM: "We hope that she will be able to focus on developing goals for herself, especially in her studies, to enable her to have something for herself and to enhance her self-esteem."

Termination in ISTDP is often quite straightforward. Since a transference neurosis is avoided, and all feelings towards the therapist are dealt with as soon as they arise, dependence on the therapist is averted. In this case, we used one more session to process the work we had done and to express the feelings about saying goodbye.

This woman, and her treatment, seemed remarkable in many ways. Given her history and the nature and duration of symptoms reported, I would have previously assumed she would be very difficult to treat and that any treatment employed would be long-term in nature. Despite horrendous abuse as a child, and a long-standing history of severe and debilitating symptoms like migraine headaches and dissociation, she had many strengths and a fierce determination to get well. The fact that she was in the midst of a current crisis contributed to the fluidity of her unconscious, which had been opened by a rise in feelings towards her husband. The circumstances, the patient's strengths, the strong alliance developed with the therapist, and the therapeutic techniques designed to liberate buried feelings all made for a potent combination.

These results lend support to a finding by Janoff-Bulman (1992) regarding recovery from trauma. She found that recovery was most strongly related to a patient's ability to construct a new life narrative that affords the patient some sense of personal efficacy and safety for the future, rather than to the severity of the trauma itself. As previously noted, ISTDP seems to be particularly effective in helping patients construct a coherent life narrative, which had been fractured by re-pressed and dissociated feelings and memories prior to treatment. These findings suggest that the patient has to come to trust herself so that she will not, as an adult, allow abuse to happen again. Trust in oneself seems to be significantly enhanced by learning to identify feelings and use them as fuel in one's own endeavours. This particular patient had already demonstrated this new-found ability in her asser-tive interactions with her husband, children, and employer. In each case, when she felt mistreated, she spoke up and behaved in such a way as to protect her own interests, while remaining on good terms with those involved. Even in the case of betrayal by her husband, she be-haved *assertively* but *without malice*. She was firm but fair-minded in ending the relationship.

Session 14—Final session

We reviewed all the massive changes she had made and how they happened. All of her symptoms were gone and had been replaced with healthy alternatives. There was ample evidence that her passivity had been replaced with self-assertion. There was no information on her sexual functioning at the time of termination, since she had decided to divorce. She still could not quite imagine liking sex, but she could imagine being tender and feeling love and support from a partner. The shift in her self-esteem and self-worth, along with the conviction that she would not settle for neglect or mistreatment from a man again, suggested that she would be able to function sexually in such a way as to increase her own pleasure. Still, this could only be ascertained by follow-up.

FOLLOW-UP

Appearance and behaviour

At the follow-up 7 years after termination, the patient entered the interview looking younger and significantly more attractive than when she entered treatment nearly 8 years previously. In this interview she was utterly sincere, at times deep into her feelings, while at other times she and her therapist shared great hilarity.

We shall deal with the evidence on each of the criteria in turn, leaving the "Essential Criterion", which depends on all the other crite-ria [1] to [8], till last.

We have included a statement of each criterion as written, first, by DM, and then by JM, in order to show the congruence between the two judges.

[1]   *Aggression*and *self-assertion*

DM: Ability to express anger appropriately and use constructive self-assertion.

JM: Increased self-assertiveness relating to her own views and needs.

There were two main incidents relevant to this criterion, the first of which concerned her relationship with her woman boss, who started being difficult and treating her badly:

> Th: One of the reasons why you came here originally was because you were in a panic that was triggered by conflict with your husband. So, here's a situation in which you felt angry. How did you deal with it?
>
> Pt: I felt that I was being taken advantage of, so rather than just staying there and taking it (*which would have been her past pattern*), I asked her to lay me off so that I could go back to school full-time.
>
> Th: So, that was in your best interest and you were taking care of yourself.
>
> Pt: Oh, totally. And she agreed to lay me off so that I could collect unemployment benefit while I was in school.

It is worth while making an addition here that was not included in our Criteria. JM wrote in her list of Disturbances "Always self-sacrificing for others", but neither of the judges included an item relevant to this in their Criteria. It would have been appropriate to have added a criterion, which we may number [9]: "*Inappropriate self-sacrifice should be replaced by enlightened self-interest, i.e. the ability, within reason, to see that her own needs are met.*" This criterion was clearly fulfilled by the above incident.

> Th: So you found a way to work it out and didn't get into a brouhaha with her or anything
>
> Pt: And I'm still kind of friendly with her.

Thus she got her own way, made a deal that was highly advantageous to herself, and she and her boss remained on reasonably good terms—constructive self-assertion *par excellence*.

The second incident involved a man named Steve with whom she has formed an important relationship (of which, much more below):

> Pt: . . . If he does something I don't like, I'm quick to tell him about it,

which is new for me with a man. . . . (*Asked for an example, she said:*)
We were at a car show together. I asked him a question about why
one truck had a windscreen that popped up. He said, "Just because", in a rather curt tone of voice. I said, "That's not an appropriate answer. I don't like that. If you don't know, just say so, but don't
be sarcastic. I don't like it. Please don't do it again". He said, "Gosh,
you're right. I can be a real idiot sometimes".

This passage illustrates how important it is to get a specific example.
The patient's statement that "if he does something I don't like, I am
quick to tell him about it" is Level 2. But here the therapist receives true,
living, Level 3 confirmation of the patient's ability to use constructive
self-assertion. If the therapist had not asked, we would never quite
have known the degree of truth in the patient's general statement.

[2]   *Her husband, or other man*
DM: We hope that she may resolve the situation with her husband, but, if
this fails, that she will form a mutually satisfactory relation with another
man.
JM: Resolution of issues related to the infidelity of her husband, and the
deepening of a meaningful, close relationship with him or another man.

It is clear that she got a divorce from her husband.
    She told the therapist that she had now graduated and that she had
met the new man, Steve, at her graduation party six months ago. He is
47, unmarried, though with at least two previous relationships with
women which came to nothing. It seems clear—as no doubt sometimes
happens—that when this middle-aged man finally fell in love, he fell
with a crash. He told the patient that he had waited for her all his life; he
phones her every day, and he remembers the day and the exact time
when he first told her he loved her.
    Almost everything that she said about him was positive. The thing
that stands out is his sense of humour. "I laugh so hard my ribs hurt. To
me, that's his most endearing quality. I love it. I love it." She loves the
way he communicates. They share all sorts of things and are very
honest with each other. They share social life and have the same
friends. Another very important factor is that her children like him, and
he likes them. She is able to be crazy, and he shares this with her, and
it's fun.
    Almost her only reservation is that he has some health problems,
which in fact did not seem to be particularly serious, but her anxiety is
highly relevant to the extra Criterion [9], formulated above, about self-

sacrifice being replaced by enlightened self-interest. Her fear was that he would become crippled and she would be left in the caring role once more:

> PT: I get scared. I don't want to take care of someone again. After all these years, first taking care of nine kids and then getting married and taking care of my own family. I just don't want to do that again.
>
> Th: All these feelings about taking care of others and having your own needs neglected . . .
>
> Pt: I'm being very selfish about that (*said in a very positive way*) . . . I didn't throw a hundred percent of myself into this but held something back, and I feel very good about that.

At this point the therapist began a major challenge of the patient's defences, just as if she were still in the main body of therapy, illustrating once more the advantage of having the follow-up carried out by the therapist herself rather than by an independent observer:

> Th: Obviously you have to hold on to yourself, but if by holding back you mean erecting a guard, that could interfere with closeness.
>
> Pt: I'm being honest with my feelings and with what I'm willing to give him right now. He knows I have big reservations because of . . . I mean, he knows everything. I remember this one moment when I told him about my father. He took my hand in his and said, "If you think that's going to make me run away, it won't. I feel so bad for you." He just held me . . .

Any reader may be forgiven for thinking of the possibility that the patient's description of Steve is a bit too good to be true. In fact, as will become clear below, it really seems that her description of him cannot be faulted. However, the same scepticism had occurred to her:

> Pt: . . . and I thought, "I've heard that before".

The therapist showed no such scepticism and continued her challenge, eventually achieving a major response:

> Th: You see, that's the way you're not letting yourself *be* in the moment and feel what you're feeling. You go to your head and to the past, and this is going to interfere . . .
>
> Pt: With my heart, yeah.
>
> Th: But what's happening in your heart if you let yourself feel what you feel in that moment? It's what you *feel*—that's where you are going to be able to tell, not in your head.

Pt: Exactly.

The therapist detects the onset of feeling:

Th: Right. So it looks as if feeling is coming over you even as you tell me about it.

Pt: My heart starts to swell.

Th: So what does that tell you?

Pt: That this is very new for me. The only thing that's made my heart swell in the past has been my children (*she starts to cry*).

Th: In that moment you felt loved, you felt understood, cared about.

Pt: YES! That was it, that was it!

Th: And now, to feel that with a man!

It is important to note that in the initial interview she was highly suspicious of nice things being said to her, linking it with her father's emotional blackmail. Here she was still suspicious, but the underlying acceptance could be reached and was intense.

This theme was repeated towards the end of the interview, where the acceptance was without reservation:

Pt: He thinks I'm the best thing since sliced bread, and, you know, that feels really nice. Really, really nice. It's wonderful.

Later in the interview they again went over the problem of her holding herself back. She said that when he gave the wrong reaction to her she got angry and "went cold" ("I still do that"); but if he apologized, as in the incident at the car show described above, then "she fell in love with him all over again".

Still later, the following dialogue occurred:

Th: So you still feel yourself holding back. Is that wise, or do you feel you hold back even when you don't want to?

Pt: No, I feel it's wise.

Th: You don't want to rush into marriage again?

She spoke first of the purely financial problem of losing maintenance from her former husband if she married. However:

Pt: I know I'm never going to marry him. I *never* want to get married again . . . I'll tell you why. I just don't want to give up every single day of my life again. I want to be able to be alone. I want to be able to go to bed at seven o'clock, or read a book.

She went on to say that this was OK with Steve, though he would like to see more of her, or at least live with her if they didn't get married. She and the therapist agreed that this was not him being a complete pushover. He was his own person, but considerate and respectful to her. But once more, this is strong evidence that the additional Criterion [9] is fulfilled—namely that she is abandoning self-sacrifice in favour of enlightened self-interest.

[3]   *Sex*

DM: Further improvement in her ability to enjoy sex.
JM: Increased enjoyment of sex.

This subject was examined explicitly and in depth, once more illustrating the importance of the kind of rapport that can, in general, only be created by the therapist herself. The result was a great deal of evidence on Level 3.

The subject was introduced as follows. When the patient spoke of standing up for herself at the car show, the therapist said:

Th: You're saying what you don't like, and he responds. Are you saying that you have a little more difficulty saying what you do want?

Pt: I'm getting better at that. I want to feel closeness. I see the difference in our sexual relationship. There is a big difference, (*slow and with emphasis*) *a big difference*.

Th: How is that?

Pt: It's very giving and accepting. I don't have the fear that I used to have. It's like two people coming together who are learning about each other. He says, "I'll never force you to do anything you don't want to do". That was so freeing. Now I know the difference.

Th: Between?

Pt: My relationship with my father or my husband, and this relationship.

Th: The difference between being used as a vehicle for the man's pleasure versus a mutual caring and respect?

Pt: Yes, respect. I don't want betrayal any more, but to be honoured and respected.

Th: Do you feel that?

Pt: Yes. I've been very careful to watch and observe.

At this point, she went on to speak of holding herself back, as described above.

Later in the interview they returned to the subject of sex. She said that Steve took a long time to feel comfortable with her, and at first he was unable to get an erection. She now had the chance to be accepting in her turn, for which he was as grateful as she had been. This, again, is clearly Level 3 evidence about the quality of their relationship:

Pt: I was very accepting of that. I said, "It's no big deal, Steve". It's holding my hand that's more important to me, so I said, 'When it happens it happens". He was very grateful for that.

Now it does happen. But she still hasn't had an orgasm with him, though she does in masturbation with a muscle massager. She has actually shown him this piece of apparatus (his response was "Great God!"), and she also has shown him where to touch her, which she likes. However, it turns out that she doesn't like to touch herself:

Th: This concerns me a little. You're still rejecting of yourself sexually.
Pt: I feel nothing when I do it. I've tried it and I don't like it *(spoken firmly)*.
Th: So you're still cut off from a very important part of you. That's something you can still certainly expand.

They then discussed oral sex, and she said she didn't like the idea of doing it to him (which is hardly surprising, in view of her history), but she was open to him doing it to her, though they hadn't tried it yet. The discussion ended with a summing up:

Th: So you're in discovery mode still, and you're open enough to tell him what you want.
Pt: Yes, yes I am.
Th: So there's nothing that you consider a problem?
Pt: No. I think as time goes by I'm starting to feel more and more comfortable with him, so I think I can tell him more and communicate to him what I'd like to try.

[4]   Children (and grandchildren!)

DM: We hope that she may be able to retain her good relationship with her children and handle difficulties with them effectively.
JM: Development of a close relationship with her children.

Th: How's your relationship with the girls?
Pt: It's really gotten better. We've come to a plateau. I'm starting to see things that I never saw before.

She has three daughters, aged 30, 26, and 21. She showed the therapist pictures, and there were exclamations of delight on both sides. She spoke positively about all three.

However, it seems clear that the middle one is her favourite. This relationship has been cemented by the fact that the daughter was diagnosed 4 years ago as suffering from a potentially life-threatening illness, for which she was successfully treated. Indeed, she recently got married. All that the patient said is Level 3:

Pt: She's very happy, and the illness has not recurred, so they'll be able to have a baby in another year or so. I feel a special bond with her, a special closeness, having gone through everything to do with the illness. I was so proud to be able to give her a beautiful wedding and to see her in her gorgeous dress. I insisted on paying every penny for that . . . (*Showing a photograph*) And that's her husband . . . I love him, he stayed by her side through everything.

Th: It sounds like your capacity to love is expanding.

This has extended to her eldest daughter's child, aged about 3, with whom she has a special relationship:

Pt: This is my granddaughter. I'm nuts about her. She's really the love of my life.

Later they came back to her middle daughter and the wedding:

Th: And you can provide all this. Didn't you feel wonderful?

Pt: Yes I did. I wanted her to have the best (*spoken almost in a whisper, with great intensity*). The only way I can describe it is, even if she was living in Italy, I would feel that she's sitting next to me. That's how I feel towards her.

[5]   *Studies (and other work)*

DM: To continue successfully with her studies, and to make use of them.
JM: She should focus on developing goals, especially in education, to enable her to have something for herself and to enhance her feelings of self-worth.

As described above, she got her employer to lay her off so that she could study full-time, and she has graduated and got a job that makes use of her qualifications. The job is concerned with people, is often fulfilling, sometimes distressing, and she is enthusiastic about it.

This criterion is clearly fulfilled.

[6]   *Her feelings about herself: self-worth etc.*

DM: The ability to assert herself constructively should lead to a great improvement in her happiness and self-confidence and her view of herself as an admirable and worthwhile human being.
JM: Improved self-esteem, allowing her to feel more respected and powerful.

There is little direct evidence on this criterion, but her improved self-confidence shines through the whole of her story, particularly her ability to assert herself with Steve and to give her daughter a highly successful wedding.

[7]   Attitude to past events, irrational guilt

DM: She should regard past events as something exceedingly distressing that happened, but which no longer adversely affect her life. She should no longer feel guilty about her part in them.

There was no evidence that she was still affected by the events of her childhood, except possibly her resistance against responding fully to Steve's love.

(This criterion was covered in Session 10, as discussed earlier, but the judges, being blind to therapy, had no way of knowing it.)

[8]   Symptoms other than dissociation

DM: Loss of all symptoms—constant anxiety, inner turmoil, pain, and heaviness.

JM: Absence of physical symptoms and lifting of depression and sense of sadness.

> Pt: I'm still on Prozac [fluoxetine, an anti-depressant]. I try to get off, but I find that after three or four days I sink into a depression— weepy, sad.

They discussed this at length, and the following emerged. During her daughter's treatment, when she was working full-time, taking care of her daughter's youngest child, and running to the hospital daily, she found it difficult to sleep. Her physician prescribed an antidepressant (Prozac) to help her sleep. When the worst was over and life began to return to normal, she stopped the medication and had an adverse reaction, feeling suddenly depressed and weepy. She assumed she needed to stay on the medication, but her response may well have been a side-effect of the sudden withdrawal and not an expression of underlying depression. The therapist encouraged her to stop medication under supervision to see if she really needs it. (A follow-up phone call six months later revealed that she had been able to taper off the medication without difficulty, had not used it in five months, and felt fine.)

Later the therapist reminded her of having to retire to bed with severe headaches, to which she replied:

> Pt: I would like to say that I'll never allow myself to do that again.

It must be obvious that other symptoms such as constant anxiety, inner pain, and so forth are no longer present.

(Note: The two judges were unaware that in Session 8 she had said that she no longer suffered from headaches or anxiety attacks.)

General criterion (with special reference to dissociation)

DM: Ability to face and express all "normal" feelings, and use them positively in her life, without resorting to her defence of dissociation.
JM: Regain control over and diminution of dissociation.

With regard to dissociation, the following dialogue took place:

> Th: These periods of dissociation. Does that still happen?
> Pt: No.
> Th: You deal with reality. You don't have to sink into a fog?
> Pt: No I don't (*very definite*).

There was conclusive Level 3 evidence of her being able to experience and express a wide range of feelings without resorting to dissociation. These included anger, humour, the ability to love a man and respond to him (with some reservation), giving and accepting sexuality, and intense love for her children and grandchildren.

COMMENT

It should be added that these major therapeutic effects were achieved in a patient who—indeed—had already shown extreme inner strength of personality, but whose background could hardly have been more traumatic.

It is also worth noting that this patient had both the *most traumatic childhood* and the *shortest therapy* of all the patients described in this book.

PART **III**

GENERAL DISCUSSION

NOTE

In the interests of both brevity and clarity, any dialogue reported in Part III has been abbreviated and simplified.

CHAPTER 8

The relation between predictions and actual events

As described in chapter 4, two judges independently drew up a "formulation" on each of the seven patients discussed in this book, which included (1) a list of problems or *disturbances* that were elicited by the therapist in the initial interview, (2) a *hypothesis* about the underlying psychodynamics, (3) predictions of the important *issues* that would need to be dealt with in therapy, and (4) a list of *criteria* for a successful outcome, which were based not only on the absence of the problems outlined in item 1, but on their replacement by the corresponding aspects of "positive mental health". Both items 2 and 3 imply predictions about the kinds of unconscious feeling that would emerge and that would lead to therapeutic effects.

The predictions were based solely on the initial assessment material, which usually consisted of a single session, though sometimes two. Of the two judges, JM was completely blind to subsequent events in all seven patients. DM was blind to all but three: The Masochistic Artist and The Reluctant Fiancée, both of whom were described in Coughlin Della Selva (1996, in which The Reluctant Fiancée was called "The Woman with Headaches"); and The Self-Loathing Headmistress, described in Coughlin Della Selva (1992). DM had read these when they were first published, but all he could remember was the heartfelt and amazingly therapeutic cry of the physically ill-treated Masochistic Artist: "It's MY body." Thus, for practical purposes, he can be counted as blind as well.

As far as this study is concerned, we need to consider two aspects:

1. which predictions that *were* made were *actually fulfilled*;
2. which important events that occurred in therapy were *actually predicted*.

The results of these two comparisons were significantly different.

WERE THE PREDICTIONS THAT WERE MADE CONFIRMED BY WHAT HAPPENED IN THERAPY?
Predictions in the Hypotheses

As will be clear from the detailed accounts of the four patients described in Part II, the comprehensive *Hypotheses* formulated by the two judges, of the dynamics underlying the problems, were not only the same in all essentials, but were completely confirmed by the events of therapy.

Predictions in "Issues to be dealt with in therapy"

Anger and guilt-laden hostility

For each patient a number of issues to be dealt with in therapy were formulated and then prioritized. These were often extremely comprehensive, but always relevant. There is no space to examine them all in detail, so we have chosen two key issues for analysis—namely, anger and grief. The information on which the analyses were based is described below.

Five of the seven patients had at least one *openly malignant* parent, and where only one parent was malignant, the patient was left unprotected by the other. For these, *buried anger* against *both* parents was predicted as the most important issue leading to therapeutic effects. The same predictions were, in fact, made for the two remaining patients, both of whose parents gave cause for anger in other ways.

Of the total of 28 predictions of the emergence of anger (one for each parent, by two judges, for seven patients—i.e. 14 patient–parent pairs), 24 (86%) were confirmed. The exceptions that never emerged as foci for anger during therapy were (1) the father of The Cold-Blooded Businessman, who colluded with the mother in sending him away to a health camp and seldom visited him, and (2) the mother of The Man Divided.

This last was the most unexpected result, since the patient made clear at initial assessment that his whole life had been dominated and controlled by his mother's severe neurosis, and he said that up to the age of 35 he "couldn't bear to be in the same room as her for more than twenty minute at a time"

Moreover, the judges predicted that the expression of anger would result in therapeutic effects. In the 12 patient–parent pairs in which anger with parents did emerge, *immediate therapeutic effects followed in 9*. The details of the violent impulses that emerged, the reasons for them, and the therapeutic effects that ensued, are summarized for each patient in chapter 10.

Grief

As described in chapter 10, close study shows that the de-repression of *unresolved grief* played a major part in all seven of these therapies and that therapeutic effects often ensued. This was an issue that *both* judges foresaw in three patients and that *one* judge foresaw in three of the others (9/14 = 64%).

Summary

The overall conclusion from the evidence described is that those predictions that were made were almost entirely fulfilled. This represents a successful scientific experiment, which largely validates both the theory and the practice of dynamic psychotherapy.

WERE ALL THE IMPORTANT EVENTS THAT OCCURRED IN THERAPY PREDICTED?

In the case of predicting the important events in therapy, the judges were only partly successful.

Anger arising from current or recent relationships

Although the two judges did well over the issue of anger and hostility in the *distant past*, they became preoccupied with this to the exclusion of *current* anger or anger in the *recent past*—which was shown during therapy by all these patients except The Self-Loathing Headmistress, and should have been obvious. JM predicted it correctly for three patients but failed to mention it for three others, whereas DM predicted it for the ones JM missed and left out the ones that she identified. For

The Self-Loathing Headmistress such hostility was not relevant. Thus of the total of 12 possible predictions (one by each judge, for 6 patients), 6 (i.e. 50%) were made correctly.

Grief

As indicated above, we learned from a close study of these seven therapies that the experience of grief not only played a major part in all of them, but that this often resulted in immediate therapeutic effects—an observation of which we previously had been insufficiently aware. Of the 14 possible predictions (one for each judge for seven patients) grief was mentioned in 9 (i.e. 64%).

This partial failure clearly resulted from the fact that grief was much less conspicuous in the initial interviews and that one of the rules for making formulations was that there had to be direct evidence on which to base the predictions.

Therefore, it is crucial that the central role of unresolved grief in psychopathology should be universally recognized.

The Criteria for a successful outcome

As was true of the Hypotheses, the Criteria formulated by the two independent judges were not only almost identical but were *always relevant*. Moreover, practically nothing important was left out. They thus formed an essential basis on which the follow-up material could be judged.

DISCUSSION

It is a tribute to the therapist that the initial interviews were so skilfully conducted that it was possible for the judges to identify accurately the patients' problems, to make accurate hypotheses about the underlying dynamics, and to predict many of the issues to be dealt with in therapy. The judges could also construct a list of specific Criteria that needed to be fulfilled for total resolution.

Our observations make clear how important it is to have more than one judge making these formulations, since often an issue that was missed by one judge was seen by the other. This means that a formulation combining the two would have been far more accurate and scientifically robust than either alone.

Now that we have studied these seven patients, it has become clear that in early life all of them suffered from *ill-treatment* and/or *neglect*, and we would know enough to predict *routinely* the following main issues for any patient of this kind:

1. anger with one or both parents;
2. grief and distress about childhood suffering, especially loss of love from one or both parents;
3. grief and anger about current or recent failed relations.

If we had conformed to this schema, we would have been able to make predictions on these issues that were almost 100% accurate.

CHAPTER 9

Aspects of initial evaluation

In this chapter we examine features that arise from the initial evaluation interview or trial therapy: first, the nature of the sample represented by these seven patients, which shows that it contains a preponderance of patients with traumatic backgrounds; then "tactical defences", the forms of resistance that are encountered in patient after patient when they are put under pressure to reveal their true feelings; and finally, when the trial therapy is successful, the far-reaching consequences—sometimes including important therapeutic effects—that follow.

THE NATURE OF THE SAMPLE

Since these therapies were chosen to show the quality of therapeutic change that can be achieved by dynamic psychotherapy at its best, it might be thought that they would contain a preponderance of "easy" patients. This is not true at all. As was foreshadowed in chapter 1, these patients lie at the more difficult end of the spectrum, which demonstrates the power of this method of psychotherapy and the therapist's skill in using it.

Traumatic early experiences

One of the most striking characteristics of the sample is the extremely traumatic nature of the patients' early experiences. As already mentioned, five of the seven patients had an openly malignant parent.

(1) The Woman with Dissociation was subjected to systematic sexual and physical abuse from her father between the ages of 9 and 15 years, together with physical abuse from her mother (e.g. hitting her with a saucepan or an iron). Her father broke her collar-bone on one occasion, and her mother threw her younger brother out of the door, crushing his skull "like a melon". (2) The Reluctant Fiancée was repeatedly and brutally beaten, emotionally battered, and sexually abused by her father. Her mother was constantly ill and made no attempt to help. (3) Clear evidence emerged during therapy that The Self-Loathing Headmistress was an unwanted child, and that her mother resented her presence and really wished she could have got rid of her. Her mother expressed this openly in the most devastating way, by deliberate neglect. The patient was often left for hours at school because her parents "forgot" to pick her up. She was forced to wear shoes and clothes that were worn out and no longer fitted. Moreover, during the summers her parents left her in the care of a maiden aunt who sexually abused her. (4). The Masochistic Artist's mother was described as a "screaming, maddening, crazy, dissatisfied bitch". The patient originally said that her father was detached and did nothing to help, but in fact he joined forces with her mother to hold her down and remove lint from her belly-button, and he also did nothing to prevent her from being subjected to painful, frightening, and unnecessary enemas. (5) The Cold-Blooded Businessman had his hands held against a hot stove by his mother until they burned, because he objected to eating something that she was cooking. From then on he refused to eat anything cooked by her. The situation ended with a traumatic separation—he was sent away to a "health camp" at the age of 10 for three years, where his parents seldom visited him. As an adult he became very severely depressed, and he only asked for therapy as a last resort to save himself from suicide, which he had planned to the last detail.

In addition, the life of The Man Divided was completely controlled by his mother's severe neurosis—for example, at the age of 13 he had to make a thousand-mile train journey to boarding-school, by himself, because his mother was phobic about flying. When he was 5 years old, his home was destroyed by a gas explosion in which they lost everything and his father was seriously injured.

Severe psychopathology

Correspondingly, the initial disturbances in at least five of these patients would seem to have made them very difficult to treat with traditional dynamic therapy. Thus The Good Girl suffered from a severe psychosomatic condition (ulcerative colitis) "only treatable by surgery"; the emotional life of The Self-Loathing Headmistress was completely destroyed by her main symptom of self-loathing; The Cold-Blooded Businessman was strongly identified with his defences, was diagnosed as a long-standing "narcissistic personality", was severely depressed, and had planned suicide down to the last detail; the Masochistic Artist suffered from florid masochistic sexual fantasies that would usually be regarded as highly refractory to treatment; and both The Woman with Dissociation and the Reluctant Fiancée had suffered from dissociation, fugue states, and severe headaches since childhood.

The patients' strengths

On the other side, it is important to note that all these patients could be described as possessing basically good personalities, and—in spite of their early traumas—all had managed to function in life without ever having a mental breakdown.

All but The Woman with Dissociation had a high level of education. Several won scholarships to prestigious universities. Their dedication to learning was a saving grace. Having a respite from home and a place to shine and develop their intellect made a huge difference to their development.

Three patients showed truly exceptional determination in dealing with extremely difficult situations: (1) in her teens, The Woman with Dissociation, with her collar-bone broken in two places by her father, crawled on all fours along the road and across a bridge to the police station; (2) The Good Girl showed extraordinary maturity in getting on good terms with the younger sister who had displaced her; and (3) The Self-Loathing Headmistress had managed to work herself up into a position of responsibility in the teeth of a potentially crippling psychological symptom.

At the time of the initial interview, all these patients were working, and all had managed to develop long relationships with the opposite sex. Of course, some of these were very unsatisfactory, but The Cold-Blooded Businessman, The Man Divided, and The Self-Loathing Headmistress had all established what proved in the end to be really good marriages.

TACTICAL DEFENCES

The subject of tactical defences is included here because, as soon as patients are put under pressure to experience their true feelings, tactical defences usually constitute the first problem that a therapist has to deal with. They lie on a complete spectrum, from being entirely conscious to entirely unconscious.

The main feelings and impulses against which patients defend themselves are *anger, emotional closeness and intimacy, distress and grief,* and *sexual feelings.* In ISTDP, examples involving anger almost always seem to be the most prominent.

The list of tactical defences found in these seven patients is given in Table 9.1. This list is based on a two-part article that appeared in the

TABLE 9.1.   Tactical defences

Avoidance
  omission
  "not remembering"
  dismissal
  changing the subject
  withdrawal
  retraction

Describing or expressing something other than the avoided feeling
  watering down
  distress rather than anger
  defence rather than anger
  "externalization"
  victimized stance

Intellectualization—or cognitive rather than affective
  intellectual discussion
  the word "because"
  generalization
  vagueness
  rumination

Partial response

Somatization

International Journal of Intensive Short-Term Psychotherapy (Davanloo, 1996a, 1996b).

Avoidance

All of the following examples lie towards the more conscious end of the spectrum. It is worth noting that many of these vignettes also illustrate ways in which the defences can be blocked or challenged.

Omission

This example is taken from The Cold-Blooded Businessman, where the patient avoids the fantasy of intimate sexuality in relation to the female therapist. The patient is describing a fantasy of taking the therapist out to dinner:

> Pt: . . . a kind of warm, comfortable sharing. . . . The next thing I see, it's the next morning. I wake up and you're next to me.
> Th: So you block out what happens between dinner and waking up the next morning . . .
> Pt: 'Cause sex has never been an intimate, close thing for me .

This eventually leads to a warm and tender sexual fantasy.

"Not remembering"

The Woman with Dissociation:

> Th: We've been talking about a tendency to have rages. Can we look at a recent example?
> Pt: With the kids. They tease me, and I get hurt.
> Th: An example?
> Pt: I can't remember.
> Th: (*Ironically*) Is this a memory problem?

It is inconceivable that the patient could not remember a recent instance of what she is describing, if she put her mind to it.

Dismissal

The Woman with Dissociation:

> Th: So you seem to be saying there's a reservoir of anger inside you. The question is where it's all coming from and who it's really meant for. Any ideas?
> Pt: No.

In this example, a less resistant patient might at least start considering the question instead of dismissing it.

A second example of dismissal comes from The Cold-Blooded Businessman:

Th: What's the feeling towards me?

Pt: Ambivalent . . . I don't know, I can't find a feeling . . .

Changing the subject ("diversification")

The Masochistic Artist:

Th: How am I going to get to know you if you keep your feelings out of the room?

Pt: Well, you see, this is the other thing. . . .

Th: This is what happens: I will say something to you and you patiently wait and listen, but pay absolutely no attention to it—you go on to something else, as if I hadn't said anything.

Withdrawal

The Man Divided:

Pt: When she started screaming . . . I just felt like withdrawing.

Th: Withdrawing is not a feeling but a way to avoid your feelings.

Pt: I don't get it.

Th: The feeling inside is a deeply painful one . . . you avoid the full experience of that painful feeling inside, as well as the feeling towards her, by withdrawing. Do you see that?

Pt: OK, I follow

In the following example, from The Cold-Blooded Businessman, this major defence is being used tactically in the transference:

Pt: I feel angry (*with you, the therapist*), but so what? I'm not going to let it get to me. I'm feeling anger and so I'm going to withdraw (*throws up his hands*).

Th: That's the way you avoid your anger.

Retraction

In her initial interview, The Masochistic Artist repeatedly gave positive responses to the therapist's interventions and immediately afterwards took them back. Speaking of her anger against her mother, the patient said, "It feels like it wells up inside me and makes me feel more powerful." Pressed for her experience of this feeling, she eventually said that she wanted to protect her mother, that it felt like a betrayal to express her anger and made her feel guilty and therefore worse.

Describing or expressing something other than the avoided feeling

In all of the examples given below, it is *anger* that is being avoided.

"Watering down"

The Man Divided:

> Pt: ... maybe she has a right to scream, ... but it *bothered* me tremendously.
>
> Th: And "bothered" means what? Clearly you have a feeling towards her—what is the feeling?

This leads to the defence of intellectualization, which is described in more detail later.

> Pt: ... having yet another brother to contend with was *very difficult to entertain.*
>
> Th: That's a polite way to put it.
>
> Pt: Right—I hated it.

Distress rather than anger

The Self-Loathing Headmistress:

> Th: Do you think you might have been frightened of your own anger as well? You end up cowering in a corner.
>
> Pt: And then I cry. I can feel it now—wanting to cry and getting smaller.
>
> Th: Yes, but to do that is to shrink away from the anger you're feeling inside.
>
> Pt: Anger—yeah, you bet. I'm very angry at my father. I felt rejected by him.

The Man Divided:

> Pt: We were always told, "Wait until your father gets home". I literally had to stand there, waiting for him with my pants down ...
>
> Th: I'm sure that stirs up a lot of feelings.
>
> Pt: Yeah, fear and pain.
>
> Th: But you leave out your anger at your father.

Defence rather than anger

The subject that The Cold-Blooded Businessman is discussing here is how he would feel and express anger with the therapist:

Pt: I would stand up, yell, tell you you're wrong.

Th: But telling me I'm wrong is not a feeling.

Pt: I want to say it's a feeling like I have towards my mother, like I don't want to have anything more to do with you.

Thus he has completely mistaken the defence for the feeling, as the therapist points out:

Th: That's not a feeling—it's a way to flee from the feeling.

"Externalization": a statement or opinion about the other person, not the feeling

The Self-Loathing Headmistress:

Th: What kinds of feeling do you have towards your parents when you go back now and can even feel them spanking you?

Pt: My parents shouldn't have done that to me.

Th: That's a statement, but it doesn't say how you feel.

The following, from The Good Girl with Ulcerative Colitis, is an example of describing distress rather than anger, followed by externalization:

Pt: I had a dream about him (*a previous boyfriend*) recently. I was furious at him.

Th: And now?

Pt: I have a sad, sinking feeling. It brings up intense pain.

Th: I'm sure that's there too, but it sounds like you haven't faced the anger.

Pt: In the end I tried to smack him, but I was too devastated. He was so narcissistic. He never really listened to me.

Taking a victimized stance

A device related to "externalization" occurs when patients put into the passive a description of what was done to them. The following two examples come from The Reluctant Fiancée:

Pt: I felt claustrophobic in that house—*trapped* (*by her parents*). School was a refuge.

Th: You were trapped. That's not a feeling. The feelings are terror and rage—also helplessness in the face of it.

In the second example, the subject is her boyfriend's sexual deviation:

Th: What are your feelings towards him as you remember that?

Pt: I was *repulsed* and *disgusted* (*by him*).

Th: But the feeling towards him?

Pt: I was scared and felt out of control, but I loved him and went along with it.

Intellectualization— or "cognitive rather than affective"

The therapist often describes intellectualization to patients as "thoughts rather than feelings".

Intellectual discussion

The following example continues one of the passages quoted above from The Man Divided:

Th: Clearly you have a feeling towards her—what is the feeling?

Pt: The feeling is an aspect of a bigger and more important feeling. You see, I'm used to my wife having tantrums in front of people.

Th: But that doesn't say how you feel about it.

The Good Girl with Ulcerative Colitis:

Pt: I don't like it that I'm the patient and you're the trained professional. I know I want to analyse it.

Th: Analysing is an intellectual process that gets you away from the feeling of irritation and resentment.

The word "because"

"Because" is a word that immediately converts a potentially affective statement into a cognitive one. The following is from The Man Divided:

Th: How do you experience this anxiety?

Pt: I experience it as nervousness because . . .

Th: (*Interrupting*) Not *why*, *how*? . . . How do you feel the nervousness?

Pt: I experience it as butterflies (*in his stomach*).

Generalization

The Good Girl with Ulcerative Colitis:

Th: . . . But then you internalize your anger and attack yourself and become depressed and helpless.

Pt: I think your portrait of me is correct in a general way. But I was not aware of that full-blown response to that doctor, though I think, in the general schema of life, that's an apt description.

Th: But we want to stay away from general descriptions.

Vagueness

The Masochistic Artist:

Th: How do you experience the anxiety?

Pt: I feel that I . . .

Th: Physically.

Pt: Agitated, frightened.

Th: How do you experience that?

Pt: I'm not sure I can answer . . . not that I feel . . . I guess, strained . . . I guess I'm not sure if it's emotional or physical.

Th: Physical.

Pt: I don't know what the physical quality is. I can't sit still.

Th: That's what you *do* (*i.e. not what you* feel).

Th: You have this tendency to circle around, to run and avoid, what you're really feeling. You stay vague and general. Are you aware, when I ask you something, that your response is always tentative?

Pt: Yeah.

Rumination

Intellectualization can reach the ultimate in the phenomenon of *rumination*—which is difficult to define but unmistakable when it occurs, as this example from The Masochistic Artist shows:

Th: You can use the drama that you create in your life to avoid the pain that you have inside—at least temporarily.

Pt: It works, it works, it doesn't work. You see, if it did work, I'd let it work, but ultimately it doesn't work at all. You see, I don't trust my feelings. I can, like, try to trust them in this kind of momentary way, but then they completely reverse themselves, and then I have a hard time sorting out what is a defence and what I am abandoning myself to . . .

Partial response

When the therapist is approaching the breakthrough of buried feelings, it is very important not to be "fobbed off" with a response that is only partial and avoids the true intensity of the experience. The following is from the Reluctant Fiancée:

Th: So, in your imagination, if you let yourself feel it, how would it go?
Pt: I would just smash him.
Th: Who?
Pt: My father. Just smash him in the face.

The therapist detects that the patient is not fully in touch with her experience; therefore, instead of asking the patient to elaborate, she asks about residual defences. The patient's response shows the degree to which these are present:

Th: Do you really feel this, or have you gone cold? We know you can shut down and go through the motions but without really feeling it.
Pt: Inside, I feel my muscles tensing.
Th: Which is still holding it in.

Somatization

When threatened with the possibility of experiencing anxiety-laden feelings, the patient may start to suffer from physical symptoms instead. Below is an example from The Reluctant Fiancée in which anger with the patient's father is felt first in the patient's abdomen and then in her chest:

Th: How do you feel inside as you go back to that?
Pt: It's in my stomach, and even my neck and shoulders are hurting.
Th: Anger was underneath?
Pt: Yes, rage. It feels like a black tornado.
Th: Where do you feel this in your body?
Pt: I feel a tightness in my chest.
Th: Tightness is the result of holding the anger in, isn't it?

This eventually leads to an extremely violent, sadistic fantasy.

Nonverbal clues among the defences

One of the things that may happen is that patients begin to express physically, but unconsciously, clues about either the *defence* or *what the defence is designed to avoid*. The therapist should immediately draw attention to this, with the aim of pushing the patient towards the experience of true feeling. The following example, from The Cold-Blooded Businessman, contains both of these phenomena together with the defence of *externalization* described above:

Th: You say you feel anger towards me, so how do you experience that inside? You are biting your finger (*unconscious expression of aggressive impulses*) . . .

Pt: I'm thinking.

Th: You avoid my eyes (*defence*).

Pt: Because I'm thinking.

Th: But it's also a way to avoid me and this angry feeling towards me.

Pt: . . . I understand what you're getting at but I'm having trouble verbalizing . . . OK, so I have this anger towards you . . . "Why are you picking on me?" (*externalization*)

Th: So you go to "Why are you picking on me?" which is not your anger towards me.

Pt: That is my feeling.

Th: How do you experience the anger?

Pt: Just by "I don't know what she's trying to do." I experience it internally.

A comment on tactical defences

As described above, an essential aim of the technique of ISTDP is to put patients under pressure to experience their true feelings. Except in the most responsive of patients, tactical defences are the inevitable result. They are very easy to miss, and anyone wishing to learn the technique needs to be thoroughly familiar with them.

THE EFFECTS OF SUCCESSFUL TRIAL THERAPY

When the patient responds favourably to trial therapy, many important effects ensue.

From the point of view of the patient

Motivation

Most patients experience relief during the trial therapy, and parallel with this there is a decrease in resistance, an increase in therapeutic alliance, and a marked increase in motivation. Below are three examples.

During the interview, The Self-Loathing Headmistress had already given evidence of motivation to face some of her most painful feelings when she said, "I'm going to have to look at this anger towards my mother". Then, at the end of the interview, the following dialogue occurred:

>Th: So, do you think that coming here and talking as we have today could be of help to you?
>
>Pt: Yes I do. As I said, it's been a long time in coming but I'm ready to deal with it.

The Cold-Blooded Businessman, who began the interview poorly motivated and soon became hostile, reacted similarly:

>Th: And the point is not to act on these aggressive feelings but to be consciously aware of them, because otherwise you keep them inside and they eat at you—you become depressed.
>
>Pt: The thought just occurred to me—some define depression as anger self-directed.
>
>Th: Anger turned inward. So you beat yourself up instead.
>
>Pt: You know, I never understood what that meant until this moment—until you said, "So you beat yourself up instead". *I'm glad I came here, you know that.*

The Woman with Dissociation:

>Pt: I've never had this kind of support before. I feel hopeful for the first time in months. I need to do this for myself, and then, if something happens down the road, I'll be able to deal with it.

The other four patients also showed positive responses, each in their own way, at the end of the initial evaluation.

Therapeutic effects

Most importantly, some patients show immediate therapeutic effects. In the present series there were three examples of *major* therapeutic effects: The Woman with Dissociation (permanent cure of headaches and anxiety attacks); The Man Divided (ability to bond with his son); The Reluctant Fiancée (ability to speak to her relatives for the first time about her traumatic childhood experiences). Further details are given in chapter 11 under the heading of "Therapeutic effects during therapy". As is discussed there, when it is possible to identify the main events leading to these effects, the result is a validation of the theory and practice of dynamic psychotherapy.

From the point of view of the therapist

Prognosis

The beauty of an interview successfully conducted as trial therapy is that the therapist has *proof from direct observation* of the patient's response to the technique that will be used. This gives a very strong indication that therapy will ultimately be successful. Certainly it was so with the seven patients presented here.

Understanding the patient

After a successful interview, the therapist should be in possession of (a) a survey of the whole of the patient's life, past and current, (b) a knowledge of how the past is affecting the present, (c) direct evidence about the defences and the anxiety-laden feelings lying behind them, and (d) an idea, therefore, about the issues that will need to be dealt with in therapy.

From the point of view of the researcher

With the knowledge summarized in the previous paragraph, researchers who are blind to subsequent events are able to create a *formulation*, as was illustrated in detail with The Man Divided in chapter 4. Scientifically speaking, two important aspects of this are (1) the ability to draw up a list of criteria for an ideal therapeutic result, which (a) can indicate the areas that the follow-up interviewer needs to cover, and (b) can be compared with the changes actually observed; and (2) the ability to make a list of the issues that will become important in therapy, and in particular to predict the nature of the hitherto unconscious feelings and impulses that will emerge and lead to therapeutic effects. As discussed in chapter 14, when this is done successfully, the result is another validation of both the theoretical and the practical aspects of dynamic psychotherapy.

Aspects of therapy

Anger, grief, oedipal feelings

The aspects of therapy examined in this first part of chapter 10 are (1) anger—particularly in relation to the breakthrough of *primitive rage*, which leads immediately to therapeutic effects—and the evidence that this provides for the validity of dynamic psychotherapy; (2) the breakthrough of *grief*, which turns out to be as important as anger and also tends to lead to therapeutic effects; and (3) oedipal feelings, which in fact figure very little in these therapies.

Apart from the therapeutic results themselves, the ever-repeated sequence involving anger—which occurs in all seven patients—probably represents the most striking observation to be found in all these therapies.

ANGER

In this section we present some extremely striking empirical observations that (1) lead, to some degree, to the rewriting of psychopathology, and (2) go a long way towards validating dynamic psychotherapy without the need for controls.

The core of psychodynamic theory

According to psychodynamic theory, neurotic disturbances arise from conflict: feelings or impulses that are kept out of conscious awareness because they are felt to be intolerable, and, if they are brought into consciousness and faced, the conflict and the disturbances arising from it can be resolved. This is the central mechanism on which all dynamic psychotherapy is based.

It is a very strange fact that this concept—which is so fundamental and which by now appears so self-evident to dynamic psychotherapists—has never been demonstrated in a way that is universally accepted. Even the existence of "the unconscious" is questioned. How can this be?

A large part of the answer lies in the gradual and time-consuming nature of most dynamic psychotherapy, during which so much occurs that, when changes do appear, it becomes impossible to say what factors were responsible for them.

Dynamic therapists might well exclaim, "If only there were a method of treatment that regularly brought about therapeutic effects immediately following the emergence of hitherto unconscious feelings!" But now there is. This is what we have tried to illustrate through the clinical material described in the foregoing pages.

The place of repressed rage in psychopathology

The two essential feelings that emerged in these therapies and led to immediate therapeutic effects were *rage* and *grief*. Of these two feelings, the breakthrough into primitive rage tends to be the most conspicuous feature of ISTDP as carried out by many different therapists, so much so that its importance tends to be overestimated. Indeed, one of the most experienced of Davanloo's ex-trainees, Robert Neborsky, circulated a summary of ISTDP which opened with the statement: "The unconscious of a neurotic adult is a primitively organized matrix of murderous and sadistic feelings overlying painful experience." Does this mean that psychopathology needs to be rewritten?

As a rigid generalization, Neborsky's statement cannot possibly be the whole truth. For instance, every dynamic psychotherapist must be able to quote many patients of both sexes whose main problems were not based on anger at all, but on oedipal problems in all their complexity. This is discussed more fully in the next section.

It might be thought that statistics on this issue would be impossible to find, but strangely enough this is not so. Allan Abbass, whose prodigious capacity for work has resulted in his having information on over 70 personally treated patients, stated that the proportion of patients in his practice who did not suffer from guilt and self-punishment over primitive murderous rage towards people close to them lay in the region of 17%.

Of course, violent impulses are nothing new to psychoanalysis and dynamic psychotherapy in general. Nevertheless, only ISTDP has revealed both their presence and their primitive quality in so many patients, so that this really amounts to a new discovery. In other words, psychopathology does need to be rewritten, though it is only the emphasis that needs to be changed.

Predictions concerning anger

Independent, blind judges predicted that the *emergence of anger*, usually against one or both *parents*, would become a major issue in the therapy of all seven patients, and that this would result in therapeutic effects.

The sequence in the breakthrough

In general these predictions were fulfilled. Not only this, but in response to the therapist's interventions in the "central dynamic sequence" (see chapter 2), patients go through an extraordinarily constant sequence of their own, as in Table 10.1. Naturally, all of the elements in this sequence do not necessarily appear in all patients, nor do they necessarily appear in the same order; however, in successful therapies, it is usually possible to discern the basic sequence of resistance→breakthrough into primitive rage→therapeutic effects.

(It should be noted that patients vary according to whether relief follows the expression of *rage* or *grief*. The order shown in Table 10.1 is the more frequent in these seven patients; in the therapist's experience with other patients, however, relief more frequently follows the expression of rage.)

The evidence is given below. "Issue by JM" refers to JM's formulation of the "Issues to be dealt with in therapy". This was based entirely on the initial assessment material. She was *completely blind* to all the events of therapy and follow-up. With every patient, the issue quoted was the first that she listed, clearly implying that she regarded it as the most important.

TABLE 10.1.   Dynamic sequence involving anger

---

(1)   Defences, resistance

(2)   Anxiety and guilt

(3)   Anger in the transference

(4)   Breakthrough of extremely violent anger,
       usually against someone from the past

(5)   Grief

(6)   Relief

(7)   Feeling of strength or power

(8)   Absence of anxiety and guilt

(9)   Love, emotional closeness

(10)   Therapeutic effects (described at once or in the next session)

(11)   Reconciliation (often reported at follow-up)

The Self-Loathing Headmistress

With this patient, all pleasure in life had been destroyed by a feeling of self-loathing and a need for self-punishment.

- Issue by JM: "Explore and experience the depth of anger in relation to her father, mother, brothers, and father's family."

(1) *Defence.* She reports a dream about being angry with her mother but she blocked it off. The therapist challenges this defence.

(2) *Anxiety and guilt.* There are clear signs of tension as she speaks of anger with the therapist. There is then intense anxiety and rocking as she speaks of anger towards her mother. Later she speaks of feeling guilty about wanting love from her mother.

(3) *Anger in transference.* She expresses anger with the therapist, who seemed impatient with her. She then has a fantasy of attacking the therapist's breast.

(4) *Breakthrough of anger with her mother.* Spontaneous transition to angry demands to be breastfed by her mother.

(5) *Grief.* Intense grief about what she has lost.

(6) *Relief.* "I felt so good" (reported in the next session)

(7) *Strength and power* / (8) *Absence of guilt and anxiety.* "She was lucky

to have me. Because I'm good. I'm a better woman than I was even as a little girl." / "It cannot possibly be wrong, what I'm feeling" (reported in the next session).

(9) *Love.* "I want to be more connected to Mum" (reported in the next session).

(10) *Therapeutic effects.* "I feel so much more alive" (reported in next session).

(11) *Reconciliation.* "My mother has shared with me parts of her heart" (reported at follow-up).

The Woman with Dissociation

• Issue by JM: "She needs to experience murderous rage against her parents, which is currently being displaced towards others."

SESSION 7

(5) *Grief.* The session began with "deep painful longings, and a sense of deprivation".

(1) *Defence.* Therapist: "Are you in touch with anger (*about her father's sexual abuse*)?" Patient: "No, . . . I just accepted it.
(*Challenge by therapist*)

(4) *Violence.* She has a fantasy of stabbing him and cutting his penis off and shoving it into his mouth.

(8) *Absence anxiety and guilt.*   "I think it would give me the greatest pleasure."

SESSION 8

(6) *Relief.* Report by therapist: "She feels much better".

(7) *Power.* Report by therapist: "She feels internally stronger".

(10) *Therapeutic effects.* She has been able to declare her needs at home and at work and is finding them getting met—though not with her husband.

The Good Girl with Ulcerative Colitis

• Issues by JM: "She needs to experience and express fully her feelings of grief and anger, especially in relation to:

(a) her father—grief and loss of his physical warmth and affection, and anger at his lack of care;

(b) her mother—grief at the absence of feeling of being loved that the patient wanted and needed so desperately, and anger at the demands her mother made on her in order to be acceptable;

(c) a previous boyfriend—grief for his loss, and anger at his inability to commit himself to her after two years of living together, and then quickly becoming engaged to someone else."

The following sequence concerns an incident with this boyfriend, who had led her on sexually and then rejected her:

(1) *Defence.* She felt "hurt" by him, but not angry. (Her defences are challenged by the therapist.)

(4) *Violence.* She now realizes she felt rage. This is followed by a fantasy of a murderous attack on him.

(6) *Relief.* "I feel ebullient, happy."

(7) *Power* / (8) *Absence of anxiety and guilt* / (10) *Therapeutic effects.* She feels powerful, happy, and fully alive. Next session: She speaks of how much better she felt after the last session, and how, instead of feeling guilty and attacking herself, and getting sick and depressed, she felt happy and alive.

The following sequence involves first the transference and then her mother:

(1) *Defence* / (2) *Anxiety.* In a previous session she had spoken of two situations at work potentially involving anger. In one she spoke of getting "filled with self-doubt"; in the other she got depressed, and she also felt it in her intestines and had to go to the bathroom more often. In the present session she said, "When I get angry I eat, if I can't express it." (Challenge by therapist.)

(3) *Anger in the transference.* She imagines being incontinent in the session and the therapist being disgusted by it, at which the patient becomes angry.

(4) *Violence against her mother.* She spontaneously moves from the transference to anger with her mother, in whose eyes she was never good enough. She has a fantasy of an extremely violent attack on her, including decapitating her and grinding her up.

(5) *Grief* / (9) *Love.* (*With tears*) "I want my mother to love me". "You're (*her mother*) so beautiful and you have so much. I wish you could have been happy."

(6) *Relief* / (7) *Power* / (10) *Therapeutic effects.* In the next session she reports feeling calmer, stronger, more grounded, and closer to the man she has started dating.

(11) *Reconciliation.* At the 10-year follow-up: "I love my mother and feel loved by her."

The Masochistic Artist

• Issues by JM: "To enable her to experience her feelings, especially anger. To face her real feelings about her mother's constant wish to hurt her."

In the following passage the issue consists of the patient's feelings about her mother's repeatedly giving her enemas when she was small.

(1) *Resistance.* The patient described feeling "rage" towards her mother, but when pressed further she said, "I go blank".

(2) *Anxiety.* She said, crying, that she felt "trapped by love"—she was not allowed to be angry because the enemas were for her own good.

(4) *Violence.* Pressed to say what happens in her body, she eventually has a fantasy of strangling her mother, hitting her "again and again and again", and dropping her on the floor by the toilet.

(5) *Grief.* Sobbing, "I don't understand how someone could do that to a child."

(6) *Relief* / (7) *Power.* "It feels like now I can have pleasure—physical pleasure. It's empowering."

(8) *Absence of anxiety and guilt.* "My body doesn't feel pushed down, it feels opened up. I'm free."

(10) *Therapeutic effects.* "I want to go out into the world now, as a woman."

Further sessions confirmed the stability of these changes.

The Cold-Blooded Businessman

This was a highly resistant patient, diagnosed as suffering from a "narcissistic personality disorder", and the process that we are illustrating took place gradually, over a series of sessions. His main problem was an inability to allow himself emotional closeness or any kind of softer feelings.

(1) *Resistance* / (2) *Anxiety* / (3) *Anger in the transference.* Some way into therapy, the therapist intervened with a head-on collision, pointing out the self-destructive effects of the patient's emotional detachment in the session. He then admitted that the therapist's intervention had made him angry with her. It required much further confrontation to get him to admit that he was afraid of expressing his anger in case he might hurt her. Eventually he had a

fantasy of becoming violent, raping her, and leaving her on the floor. His feeling was "total indifference".

(6) *Relief.* He said he felt "released" and, later, "relaxed".

(5) *Grief.* Further challenge led to his saying that he was "overwhelmed with regret" at what he had done in his fantasy. He had hurt her intentionally—whereas, though she had hurt him, it was not intentional.

(8) *Absence of anxiety and guilt.* He said that he felt he had done something "horribly wrong". It is arguable that although this was an expression of *guilt*, a more appropriate word would be *remorse*, which contains an element of *compassion* and is one of the "softer" feelings which should be welcomed.

(4) *Anger with his mother.* The therapist asked whether there was any previous situation that came to mind. He immediately spoke of his mother. "I want to smash her body and leave her in the sewer to die alone."

(9) *Love* / (10) *Therapeutic effects.* Over the next many sessions, he worked over rage against his mother, and, as he did so, more and more tender and loving feelings came to the surface—though not for his mother. In a session after he had attended a funeral, he said, "I feel like a human being. I'm experiencing all kinds of feelings. . . . I felt very close to the family."

The Man Divided

Something always went wrong in this patient's close relations with women, which he coped with by developing extramarital affairs. In his background, his mother was rigid and domineering.

• Issue by JM: "To enable the patient to experience fully the rage directed towards his mother." This was the only prediction concerning anger that was not confirmed. However, the sequence did occur in relation to his wife.

(6) *Relief from expressing aggression.* In Session 5 he reported having been assertive with his wife. He said he felt "liberated" from his fear of speaking out.

(1) *Resistance* / (2) *Anxiety.* The therapist tried to get him to "portrait" his anger with his wife, but he became anxious and tried to get her to back off.

(4) *Breakthrough of violence.* Eventually he was able to have a fantasy of

slapping his wife, pushing her down, "fucking" her, and throwing her down the stairs.

(5) *Grief.* He said (Session 6) that he had been very upset by facing his mixture of sexual and aggressive feelings.

(3) *Anger in the transference* / (1) *Defence.* He then said that he was angry with the therapist for encouraging him to face these anxiety-provoking feelings. He had the impulse to phone a previous therapist. The therapist pointed out that this was an example of his ever-repeated pattern of coping with anger with one person by turning to someone else.

(9) *Love* / (10) *Therapeutic effects* / (11) *Reconciliation.* In Sessions 7–9 he reported "wonderful feelings of closeness" with his family over the holidays. Also, he had phoned his mistress and told her he was ending the relationship once and for all, as he intends to preserve his marriage.

The Reluctant Fiancée

This patient had been systematically physically abused by her father. She loved her mother, but she also described her as "totally ineffective"—unable to protect her from her father, to stand up to him, or to leave him.

• Issue by JM: "To enable the patient to experience fully the hatred and rage directed towards her father."

(1) *Resistance* / (2) *Anxiety.* "I feel my muscles tensing." As a child, "I would just go cold." "I feel like crying." "I'm afraid all the ties with my family will be destroyed." "This is terrifying to me."

(4) *Violence.* After a long passage in which she spoke of anger with *children*—who seemed to represent herself and her own reaction to abuse, she had the following fantasy about her father: "I knife him and knife him and knife him."

(6) *Relief.* "All I see now is me sitting on the couch and feeling very peaceful." "All of a sudden I see sun. There's sunlight streaming through the windows."

(8) *Absence of guilt and anxiety.* "Now I see my mother, with the car full of kids, coming into the drive . . . I say, 'He's dead'. I don't think they're sad. It's a celebration."

(10) *Therapeutic effects.* She had begun the session with: "I've had a headache all week, which is killing me right now." At the end, the

therapist asked her about her headache: She said: "It's better. That's funny, it's nice." At the 8-year follow-up she said, "I never get headaches any more".

(11) *Reconciliation*. At follow-up: "I can accept him as he is. I don't forget what happened, but I don't carry all those feelings around. We don't get into conflicts any more. He's a tired old man and I do the obligatory visits, but I don't let it get to me any more."

Later, the issue became anger with a previous boyfriend, who had abused her:

(1) *Defences* / (2) *Anxiety* / (5) *Grief*. At the time she had "shut down and gone on automatic pilot". In the session: "I have a sad, sinking feeling. It brings up intense pain." "I got depressed. There was so much anger."

(4) *Violence*. Eventually she says: ""I would incinerate him. It would be brutal. Knocking him to the floor and stomping on him."

(6) *Relief* / (5) *Grief*. Therapist: "What is your feeling now?" Patient: "Relief. There was no possibility with him. It's sad, but that's the truth."

(10) *Therapeutic effects*. These had started before this session, but it seems clear that they were now being consolidated and strengthened. "In the past few weeks, I've felt this opening with my fiancé. I feel closer and warmer." In the next session she reported a very happy weekend with her fiancé, "almost euphoric".

• Issue by JM: "To recognize and experience her mixed feelings towards her mother."

The therapist summarized work on this issue in Session 11: "I began to exert pressure to feel the anger towards her mother. She began to feel angry with me [*(3), anger in the transference*], but started to back-pedal [*(1), resistance*]. I pointed out that she defeats herself when she backs off from her anger [*challenge to resistance*]. 'How would you declare the anger?' She was equivocating [*(1), resistance*] and I challenged her to be direct. I made the link between myself and her mother, who was always telling her to 'Speak up, stand up straight' and so on. [*This led to (4), anger, directly expressed*]: 'I am so angry with her. Where were you? What kind of role model were you?' The rage was expressed verbally, but she still avoided any physical impulses towards her."

No consequences of this passage were recorded, but the following is a passage from the follow-up:

(9) *Love and closeness* / (11) *Reconciliation*. "It was very sad when she died, but also very moving. I went to take care of her in the last few weeks, and there was a closeness. She died in my arms. Even though she's gone I still feel deeply connected to her. I have forgiven her and I hold onto the love."

Discussion

The history of these observations

The essence of this dynamic sequence was originally worked out in response to a series of videotaped interviews presented by a variety of therapists at the International Conference in Amsterdam in 2002, mentioned above. The present series has confirmed the original sequence (resistance→breakthrough into primitive rage→therapeutic effects) and enabled it to be expanded (Table 10.1)—thus leading to a kind of cross-validation—and there is very little doubt that it is a general phenomenon, regularly observed in this method of therapy.

The question of "unconscious"

We need to ask whether the material that emerged from these patients had originally been truly unconscious.

It might seem that this is self-evident, but apparently it is not. When a draft of the present book was first submitted to a publisher, one of the reviewers asked, "What evidence is there that the material that emerged [from The Self-Loathing Headmistress] had been unconscious?" This is almost unanswerable. It is always arguable that these patients had been harbouring quite conscious, violently sadistic fantasies since early childhood, that they were tenaciously defending themselves against admitting them, and that therapeutic effects followed simply from finally being able to share them openly with another person. Does anyone believe this?

The significance of these observations

The following is a simplified summary of the scientific experiment that has been carried out:

1. Predictions were made that certain originally unconscious feelings would emerge into consciousness, and that this would result in therapeutic effects.

2. These feelings did emerge in an unmistakable form.

3. The result was a sequence, repeatedly observed, which contained much more detail than the simple phrase "therapeutic effects"—namely:

    Relief→Power→Love→Therapeutic effects→Reconciliation

Surely the result is a confirmation of the core of psychodynamic theory described at the beginning of this chapter.

GRIEF

The lower corner (I/F) of the Triangle of Conflict (Figure 2.1) represents three main categories of feeling against which patients defend themselves: *anger*, because of anxiety and guilt; *oedipal feelings*, also because of anxiety and guilt; and *grief* because of the accompanying pain. We have already dealt with anger in the previous section. Strangely, oedipal feelings (discussed in the next section) figured very little in these therapies. On the other hand grief, which we consider now, figured very prominently. The therapist stated categorically: "All these patients expressed the deepest grief." Below are the details, together with evidence about the therapeutic effects that immediately followed. It is important to note, however, that many examples involve both grief and anger, so that it becomes impossible to separate one from the other.

The Masochistic Artist

After the session in which this patient got in touch with her grief about what she had not received in her marriage, she decided to end the relationship with her lover.

In a later session she was in tears, as she had sadistic fantasies about her father. At home after this session she burst into tears, felt better, and for the first time found the capacity to comfort herself. She then reported that she felt "inside herself" and no longer alone—in other words, that she felt at peace with her inner world—and that her masochistic fantasies no longer excited her. In a passage not recorded in this book, she also experienced the most intense grief as she re-lived her experience of her mother's death from cancer 20 years before and the cremation ceremony at sea.

The Cold-Blooded Businessman

The patient expressed grief and concern about his rape fantasy against the therapist. Over the next many sessions, more and more loving and tender feelings came to the surface.

The Woman with Dissociation

In Session 6, this patient experienced a violent fantasy against her husband because of his current infidelity. This was followed by deep waves of grief about all that had been lost between them.

In Session 7, she experienced a "searing sense of deprivation of her most basic needs" in childhood. This was followed by memories of her father's sexual abuse, and her mother's relative ineffectiveness in helping her, which was accompanied by waves of grief. Later in the session she had an extremely sadistic fantasy directed against her father. In the next session she reported that she felt "much better and internally stronger" and had begun asserting herself with her children

The Man Divided

In Session 2, the patient became very choked up at the thought of his children dying. This led to the link between the birth of his second son and the younger brother who had died as a baby, with the interpretation of his death-wishes towards the latter. In Session 3 he reported the moving incident with his second son, when his son opened his arms to hug him—the first time ever that he had been able to bond with his son.

In Session 15 he reported having woken up crying. This was about the current loss of his grandmother, and also about his father's total withdrawal from the very beginning. There was then a major breakthrough of longing and grief about his loneliness as a child. In the next session he reported that he felt much better and was able to make sense of his life in a deeply meaningful way.

The Reluctant Fiancée

On three occasions, the patient's experience of anger with a particular person was followed by the de-repression of intense grief, but on no occasion was this followed by clear-cut therapeutic effects (the session that resulted in recovery from a fortnight-long headache contained violent fantasies but no grief):

1. She de-repressed anger with a previous boyfriend. In the next session she reported sobbing for two hours about the loss of him.
2. She experienced deep sadness and tenderness for her father after her fantasy of murdering him.
3. After murderous fantasies directed against her elder brother, she expressed "waves of grief—deep pain over the loss of him."

The Good Girl with Ulcerative Colitis

The patient began her therapy on the twentieth anniversary of her father's death, and she felt the need to resolve her feelings of grief about this profound loss. She came to Session 2 reporting that she had been experiencing waves of grief about his death. In the next session she reported having felt "sad, but also grounded" during the past week. After her violent fantasy directed against her mother, she exclaimed with deep grief, "I want my mother to love me".

The Self-Loathing Headmistress

Late in therapy, the patient came to the angry realization that her mother never wanted her, which was accompanied by waves of grief about what she had never had. At this point, for the first time in her life, she was able to feel a strong desire to live. This was a turning point in her therapy.

Summary

The following is a summary of the observations described above:

— Grief about *loss of a loved one* was expressed by five patients (The Masochistic Artist, The Man Divided, The Woman with Dissociation, The Good Girl with Ulcerative Colitis, The Reluctant Fiancée).
— Grief about *suffering in childhood* was expressed by all seven patients.
— Grief *about violent impulses* was expressed by four patients (The Masochistic Artist, The Cold-Blooded Businessman, The Man Divided, The Good Girl. Violent impulses *led to* grief-laden love in two patients (The Reluctant Fiancée, The Good Girl) and to grief about loss or suffering in two (The Woman with Dissociation, The Self-Loathing Headmistress).
— Grief *unaccompanied by anger in that session* was followed by therapeutic effects in four patients (The Masochistic Artist, The Man Divided, The Good Girl with Ulcerative Colitis, The Woman with Dissociation). Grief *accompanying or following anger* was followed by therapeutic effects in six patients (The Masochistic Artist, The Cold-Blooded Businessman, The Man Divided, The Woman with Dissociation, The Self-Loathing Headmistress, The Good Girl with Ulcerative Colitis). In the Reluctant Fiancée, therapeutic effects were not clear-cut. (It is worth noting that *anger*, whether or not

accompanied by *grief*, led to therapeutic effects in all seven patients.)

Discussion

Just as was true of anger, every one of these patients de-repressed the deepest grief. On the other hand, we have been unable to detect a clear-cut sequence involving grief, unlike that involving anger described in the previous section.

In order to separate the effects of expressing these two feelings from one another, we need to list therapeutic effects immediately following *anger unaccompanied by grief* and those following *grief unaccompanied by anger*. The former was represented by one patient only (The Reluctant Fiancée), the latter by four patients (The Masochistic Artist, The Man Divided, The Woman with Dissociation, The Good Girl with Ulcerative Colitis). This emphasizes the importance of grief.

The overall conclusion from all these observations is that it is just as important therapeutically to reach patients' grief as it is to reach their anger.

OEDIPAL FEELINGS

In these therapies, oedipal feelings figured very little. The only exceptions were as follows: (1) The Good Girl with Ulcerative Colitis mentioned, at follow-up, guilt about fantasies of sexual possession of her brother and her father. (2) The Masochistic Artist said that she was always aware of her father's jealousy—"I felt somehow I was betraying him by being interested in other boys". This was said in connection with a dream in which her father, as a *handsome young man*, subjected her to anal intercourse—which was a distorted reference to her mother's *actual* mistreatment of her. (3) The Man Divided described his jealousy of his younger brother, whose penis was being held by his mother in the bath—and in the next sentence he mentioned childhood masturbation.

The Masochistic Artist's dream did suggest that there was some pleasure in her reaction. However, the reactions of the other women patients to awareness of their father's hidden erotic feelings, or to overt sexual abuse, consisted only of anger and never of any kind of pleasure.

It would seem that in The Woman with Dissociation, The Reluctant Fiancée, and The Cold-Blooded Businessman, the relationship with the parent of the opposite sex was so bad that there was hardly any room for "positive" oedipal feelings, but their absence in the others is surprising.

PCDS has, in fact, treated other patients in which oedipal problems were the main issue. Equally, Davanloo has presented videotapes of several therapies in which the central issue consisted of guilt-laden eroticized feelings for the parent of the opposite sex, and/or hostile rivalry or guilt-laden triumph involving the parent of the same sex. More recently, other ISTDP therapists (Robert Neborsky, Jon Frederickson, personal communications) have found it possible to take a female patient, in a state of "dreaming while awake" (discussed below), through a fantasy of sexual intercourse with her father, in an exactly parallel way to that used with the murderous fantasies expressed by the patients in the present book.

All this means that oedipal problems are, indeed, dealt with in ISTDP, and therefore their relative absence in our seven patients can only be regarded as a chance result in a small sample. Nevertheless, we may contrast the relative absence of oedipal problems in ISTDP with Freud's view—which he apparently held to the end of his life—that the Oedipus complex was the central cause of all neurosis. Thus, once more, the *emphasis*, though not the substance, of the dynamic theory of psychopathology needs to be rewritten.

Further aspects of therapy

This second part of chapter 10 begins with an examination of the nature of fantasy in the breakthrough and the almost hallucinatory experience of "dreaming while awake", which seems to be a hitherto unrecognized state of consciousness. There then follow examples of the links that were made in these therapies among the three corners of the Triangle of Person—namely, Current, Transference, and Past (Figure 2.1)—and a discussion both of the therapeutic importance of these links and the way in which they validate the theory and practice of dynamic psychotherapy. We then present the unique and striking evidence provided by these patients on certain aspects of psychopathology. The chapter continues with a consideration of the therapeutic mechanisms involved in ISTDP, with special reference to the importance to patients of understanding their own life history. Finally, we describe, with evidence from these patients, how termination usually presents no problem in this form of therapy.

THE NATURE OF FANTASY IN THE BREAKTHROUGH
"Dreaming while awake"—a hitherto unrecognized state of consciousness?

As was described in Chapter 9, the main therapeutic effects in all these patients followed when hitherto buried feelings of anger and/or grief came to the surface. Of the two, the breakthrough of anger appeared in the form of intense and violent fantasies, often of a murderous and sadistic nature.

In real life, if one loses one's temper and attacks someone, there are two elements present: (1) intense inner experience, and (2) violent physical movements.

If the breakthrough in ISTDP is to be truly therapeutic, it is very important that the *inner experience* must be felt in the body, viscerally. The indications that this is happening, which the therapist must watch out for, consist of the *physical movements*—in the jaw, arms, or legs, according to the nature of the impulse—but *always much more muted* than they would occur in real life.

Some histrionic patients may wish to use violent physical movements, or shouting and screaming, as a way of discharging their impulses without really experiencing them; for these patients, it is far more beneficial to concentrate on the inner experience while remaining still. On the other hand, patients who become frozen and immobilized in face of anxiety over anger need to feel their impulses fully in their body.

During the breakthrough the patient's state possesses very special characteristics, some of which are not easily explained. It is clear that in this state the patients' experience is overwhelmingly powerful, and, moreover, although their experience is *inner,* they are not in a state of trance or withdrawal but are intensely sharing their feelings with the therapist. Indeed, this state seems almost to have been specifically designed to be therapeutic, since the forces that might abort it are left in a state of abeyance: *guilt* and *anxiety* are expressed at first, but evaporate under pressure; the *victim's* horrified reaction or appeal for mercy, leading to the opposing force of *compassion,* is simply not part of the scene; and *grief* about having such impulses against someone potentially loved only occurs after the violence has run its course.

The fantasy is a vivid experiencing of buried feelings, timeless and often near-hallucinatory, as befits any kind of feeling just emerging from the unconscious. It also may appear to be seen through a child's eyes. The following is an experience—away from the session—reported by The Masochistic Artist:

"I was in the kitchen, preparing dinner. I picked up a knife and suddenly thought, 'You bitch. How can you do this to me? You wanted to murder me.' *I got an image of my mother's face, which was very large, as it would appear to me as a child.* I imagined taking the knife and chopping my mother to bits. . . ."

The following is an example from The Self-Loathing Headmistress, who went through the quite amazing experience of *re-living* what it was like being breastfed by a mother who wished she did not exist—but now the patient's experience was different, for in her fantasy she was determined to demand her rights as a baby:

> Pt: I'm going to have your breast whether you like it or not. Stop fussing! Sit there, stop your squirming! I am going to be in this world whether you like it or not!

This is an example of the essence of dynamic psychotherapy—the early traumatic experience, now faced, surmounted, and detoxified with the insight and determination of a mature adult.

Similarly, the fantasy may take on a life of its own, as was shown by the following sudden transition from darkness to light, once the murderous impulses of The Reluctant Fiancée had been expressed against her father and the guilt had been overcome:

> Th: Then what would happen?
>
> Pt: I guess I'd be arrested. . . . That's funny, I don't see anyone else in the house. But I'll tell you something, there's sun in the living-room. Whenever I'm in the kitchen it's dark. All of a sudden I see sun. Now I see my mother, with the car full of kids, coming into the drive. They are all chatty and happy.

It really does seem as if these phenomena represent a hitherto unrecognized state of consciousness, which possesses the property of *quiet intensity*—one in which there is an *intense inner experience* of feelings and impulses, but without connection to the opposing forces mentioned above, and with limited expression in physical terms. Davanloo recognized it, using the term *dreaming while awake*, but he did not give it any special theoretical emphasis.

Here we may raise another question, as follows. Of course, unconscious hostility is part of the bread-and-butter of all dynamic psychotherapy, so why has this "quiet intensity" not been discovered by traditional dynamic therapists and adopted as a standard aim of therapeutic technique? The answer must lie in their failure to recognize the crucial role of *true experience*. This may be illustrated by the following clinical story:

The Architect Who Loved Kipling

Like The Good Girl with Ulcerative Colitis in the present series, this 50-year-old man had good reason to be angry with his mother, who—whatever his current achievement might be—had always been dismissive of it and demanded more. The therapist pressed him to describe what he felt, blocking each evasion as it appeared. Finally, the patient got as far as saying: "There was a bridge over a river not far from home, where the water ran still and deep. The parapet was low, and we used to walk there quite often. . . ." The therapist was content with this open allusion to murderous feelings and left it there.

At follow-up a year later, the patient was little improved. What had gone wrong? If we make use of the clinical material described in the present chapter, it seems clear that an *allusion*—however open—does not face the patient with the *true experience* of his impulses, and that what the therapist failed to do was to press him to describe *the explicit murderous fantasy*, in living detail.

Exactly the same applies when the therapist remains content with a *response to interpretation*, however strikingly confirmatory this may be.

Comment

It seems probable that this kind of experience of "dreaming while awake" also occurs in the form of therapy named "accelerated experiential dynamic psychotherapy" (see Fosha, 2000). The author uses the term "true self-experience", writing that this "may be accompanied by feelings of happiness, well-being, and relaxation, and by a sense that everything is simple, easy, and beautiful" (p. 148).

The effect resulting from this state is one of the totally unexpected—and seemingly miraculous—empirical discoveries stemming from Davanloo. Although it looks easy, bringing the patient to this state requires great skill and experience.

LINKS IN THE TRIANGLE OF PERSON

One of the basic observations in dynamic psychotherapy is that neurotic patterns that originated in the relationship with people in the distant *past* are repeated in the relationship with people in more recent or *current* life, and are then repeated in the relationship with the therapist—that is, the *transference*. These three categories of people are represented by the corners P, C, and T of the Triangle of Person in Figure 2.1.

In consequence, one of the most important principles of technique is to bring the patient to insight about the similarities in these patterns—that is, to realize that *transference* patterns, T, are similar to *current* patterns, C, and that both are similar to, and thus *derived from*, patterns laid down in the past, P. This means making the *links* among the three categories—that is, transference–current (T–C), current–past (C–P), and transference–past (T–P)—thus completing the triangle.

Clinical experience makes clear that all three links are important, but there is also *research* evidence supporting the therapeutic effectiveness of the T–P link in particular. Malan (1976b) showed, by statistical work on brief psychotherapy, that the therapist's emphasis on interpretations making this link between transference and past correlated significantly with favourable outcome. Examples are given below of these three links from the current series.

In the present series, close examination of the events surrounding insight into these links can provide objective validation of dynamic theory and practice, as in the examples below.

T–P link

The Cold-Blooded Businessman

> Th: But the anger is towards me. So if that came out, no holds barred?
> Pt: I would stand up, yell, tell you you're wrong.
> Th: But telling me I'm wrong is not a feeling.
> Pt: I want to say *it's a feeling like I have towards my mother*, like I don't want to have anything to do with you.

This was a forerunner to the breakthrough of violent feelings against the therapist, from which there followed major therapeutic effects.

The Good Girl with Ulcerative Colitis

This is part of the therapist's summary of an early session:

> "She came in saying she got a bill from me in which she was charged for a missed session. She claimed to be irritated but avoided the *experience* of it by intellectualizing. As her stubborn defiance was identified and challenged, the experience of anger towards me emerged. She had the impulse to lash out, beat my shoulders, and punch my face. As she faced me on the floor *an image of her mother emerged*. She realized this was the link. She experienced me, *like her mother*, as demanding of her.
>
> "In the next session she said that the last session was a pivotal one for her. Her mother was demanding, so she could express her anger indirectly by withholding what her mother wanted."

From a later session (a second example of the same T-P link):

> Pt: So let's say I had an accident [i.e. was incontinent] and you did reject me. I would feel really bad, but also angry.

Th: Did you imagine that?

Pt: Yeah, well, it's my mother actually.

Still later (a third example):

Pt: We're going to get into it and have a fight . . . I push you, and you push me back.

Th: So this is where I become . . . (*The patient completes the sentence:*)

Pt: It's my mother!

Violent fantasies against her mother proved to be the main event in therapy leading to therapeutic effects.

The Self-Loathing Headmistress

The therapist described a session in which the patient suggested that "she was afraid I'd view her as a burden, get sick of her and want to be rid of her. I looked for the feelings underneath, she got to anger and then immediately said, '*It's not you, it's my mother*'." This was a forerunner of the final breakthrough, in which the patient realized how much her mother wanted to get rid of her and that her own self-loathing was an identification with her mother's view of her.

A second example, from a later session:

Pt: The last time I came, you were wearing your red dress, and I was focusing on where the V of the dress comes down, by your breast and your heart.

Th: You want to go for my heart?

Pt: (*Intense anxiety and rocking*) I had that feeling of transference and all that stuff. *Mum, and going for her breast and her heart.* I had that image of biting her breast.

The therapist wrote: "What seemed so striking was the profound effect this session had on her ongoing sense of being. She felt better able to connect emotionally with others and had a desire for greater closeness with her mother."

C–P link

The Self-Loathing Headmistress

In the session following the one just discussed, and illustrating further her increasing ability to connect emotionally to others, the patient spoke of a woman friend who had had a breast removed and had also been bereaved by the death of her grandmother:

Pt: I almost feel I was better able to experience this poor woman's pain than she was. It's like the sadness of wanting to get to the pain they can't deal with. I see how heavy it is and how much they defend against it. *It reminds me of Mum and wanting to get through to her, to break through her defences.*

At the 7-year follow-up she spoke of her reconciliation with her mother—deeply felt on both sides: "My mother has shared with me parts of her heart, her places of panic. There's more depth there, in seeing her vulnerability."

The Reluctant Fiancée

Using the phrase "it would be a life-and-death struggle", the patient had described her fantasy of a murderous attack on a previous boyfriend who had abandoned her:

Th: What is your feeling now?

Pt: Relief. I've survived. There was no real possibility with him. The relationship was really awful, abusive actually.

Th:　Does anyone else come to mind?

Pt: *My father, actually.* I had a flash of him. When I talked about the life-and-death struggle, I thought of my father. It's like I was repeating all that with Jim. I was abused by him like I was by my father.

The patient's main problem had been an extremely tenacious unwillingness to commit herself to marriage. In the next session she reported a very happy weekend with her fiancé. They met with a priest about a wedding and went out looking for furniture. However, later follow-up (see chapter 1) showed that this effect was temporary, although the situation was finally resolved.

The Woman with Dissociation

From the therapist's summary of Session 4:

"She then raised the issue of anger with her daughter. When she got to the experience of anger, she made a spontaneous link to her mother. When she saw how she was reacting to her daughter as a stand-in for her mother, she immediately differentiated one from the other. She imagined telling her daughter directly what she was upset about and had the sense it would go well.

T–C link

The Man Divided

The following are extracts from the therapist's summary of Session 16:

"The patient noticed sexualized feelings and fantasies about me after the last session, which he connected to the possibility of losing me (*termination was in the air at this point*). He was able to see that the affairs he used to have had always occurred during a separation from his primary attachment figure (*i.e. both his previous and his present wife*). The patient is doing nearly all the work in these sessions, just working the conflicts through and making connections to solidify the insights he's gained."

Discussion

The vignettes shown above make certain that establishing these links—and especially the T–P link—played an important part in therapy, leading directly or indirectly to therapeutic effects. This observation confirms both the statistical work by Malan mentioned above and long-held principles of psychoanalytic technique based on generations of clinical observation.

Malan (1976b) quoted four well-known authorities who wrote of the importance of these links many years ago, two of whom are quoted here. Glover (1955) wrote:

> We are never finished with a transference interpretation until it is finally brought home to roost. To establish the existence of a transference-fantasy is only half our work; it must be detached once more and brought into association with infantile life [we would say, better, "early life"]. [pp. 132–133]

Alexander (1957) brought in the third corner of the Triangle of Person:

> Interpretations which connect the *actual life situation* [i.e. the C corner] with *past experience* [P] and with the *transference* [T] . . . are called *total interpretations*. The more that interpretations approximate to this principle of totality the more they fulfil their double purpose; they accelerate the assimilation of new material by the ego and mobilize further unconscious material. [p. 68]

This statement by Alexander makes clear the importance of *completing* the Triangle of Person—that is, the importance of including the C corner (current or recent relationships). It is essential that patients should understand the way in which patterns laid down in the past permeate all their relationships, including those in their current life or more recent past.

However, there is more to the evidence than this. First, all these authors refer only to progress in the *process* of therapy, and Malan's observations are concerned only with *eventual* outcome. In the present series, therapeutic effects were observed *within* therapy, sometimes described immediately, and sometimes reported in the next session.

Second, all four of the above authors, together with the statistical work by Malan, are concerned entirely with insight received through *interpretations*—that is, through therapists *telling* patients what seem to be their underlying feelings—which is always open to the objection that any response, however confirmatory, is simply the result of suggestion. But, as the reader may have noticed, every single one of the links described above was reached, not through any direct statement from the therapist, but through *spontaneous insight by the patient* leading to direct experience. It seems that the defences have been so weakened that these patients are ahead of the therapist, and they make the links themselves as a result of pressure from their unconscious therapeutic alliance. Scientifically speaking, this is far more convincing.

Thus these therapies confirm, with objective clinical evidence, two principles of dynamic theory and practice: (1) the observation that patterns formed in early life are repeated in current relationships and in the transference; and (2) the therapeutic effect of insight about the resulting links in the Triangle of Person, leading to the true experience of the feelings and impulses involved. The fact that patients reach this insight spontaneously is yet another illustration of the power of the technique of ISTDP.

EVIDENCE ON PSYCHOPATHOLOGY

An immensely valuable property of a really powerful method of dynamic psychotherapy is that it can provide conclusive evidence bearing on certain aspects of psychopathology. In particular, some theoretical ideas are unmistakably confirmed, while others need to be treated with greater caution.

The meaning of a phobia

Suppose that a patient is presented at a case conference suffering from a *fear of knives*. For this symptom the members of the conference might well offer a standard psychodynamic equation: patients' fear of knives = a fear of what they might do with a knife—that is, a fear of their own violent impulses. In routine clinical work, no one would be likely to report on whether or not this speculation was confirmed by subsequent therapy.

We may now quote from the therapy of the Reluctant Fiancée, the topic consisting of links between fantasies about anger with her father and pain in her head and eyes:

Pt: I would send daggers out of my eyes to pierce him, icicle daggers— I see icicles sticking out all over him, like puncture wounds.

Th: If your fight is just with hands and fists, he might overpower you. So, what would you have to do?

Pt: The thing that entered my mind is a knife. I can't watch movies with knives. I can't watch knives going into people. *In the movies I absolutely hide and shake if I see that.*

Th: Like the daggers, right.

Pt: I didn't even think of that. . . . I have a knife and I keep plunging it into him. It would be frenzied—just over and over.

It is important to state that the link between fear of knives and murderous impulses was not suggested to the patient by *interpretation*, but emerged spontaneously from her unconscious. The evidence could hardly be more convincing.

Breastfeeding

There has always been a tendency among psychoanalytically trained professionals, following Freud's formulation of "oral, anal, and genital", to reduce psychopathology to its earliest possible origins and in particular to *parts of the body*. This applies, for instance, to theories involving *breastfeeding*. The material presented here offers evidence that confirms its importance in one patient only. The other six patients demonstrate that complete recovery can occur without this issue being mentioned.

In one of the most moving passages in all these therapies, The Self-Loathing Headmistress actually *re-lived* her experience of being breastfed by an unwilling mother, but now with a difference, for in her fantasy she expressed what she could not have done as a baby— namely, her angry determination to get what she needed, come what may:

Pt: I'm going to have your breast whether you like it or not. Stop fussing! Sit there, stop your squirming!

As described below, it became clear later in therapy that her main symptom of self-hatred arose from an identification with her mother's hatred and wish to get rid of her. Her experience in the session now revealed that the roots of this symptom could be traced back to the earliest possible relationship with her mother—indeed, before she was born. She was conceived within a year of her elder sister's birth, and her mother had more recently said to her, "Don't think breastfeeding will prevent pregnancy", thus making clear that she was an unwanted child.

Thus, for her, the crucial significance of breastfeeding was unmistakably confirmed. Yet it is important to note that the traumatic situation to which she was reacting was not breastfeeding itself, but the whole of her mother's relationship to her, which had continued throughout the years and up to the present.

The evidence suggests that there were two quite separate mechanisms at work in this patient's self-hatred—namely, not only (1) an identification with her mother's negative view of her, but (2) the operation of her "superego", consisting of her own angry and guilt-laden impulses redirected against herself. This leads immediately to the next subject.

Self-directed aggression

The earliest mention of this crucial aspect of human psychopathology occurred in "Mourning and Melancholia" (1917e [1915]), where Freud wrote that self-reproaches in severe depression appeared to consist of displaced reproaches against someone whom the patient "loves, has loved, or should love". In *The Ego and the Id* (1923b) he wrote: "the more a man controls his aggressiveness, the more intense becomes his ideal's [i.e. in later terminology, his superego's] inclination to aggressiveness against his own ego."

The present series of patients offers convincing evidence of the inference that self-directed aggression—which can take many forms—may consist of displaced impulses unconsciously directed outwards. Examples are given below.

Self-hatred

Here is a further passage from The Self-Loathing Headmistress, the topic being physical punishment by her parents:

    Th: So what kinds of feelings do you have towards them?
    Pt: I feel deep self-loathing.

This reaction is apparently quite paradoxical, but it becomes entirely understandable in terms of the mechanism lying behind self-reproaches described above.

The evidence in the following vignettes comes from the coincidence of detail between self-directed impulses and those that are directed outwards.

Identifying with the victim of the patient's own impulses

The Good Girl with Ulcerative Colitis had suffered from attacks in which she felt she was choking. During therapy the following occurred:

> Pt: I want to strangle my mother . . . I still feel I'm controlling myself (*she puts her hand round her throat*) . . . I just squeeze the life right out of her . . . I choke the life out of her.

Interestingly, Abbass (personal communication) reports that he has seen a large number of patients complaining of choking sensations, in whom impulses to strangle were revealed during subsequent therapy.

Self-punishment

The Self-Loathing Headmistress:

> Pt: I'm very angry with my father. He turned off when I entered puberty.
>
> Th: And the anger?
>
> Pt: I kept the anger inside and pounded myself (*she had the fantasy of pounding herself into the ground with a hammer*).

The evidence that this was her own outwardly directed impulse comes from a later session. There she described an incident in which she had become enraged with a man who had behaved awkwardly to her over the phone, after which she had the fantasy of "really pounding him" with a baseball bat.

Suicide

The method of suicide chosen may sometimes be clearly seen as an impulse directed against someone else, now directed against the self. Early in therapy The Good Girl with Ulcerative Colitis mentioned that after having been rejected by a boyfriend she became depressed and had the impulse to kill herself by slashing her neck. In later sessions she de-repressed the fantasy of slashing her boyfriend's neck, and later that of her mother.

The mechanism by which self-directed aggression may be relieved

Of the above examples, The Self-Loathing Headmistress's fantasy of pounding herself and The Good Girl's impulse to slash herself both confirm unequivocally that anger felt towards someone else can become directed against the self. It is a natural prediction, therefore, that this self-directed aggression will be relieved if anger at the other person can be expressed openly. This prediction was confirmed by two patients.

Late in therapy, The Good Girl with Ulcerative Colitis expressed a fantasy of being incontinent and the therapist being revolted by it:

Th: You feel anger towards me and imagine my reaction to your accident with disgust—and imagine that I would reject you.

Pt: Uncontrollable rage.

Th: That *I* would experience uncontrollable rage?

Pt: That I deserve to die. As you speak, though, I don't feel like dying. I feel angry and I feel like striking back.

Here we see before our eyes the moment in which self-punishment turns into outwardly expressed aggression.

The evidence provided by The Man Divided was less spectacular, but still thoroughly convincing. One of his patterns was to drink too much and then drive out on his motor cycle, thus putting his life in danger and potentially fulfilling his need for self-destruction to the ultimate. During therapy he reported that—for the first time—he had expressed anger openly to his wife, that she had responded favourably, and that afterwards he had no longer felt the need to drink and drive.

Anger and depression

These examples of self-directed aggression raise the whole question of the link between unexpressed anger and depression. There is an often-quoted psychodynamic equation that "Depression is anger turned against the self". It needs to be said immediately that, as a rigid generalization, this cannot possibly be the whole truth. Surely one of the primary explanations for depression consists of unexpressed feelings about loss, in which case unexpressed anger is not necessarily present—though, of course, it may be. The Reluctant Fiancée made the link between depression and anger explicitly: "I got depressed, there was so much anger."

There may be evidence that this mechanism is at work in patients who suffer from self-punishment or self-destructiveness, which may be described, once more, as the operation of the "superego".

In the initial interview with The Cold-Blooded Businessman, whose depression was severe and involved detailed suicidal planning, the following passage is worth quoting again:

Pt: Am I unconsciously wanting to hurt someone physically? The thought just occurred to me—some define depression as anger self-directed.

So far one might well interpret this as a piece of intellectualized insight offered for the therapist's benefit, but . . .

Th: Anger turned inwards. So you beat yourself up instead.

Pt: You know, I never understood what that meant until this moment—until you said "So you beat yourself up instead".

In this previously poorly motivated patient, there was then a sudden transition:

Pt: "I'm glad I came here, you know that."

Thus this insight marked the transition from open resistance to therapeutic alliance, which suggests strongly that it was genuine.

The meaning of masochism

Of all the phenomena that are encountered in psychotherapy, masochism is one of the least understandable to common sense. How can anyone derive pleasure from fantasies of being tortured? Yet this was true of The Masochistic Artist, who, without such fantasies could not reach orgasm and, moreover, played out her need for suffering in the men whom she chose as partners.

The patient's background involved the following: The family included two sets of children, one from her parents' current marriage and an older set from her father's previous marriage. Her mother, who clearly resented the patient's very existence, vented her hostility and sadism on her by finding ways of hurting her both emotionally and physically. In order to get love, the patient had to be submissive and perpetuate the role of victim. Her father made no attempt to protect her, and he expressed erotic feelings for her instead of caring for her. She married a man who ill-treated her, and she said openly that she knew that she had "married her mother".

Her florid sexual fantasies had started at the age of 6 years and involved being *raped and tortured* by an *older man*, in the presence of *his wife*, and *older children and younger children*. Although the resemblance to the situation in her own family is unmistakable, and although this is clearly an example of the well-known phenomenon of the "compulsion to repeat", the underlying mechanism is far from clear.

During therapy she experienced, with much distress, a highly *sadistic* fantasy about her father. In the next session she reported that she had been overcome with *tears*, which gave her tremendous relief, and then that she had tried to use her usual fantasy but found that *it was not arousing any more*—"it was too obvious, too painful"; finally, she converted it into a *tender fantasy* with her lover. Shortly after this, she herself said that she realized she had been "actually re-living a trauma". The therapist's comment was: "It's as if these parental introjects have been ousted and she's claimed her true self."

Even after this evidence, the actual mechanism is still very difficult to formulate; however, what is clear is that her need to re-live her trauma was eliminated by the expression of hitherto unconscious *anger* and *grief* about what she had suffered. This suggests the possibility that another part of the mechanism may be related to the flashbacks and recurrent nightmares observed in the post-traumatic syndrome, which may consist of the pressure from *unassimilated and overwhelming feelings* pressing to emerge into consciousness.

In any case, this exceedingly striking episode from therapy offers additional evidence about the whole question of the meaning of masochism.

Psychosomatic symptoms and their meaning

The cumulative evidence for the efficacy and effectiveness of dynamic psychotherapy in the treatment of psychosomatic conditions is extraordinarily strong—an observation that needs to be more widely known.

1. In a review article on the history of research in psychotherapy, written in 1973, DM concluded that the only tangible evidence to be found in the literature for the validity of dynamic psychotherapy lay in the treatment of peptic ulcer, asthma, and the palliative treatment of ulcerative colitis (Malan, 1973).

2. Luborsky, Singer, and Luborsky (1975) found strong evidence for the efficacy of dynamic psychotherapy in psychosomatic conditions, which was one of only two exceptions to their observation that all forms of psychotherapy were equal and "all must have prizes".

3. In Abbass's list of controlled studies (personal communication), three of the most strikingly positive results involved the comparison

of *medical treatment plus traditional dynamic psychotherapy* with *medical treatment alone.* These are Guthrie, Creed, Dawson, & Tomenson (1991) and Svedlund (1993), both on irritable bowel syndrome, and Sjødin, Svedlund, Ottosson, and Dotevall (1986) on peptic ulcer.

It is interesting to speculate on the reason why these conditions should give positive results in controlled studies. It seems possible that the relief of psychosomatic symptoms is a more reliable indicator of true resolution than, for instance, the relief of depression or anxiety—which can occur by "spontaneous remission" or "flight into health".

In our own series, two patients (The Reluctant Fiancée, The Woman with Dissociation) were *cured* of attacks of severe headache that had lasted since childhood; one (The Cold-Blooded Businessman) was cured of erectile dysfunction; and one (The Good Girl) was cured of ulcerative colitis. Two of these patients gave extremely interesting evidence on the meaning of their symptoms, as now discussed.

The Good Girl with Ulcerative Colitis

It is clear that this patient's intestinal system was extremely vulnerable, since she began to suffer from abdominal symptoms from an early age, diagnosed as irritable bowel syndrome. This progressed to two severe attacks of ulcerative colitis, at ages 27 and 31, the first of which followed the break-up of a relationship with a man.

In Session 16 the patient spoke of a man connected with her work who had made her very angry (in the examples given in this section the dialogue is highly abbreviated and edited):

Th: It sounds like you don't allow yourself to experience the anger. You internalize it and become depressed.

Pt: I felt it in my stomach—my intestines get clenched and then I have to go to the bathroom more often.

This is a very clear description of inner stress being expressed through the involuntary (smooth) muscle of her intestines. Davanloo emphasizes that it is the therapist's task to block this and to get the patient to express, first, the anxiety and, then, the impulse, through voluntary (striated) muscle instead. This is the aim of the therapist's next intervention:

Th: So do you want to focus on the anger instead of making yourself sick?

Pt: Yeah, well, I imagined really pounding this guy, visualizing him up against the wall.

At this point her voluntary muscles become activated, and she demonstrates her action with her arms.

Th: Where did you pound him?

Pt: Hitting him in *his* stomach—that's interesting!

This could certainly lead to the inference that her abdominal symptoms represent *turning her impulses against herself.*

One year after termination of her 68 sessions, her surgeon—who had told her she "over-psychologized"—was amazed to find not only that she was quite symptom-free, but that although her colon showed scarring, there was no longer any sign of active inflammation. This situation was maintained at the 10-year follow-up.

At this follow-up interview, she made absolutely clear the way in which her feelings had formerly affected the vegetative system of her gastro-intestinal tract and that this link had now been broken:

Pt: I deal with my feelings very differently . . . when I get nervous, I don't feel it in my gut. It's amazing. Symptomatically, I FEEL FABULOUS. It just doesn't go to my stomach any more.

The Reluctant Fiancée

One of this patient's main symptoms consisted of excruciating tension headaches, occurring about every week, from which she had suffered since an early age. She came up to Session 6 with a headache that had lasted for a week, which she described as "killing her". In a search for the precipitating factor, the patient mentioned an incident involving her father and her brother. This led to the following dialogue:

Pt: I could just smack their heads together.

Th: And the feeling inside of you?

Pt: Hatred towards my father and disgust with my brother. I would send daggers out of my eyes to pierce my father, icicle daggers—I see icicles sticking out all over him, like puncture wounds.

Th: Do you see? Inside of you is this terrific rage, with an impulse to attack and puncture and pierce him, and yet you keep this tightly controlled inside and you end up by experiencing the very thing you wanted to do to him—the piercing in your eyes, the pain in your head, but at that moment the impulse was to have *him* experience this pain. You see, unless this gets faced directly and you feel what you want to do to him, this mechanism takes hold, in which you internalize it and end up suffering. Both these impulses—to smash their heads and pierce his eyes—show exactly a one-to-one correspondence with your symptoms.

Pt: Oh, I didn't even think of that. We're talking about heads and eyes, and my head and eyes hurt. I see that.

This was followed by a long passage in which the patient experienced her violent and sadistic impulses against her father directly—after which she reported that *her headache had gone*. (It is interesting that her original impulse had been to "smack their heads together".) At the 10-year follow-up she said, "I don't get headaches any more. It's a distant memory." People suffering from headaches sometimes describe them as "piercing", which makes some sense of the impulse that this patient described.

Interpreting the evidence

In both these patients there is a kind of "chicken-and-egg" problem, which means that one has to be careful in making any theoretical inference. What is not in doubt is that the physical symptoms and the impulses are in some way connected or "correlated", and correlations say nothing about the direction of causation. Another possibility, therefore, is that the physical symptoms came first and that the patients then incorporated them into their impulses, taking revenge on the other person, "in kind", for their own pain. From a therapeutic point of view, however, this does not matter, since in both patients the process of making the impulses conscious did, in fact, relieve the symptoms permanently.

Comment

All neurotic symptoms result in suffering, and it is sometimes difficult to distinguish between those that are a manifestation of a "punitive superego" and those in which the suffering, so to speak, is simply a by-product of the neurotic process. But in the later examples quoted in this chapter, there was strong evidence for impulses being turned against the self. This suggests that self-directed aggression involves the fusion of the following needs: (1) the need to defend against becoming aware of outwardly directed impulses; (2) the need to protect loved ones, against whom these impulses are directed; and (3) the need to express guilt about the impulses through self-punishment.

THERAPEUTIC MECHANISMS

It is important to emphasize that, as a form of treatment, ISTDP is not a cathartic method—or rather, it is not *only* cathartic: one cannot dismiss the observation that major therapeutic effects often follow *immediately* from the catharsis of expressing hitherto buried feelings such as anger and grief. It seems likely that two further important factors that help to prevent relapse are *insight about defences* and the ability to *make sense of their lives*, or, in other words, to *construct a coherent life narrative*.

This is a highly subjective aspect of outcome that would be unlikely to appear in any list of criteria, and yet it is of immense importance to a person's whole outlook. Most of these patients came to therapy confused and bewildered by their lives and their history, but by the end of it they were able to make sense of all that had happened.

Four patients described this explicitly. (1) In Session 15 of The Man Divided, there was a major breakthrough of longing and grief about the loneliness and isolation of his childhood. The therapist wrote of the next session that "he felt much better and was able to make sense of his life in a deeply meaningful way". (2) After the link had been made between The Masochistic Artist's father and her sexual fantasies, she said that "this had de-mystified" them. (3) The therapist wrote of The Reluctant Fiancée's last session that "she was no longer in a muddle but could see herself and others clearly, now that her feelings from the past had been worked through". (4) Finally, the most explicit statement on this theme was made by The Woman with Dissociation:

> Pt: It's wonderful and it's a way of confirming, Yes, this happened, Yes you *do* have these feelings and you *were* burying them, and Yes, this is the way you were handling them. Yes, it's . . . another clue as to this big picture, or proof—it's like proof.

TERMINATION

The following is a quotation from the therapist's account of Session 18 with The Man Divided:

> "Given the healthy ways he had dealt with some very difficult situations, the patient wondered about ending therapy. He had exceeded his own expectations and felt capable of going out on his own."

In many forms of dynamic psychotherapy, it is usually the therapist who suggests termination, which results in the need to devote considerable time to working through the patient's transference feelings of loss and anger. Much more satisfactory is a situation like that quoted above, in which not only have transference feelings already been brought into the open and resolved, but *patients suggest termination themselves because they have received in full what they came for*. The same applied to at least two other patients—The Masochistic Artist and The Woman with Dissociation (records are not complete for the others). With properly conducted ISTDP, this is the rule rather than the exception.

CHAPTER 11

Aspects of outcome

The aspects of outcome considered in the chapter are as follows: therapeutic effects during therapy, which provide validation of dynamic psychotherapy without controls; changes in the patient's appearance; the attainment of "happiness"; facing stress without relapse, which is one of the tests of "total resolution"; and what may be called "transcendental" experiences during the follow-up period. All these aspects of outcome illustrate the depth of the changes that can be achieved by this method of treatment. The chapter concludes with a series of comments from the patients on the therapeutic factors in their therapy, which show extraordinary accuracy, and, finally, the important observation at follow-up of the absence of unresolved transference.

THERAPEUTIC EFFECTS DURING THERAPY

When disturbances that have lasted for many years—despite the patient's best efforts and many therapeutic interventions—are resolved within a few sessions, we can infer that the therapy itself was responsible. At termination, all these therapies showed such evidence. Follow-up revealed that these changes were maintained and often strengthened over time. This suggests that dissolving and restructuring defences removes barriers to growth, which can then continue unimpeded after termination. The patients in our series repeatedly show both kinds of evidence, as summarized below.

The Woman with Dissociation (age 42, 14 sessions)

In Session 8 she spoke as follows: "I don't have any more anxiety attacks. *I haven't had a headache since that first day I came to see you, and I know because I chart them.* I've had headaches since I was 8"— headaches for 34 years, gone in one session! Moreover, this occurred after an interview in which, for the first time in her life, she had truly faced her rage and pain about early deprivation and abuse. By Session 14 she had reported major improvement in her ability to assert herself and to cope with difficulties, without anxiety.

The Reluctant Fiancée (age 36, 16 sessions)

In Session 6 she had a murderous fantasy about her father, followed by anger and violence against a previous boyfriend. In the next session (Session 7), she reported many improvements in her relationship with her fiancé—but there was no change in her severe inhibition against marrying him. In the same session she de-repressed her feelings about her father's sexual abuse. She then had a murderous fantasy about him, which was followed by deep feelings of sadness, and tenderness to-wards him. Although there were no improvements reported in Session 8, in her final session (Session 16) she described how she was no longer anxious or depressed—she had first felt she wanted to die at age 8 (28 years previously). She also described how she was now able to be self-assertive without anxiety, was able to express the full range of her feelings both at home and at work, and no longer suffered from head-aches, which she said had been "excruciating" since childhood (say, 26 years).

The Man Divided (age 44, 20 sessions)

This patient complained of depression since the birth of his second son, who at the time of the interview was aged 2½. He had been quite unable to bond with his son. He had also withdrawn emotionally from his wife and had become involved in an affair with another woman.

In the first interview the therapist made the link between his *second* son and his *second* younger brother, who was born when the patient was 9 years old and had died two weeks later. In Session 2 he reported having felt closer to both his wife and his son. In this session the therapist explicitly interpreted guilt about death-wishes towards his brother. In the next session the patient reported not only further improvement in his relationship with his wife, but also a most moving incident demonstrating closeness with his son (see chapter 4). In Session 6 he expressed a violent fantasy against his wife, about which he was extremely distressed. In Session 7 he expressed his anger with the therapist for making him face these mixed feelings. In the next session (Session 8) he reported "wonderful feelings of closeness" with his wife and family. He had also phoned his mistress and told her he was ending the relationship once and for all.

The Masochistic Artist (age 39, 32 sessions)

In a session beyond the middle of therapy she reached a violent and sadistic fantasy against her father, accompanied by deep grief. In the next session she said, *"I feel free for the first time in my life"*, and she reported that *she could no longer get any arousal from her masochistic sexual fantasies*, which she had had since the age of 6 (for 33 years).

* * *

All three of the remaining patients, who were given between 58 and 68 sessions, suffered from disturbances dating from childhood which showed major improvements during therapy.

The Self-Loathing Headmistress (age 29, 58 sessions)

Late in therapy this patient de-repressed the experience of being breastfed by an unwilling mother, together with her determined rebellion against this situation. The therapist wrote of the profound effect that this session had had on the patient's "sense of being". She was now able to connect emotionally with others, and she could now trust her own feelings rather than dismissing them and accepting the views of others.

The Cold-Blooded Businessman (age 58, 58 sessions)

This patient had developed a "narcissistic personality"—involving complete inability to have "softer" feelings such as tenderness, compassion, and remorse about the pain and harm that he had caused to those closest to him—in response to serious abuse by his mother (starting at least by age 7 years) and separation (between ages 10 and 13). Late in therapy the following sequence occurred: (1) between sessions he had a violent rape fantasy against the therapist, after which he felt overwhelmed with regret. (2) In the next session he reported feeling "like a human being", he felt close to other people, he was at times moved almost to tears. (3) In the next session after this he had a fantasy of loving sex with the therapist. (4) He then was able to have loving sex with his wife, and he reported *"feeling alive and happy for the first time in his life"* (at least 51 years).

The Good Girl with Ulcerative Colitis (age 34, 68 sessions)

This patient experienced violent fantasies first against a former boy-friend who had rejected her, and in a later session against her mother, together with deep grief. After each of these sessions she reported feeling powerful, happy, and fully alive and no longer feeling guilty and attacking herself. This tendency towards self-attack probably went back to her childhood—say, 24 years.

Comment

We feel that this evidence speaks for itself.

CHANGES IN THE PATIENT'S APPEARANCE

The following are the therapist's comments regarding The Self-Loathing Headmistress, written at the end of the patient's final session: "She had entered treatment looking tense and timid. Although statuesque, she tended to crouch and seemed to want to make herself disappear. Her voice was low and constricted. As she became able to tolerate all of her intense and conflicting feelings and to perceive those in others accurately, without needing to defend against them, her whole body-presence became relaxed. While she had previously looked almost boyish, by the last session her hair was flowing and her clothing was feminine and sensuous."

Such descriptions occur towards the end of therapy or at follow-up for all seven of these patients. Some other examples are given below.

The Reluctant Fiancée, 7-year follow-up

"The patient entered the interview looking wonderful—young, vital, and alive—and considerably younger than her current age of 45."

The Woman with Dissociation, 7-year follow-up

"She entered the interview looking younger and significantly more attractive than when she entered therapy."

The Masochistic Artist

The following was written by the therapist at the end of the next session after the breakthrough of violent feelings against her father: "It was not only the content of the changes reported that was so remarkable, but the way the patient carried herself and interacted with me that revealed the depth of the changes in her. She looked calm and very pulled together, Instead of speaking in a disjointed way that made her seem scattered, she was direct and confident."

Comment

Of course these are highly subjective judgements made by a therapist who might well wish to put the best face on her results—But wait! The following is taken from the therapist's description of her work with The Cold-Blooded Businessman:

> "It should be noted that the patient not only reports feeling very different, but in fact looks very different. By this time (40 sessions of therapy), he has lost 30 pounds and looks considerably younger and more attractive than he did when he started therapy.
>
> "The first time I presented this patient at a conference, I noticed a significant 'buzz' in the audience when I played a portion of this tape. In fact the mumbling was so loud and disruptive that I stopped the tape and asked the audience what was going on. Someone said, 'You've got the wrong tape—this is a different patient'. I responded, 'No it's not, it's the same man'.
>
> "These are the kinds of change that occur in ISTDP, but can't be quantified or adequately described on paper. Patients' entire look and demeanour can change drastically as their internal world gets reorganized. The loosening and dropping of defences often has a physical component. Patients become more relaxed and fluid and, frequently, more attractive."

It is not often that such a "natural experiment" can give objective evidence for a subjective judgement.

"HAPPINESS"

Evidence for "happiness" was apparent in material from the follow-up interviews of all seven patients.

The Cold-Blooded Businessman

18-month follow-up: "I'm a different person and I'm much happier."

The Good Girl with Ulcerative Colitis

8-year follow-up: "I'm very happy." She said that if she never found a man and was never really professionally happy, she would still have a good life. Of the effects of her relationship with her new man-friend, she said, "I was happy before I met him".

The Self-Loathing Headmistress

7-year follow-up: "I feel it's like a garden inside. It's growing and thriving and it's beautiful."

The Reluctant Fiancée

8-year follow-up: "Now I'm happier than I ever imagined possible. . . . I don't have any of those symptoms any more. I'm happy. I feel wonderful—my life is blessed."

The Man Divided

"I feel so much better. Life is good."

The Masochistic Artist

After the breakthrough of rage towards her father, she said, "It's a miracle really—that I can let go of suffering and experience pleasure, real pleasure", and late in therapy she says she is "really happy and has the idea of terminating."

Follow-up at a few months: "Life has become rich." At the 3-year follow-up: "I cannot imagine ever being unhappy again."

The Woman with Dissociation

Concerning the 7-year follow-up, the therapist wrote: "We're not talking about her being less depressed or less anxious or even 'within normal limits', but being truly happy." The therapist went on to quote David Schnarch (1991), who divides people into three groups: the pathological, the normal, and *the blessed few*. She wrote that this patient clearly comes into the third of these.

Comment

Strangely, "happiness" never appeared explicitly in our criteria, and we do not remember it being mentioned in work by other authors. Perhaps it seems to be too vague a term and also too easily used without supporting evidence. Yet in these seven patients it clearly comes from the heart, and then it sums up something that shines through the whole of the follow-up material.

FACING STRESS

One of the true tests of "total resolution" occurs when patients have not only become free from all their original disturbances, but have experienced *psychodynamically significant stress,* which they have coped with in a new way without relapse.

In her final session The Reluctant Fiancée said that her greatest fear was of her mother's death, but she felt that facing her anger with her would enable her to cope with it. At follow-up this was shown to be fulfilled. The Self-Loathing Headmistress went through a serious falling-out with her husband, to the extent that she was not sure she wanted to continue in her marriage, but she was able to work through this experience and repair the relationship with him. The Masochistic Artist was precipitated into intense guilt at the very thought of leaving her husband, but in the end she was able to divorce him without relapse. Finally we can add The Good Girl with Ulcerative Colitis. For her physical condition the original precipitating factor had been the loss of a boy-friend, which repeated the loss of her father, who had died when she was 14. During the follow-up period she suffered, without relapse, the loss of her stepfather and her father-in-law, both of whom she said she adored. Moreover, she then suffered the extremely severe stress of the sudden and unexpected death of her younger sister, with whom she had had an intense love–hate relation. After this she did become depressed, but this was permanently resolved in a single therapeutic session, and, moreover, she suffered no recurrence whatsoever of her ulcerative colitis.

"TRANSCENDENTAL" EXPERIENCES
AND THE DEPTH OF CHANGES IN THESE PATIENTS

There were three examples of experiences reported at follow-up which could be described as "surpassing the natural plane of reality or knowledge", which is one of the dictionary definitions of the word "transcendental". Two of these have already been described in chapter 1. The first is the Self-Loathing Headmistress's experience with her daughter, for which she used the words "a moment of such profound joy, just beyond the limits of this universe, beyond words". The second is the vision that came to The Reluctant Fiancée in the church, "as if I was crossing a bridge from my old life into a new one. . . . Since then there's been no looking back." And the third was also experienced by The Self-Loathing Headmistress, who described how, during her second pregnancy, the doctors told her that they could not hear the baby's heart and gave her an appointment for an ultrasound test. "I felt like shit, sick as a dog. But then, the night before the test, I had a wonderful dream about two full moons, and I woke up and just felt *life*, and I knew this was a fine pregnancy." And this was a patient who came to therapy with such a sense of *inner badness* that she had to punish herself by fantasies of pounding herself into the ground with a hammer. Whether or not "transcendental" is the right word, such experiences lie beyond what one could possibly hope for in a therapeutic result.

This leads to the question of the *depth* of changes. Here we may add to the three examples quoted above. Thus the Masochistic Artist, describing the sexual relationship with her husband, used the phrase, "It's an enraptured sense of this other being". The Man Divided, finally asserting himself with his wife, used the inspired phrase, "Just tell them you'll call them back because your abusive husband can't stand it"; his feeling after he had said this was, "The only thing I can liken it to is how you feel after sex". The Good Girl's ulcerative colitis—"only treatable by surgery"—was not merely halted but *healed*, and she described herself as "radiating good health".

The point that these examples illustrate is that the patients reached something beyond what is so dryly called "positive mental health": they reached the full potential that human beings are capable of *when they are in harmony with their unconscious*. This is a measure of what dynamic psychotherapy can achieve at its most powerful. Only someone steeped in long-term follow-up can say with conviction that these results belong to a *different order of magnitude* from anything seen—or at least published—before.

PATIENTS' COMMENTS ON THEIR TREATMENT AND THE ISSUE OF RESIDUAL TRANSFERENCE

In follow-up interviews, it is routine to ask patients what they felt about their treatment, and in particular what factors they thought were responsible for any changes that may have occurred. Experience shows that, even with those patients who are most improved after traditional dynamic psychotherapy, one often receives answers that completely miss the point and sometimes are quite distorted. An example is a patient, saved by his 5-year analysis from the inferno towards which his sexual deviation had been drawing him, who remarked at follow-up that "he supposed it had been useful to lie and relax on a couch for fifty minutes a day". With this patient, the residual malignant transference could hardly have been more blatant.

Another patient—who had given one of the best therapeutic results of all—when asked about things her analyst had said to her, said she remembered no interpretations but spoke above all of his humanity: she had been complaining about having to do her husband's ironing, to which he said, "Have you ever thought of using drip-dry shirts?"

With many other patients it seems that the events of therapy are like dreams, which rapidly sink back into unconsciousness in waking life. In the present series, the remarks of four patients were recorded.

The Good Girl with Ulcerative Colitis

> Pt: (*At 10-year follow-up*) What was really responsible was getting to the core—to get out all the crap (*for this particular patient, a significant word!*) I had stored inside, so that I could become healed.

In her summary the therapist wrote: "The patient went on to say that the relationship with me was essential. It was essential that she let me in, and that once I was in (which she acknowledged fighting against for some time), I stayed there steadfastly through it all. Being there with her through it all facilitated the process of healing. She realized, quite spontaneously, that the eye contact and capacity for closeness that was established with me was the very thing that enabled her to reach this kind of closeness with her future husband. They made eye contact during their first interaction, and that this was the immediate connection between them."

The Man Divided

The therapist's summary at the 1-year follow-up reads as follows:

> "I asked him what the important factors were in our work together. He said it was my willingness to focus on the difficult feelings, and then ride the roller-coaster with him, that made all the difference."

At the 10-year follow-up:

> Th: What do you think helped you?
> Pt: Without question it was dealing with all the feelings I hadn't re- solved about my own family. I haven't thought about it now for a long time.

The Reluctant Fiancée

Th: (*At 8-year follow-up*) What was it about what we did together that finally helped?

Pt: Being able to talk, really talk freely, about what happened and how I felt about it. It was healing, in a sense, to get it all out. Before, I kept it in and made myself sick. I used to shut down, freeze, and curl up in a ball when it all got too much. So, I think, having a place where I could get it all out and deal with it was what helped.

She also said that she always felt safe in the room with the therapist. She had always remembered the abuse and trauma but had never had anyone to help her with her feelings about it. That was the key or clue to it all

The Cold-Blooded Businessman

The reader is referred again to this patient's moving and heartfelt description of his experience of therapy, which is too long to re-quote here (see the follow-up section in chapter 5).

Comment

What is striking is the accuracy and relevance of every one of these statements from the patients. If we take the four sets of comments together, then the following themes were included:

1. reaching their true, painful feelings about the past;
2. the nature of previous defences;
3. the therapist's steadfastness in staying with them;
4. the therapist's determination to focus;
5. the importance of the transference relationship;
6. generalization of events in the transference to outside life.

If any therapist were asked to name the important factors in dynamic psychotherapy, this list could hardly be bettered.

It is interesting, however, that none of these patients specifically mentioned their murderous feelings.

Above all, what shines through these comments is the *absence of residual transference problems*. It seems that, whenever the transference became an issue in therapy, the fact that the therapist brought it into the open at once was enough to *resolve* it permanently. This absence of residual transference can be illustrated *par excellence* by part of the dialogue from the 10-year follow-up of The Man Divided:

Pt: I was looking forward to seeing you, and now that it's been several years since you got involved in that project with that businessman, I'm at peace.

Th: So you heard about that. (*It's a small town!*)

Pt: I have tremendous animosity towards him, and I was very disappointed to hear that you contemplated collaborating with him.

Th: Well, it was brief. As soon as I began to see through him I withdrew.

Pt: Good for you. I'm glad to hear it. He could charm the pants off anyone, but he's a nasty human being. Having encouraged me to apply for that job here, he stabbed me in the back . . .

This passage shows genuine concern for the therapist as one good friend to another, and it has nothing to do with "transference" whatsoever.

PART IV

RECAPITULATION AND CODA

CHAPTER 12

The present work, traditional dynamic psychotherapy, and psychoanalysis

THE CHARACTERISTICS OF THESE THERAPIES

A reader who refers back to the beginning of chapter 1 can see that every aspect of the fantasy described there has been fulfilled: the method of therapy is entirely psychodynamic; it is applicable even to severely disturbed patients; therapeutic effects occur within "short-term" or "medium-term" therapy as conventionally defined; the whole neurosis has disappeared by termination; this position is maintained at 4- to 10-year follow-ups; and adverse phenomena such as regression, intense dependent transference, and difficulties over termination do not become a problem.

A well-known authority on psychotherapy was heard to say, in connection with the work of Davanloo, something like, "I've been in this business too long to believe in that sort of claim"—and, indeed, therapists who read no more than the above summary would be likely to make a similar response. Yet, for psychoanalysts laboriously working through the transference neurosis, and for those dynamic therapists struggling to make short-term therapy applicable to more than a small minority of patients, these results do appear to be nothing short of a miracle.

COMPARISON WITH PSYCHOANALYSIS

The results may indeed be miraculous, but in a sense there is nothing miraculous about the method, every aspect of which is based on the fundamental principles of dynamic psychotherapy. Moreover, both the events of therapy and the way in which therapeutic effects occur entirely confirm psychodynamic theory. Since this is so, we have to ask, what is the difference from psychoanalysis? What has gone wrong with analysis that makes it necessary to treat patients for years at several times a week? Here it must be remembered that Davanloo began his therapeutic career as an analyst in training. Therefore, we may ask, what technical changes did he introduce into psychoanalytic technique that resulted in such an overwhelming difference?

There are many answers, the first of which is the replacement of *free-floating attention*—a central principle of psychoanalytic technique—by *focused activity*. It is quite clear that the *passivity* implied by "free-floating attention" is anathema to any therapist who wants to get results in a short time. The danger is that it allows patients to continue in a state of resistance, and thus avoid the central issues, almost indefinitely; in addition, it tends to lead eventually to the *transference neurosis* and to "analysis interminable".

Of course, those who have investigated other forms of short-term psychotherapy are likely to answer that focused activity or "focality"—that is, planning therapy in terms of a central problem and then concentrating interpretations on this focus—is essential to their technique. Yet it is clear that the kinds of therapeutic result achieved by ISTDP can only very rarely be matched by other forms of short-term therapy—and probably not at all with patients as disturbed as those described here. Moreover, psychoanalysts might well answer that, if the patient is in a state of resistance, then—ever since Freud—interpretation of resistance has always been central to analytic technique. Why are the results not the same?

This mystery is solved by the statement of a principle that is both amazingly simple and quite revolutionary. It can be regarded as one of the most important innovations introduced by Davanloo, and it is so simple that it easily escapes notice: the mistake made by both analysts and all other dynamic therapists is to rely on *interpretation*—that is, *telling* patients what you think they feel—as their principal therapeutic tool. This allows patients to give confirmatory responses without actually *experiencing* the feelings described in the interpretation. What Davanloo did was to replace *telling* them by *asking* them what they feel, and then dealing with their *resistance* against answering the truth in any depth.

What about the nature of this resistance? Again, this is something that tends to be missed in other forms of dynamic psychotherapy. The resistance takes the form of *tactical defences,* a subject that was dealt with at length in chapter 9, but it plays no part in psychoanalytic or traditional psychodynamic training. As a single example, analysts in training have never been taught to recognize the subtle tactical defence being used against anger in a response like this, which occurred in a patient of Davanloo's:

Th: What did you feel about that?

Pt: I felt he was being unfair.

Although the patient is using the word "feel", she is actually not describing her feelings at all, but is making a statement about the other person, as is shown by the next obvious question, "What do you feel about his being unfair?"

THE FURTHER COURSE
OF THE CENTRAL DYNAMIC SEQUENCE

In practice the therapist does not ask this question, but—in accordance with a general principle—goes straight for the defence, *pointing it out* and *blocking it*: "That's a thought, not a feeling", or "But we still don't know what you feel."

The example above can be used to illustrate the further course of a typical therapeutic session. The patient often goes on to use other tactical defences, each of which is blocked in a similar way, until eventually she admits to some form of anger.

This leads in the direction of the innovation towards which all interventions have been aiming, which is the emphasis on *bringing the patient to the true experience of feeling*—because the next question after receiving an answer such as "Angry" is "How do you experience the anger?" or "What does the anger feel like inside?" This usually leads to resistance in the form of further tactical defences, which in turn must be clarified and blocked.

As was described in chapter 2, this pressure on the patient to experience her true feelings arouses intense and complex mixed reactions in the transference. Usually uppermost is anger at not being allowed to use her customary defences, which of course she tries to conceal. The result is likely to be the appearance of yet another kind of resistance—a phenomenon that, strangely enough, is also central to the classical psychoanalytic process—namely, *resistance in the transference*. Freud's recommendation was that analysts should refrain from making inter- pretations until this form of resistance has crystallized. Davanloo em- phasizes its importance even more, but he recognizes this kind of resistance as having its roots not only in the avoidance of anger but also in the avoidance of *emotional closeness* with the therapist (interestingly, the word "closeness" does not seem to be part of psychoanalytic termi- nology).

The resistance in the transference is often quite refractory, in which case the therapist may introduce the *head-on collision*—yet another inno- vation—confronting the patient with the consequences for the therapy of maintaining this position indefinitely. Analysts would quite rightly say that this is an example of *exhortation*, which has been proved in analysis over and over again to be utterly ineffective. But in ISTDP, if correctly timed at a point where the patient's unconscious has already been partly loosened, it has been conclusively shown to be effective in the extreme. In fact, Davanloo would say that, rather than an "exhorta- tion", it is an *appeal to the therapeutic alliance* to turn against the defences, and that the power of this aspect of the therapeutic relationship has never been fully recognized.

This issue is so important—and such a distinguishing factor—that it needs to be emphasized. In ISTDP we appeal to the healthy part of the ego. It is our partnership with the strength, will, and fortitude of the patient that constitutes the therapeutic alliance. The drive towards health and wholeness can also be unconscious, and we deal actively with both the unconscious alliance and the unconscious resistance. I do not know of any other dynamic therapy that speaks directly to these two parts of the patient in the same way. This is a very powerful technique.

When all goes well, the patient is able to acknowledge her anger with the therapist, which leads to her allowing emotional closeness. She may then spontaneously link the transference situation with her feelings about someone in the distant past (as described in chapter 2).

Even now, however, the therapist may encounter yet another tactical defence—namely, the *partial expression of feeling*, avoiding the true depth of experience. In chapter 10 we gave an example of this, taken from a therapy that was not ISTDP. In connection with anger against his mother, the patient said "There was a bridge over a river not far from home, where the water ran still and deep"—and the therapist thought that this *indirect reference* to murderous feelings was sufficient. However, follow-up showed that the patient was largely unchanged. Any-one fully versed in the principles of ISTDP would have made him go through his fantasy of the murder in living detail, which might have made the difference. This is what the actual therapist missed—and what is usually missed in all other forms of dynamic psychotherapy, including analysis.

The defence of "partial response" must be blocked in its turn. Even-tually—and here is the fundamental discovery to which all these inno-vations have been leading—patients are forced back into the state of consciousness described in chapter 10, "dreaming while awake", in which they experience their true feelings and impulses in fantasy in a way that leads to immediate therapeutic effects. This is the true miracle.

SUMMARY AND CONCLUSION

The really essential steps in the technique of ISTDP can be formulated most simply as follows:

1. *Ask* patients what they feel.
2. Block the tactical defences.
3. Deal immediately with the *transference resistance*.
4. Do not let up until they have *experienced viscerally* their underlying feelings and impulses to the full.

As we have made clear many times, no one is pretending that this is easy in practice. But even the limited awareness of some of these ideas might well result in making traditional methods shorter and more effective.

CHAPTER 13

Conclusions

Davanloo (1990) has developed a systematic method of intervention that provides us with "an unrivalled opportunity not to make inferences about the unconscious, but to observe what lies there directly, and thus to test the validity of many concepts that form part of psychoanalytic theory" (pp. 169–170). While relying on his understanding of psychoanalytic theory, Davanloo pioneered a new series of techniques aimed at the rapid dismantling of the defensive system in a way that brings the patient's core conflicts to the surface in an unmistakable way.

Following some initial treatments of short duration, Freud and his followers became increasingly passive as therapists, resulting in long and protracted therapies in which cause and effect were nearly impossible to ascertain. Since analysis took so long, therapists could not obtain a very large sample in their own practices, making it difficult for them to reach their own conclusions regarding the nature of psychopathology and the process of therapeutic change. With the advent of ISTDP, we have been given a unique opportunity to study both the immediate and long-term effects of intervention on patients' functioning and to draw some conclusions based on the many patients who can be treated by this method.

A review of the scientific literature (chapter 3), along with the material from the detailed case studies contained therein, strongly supports the contention that Davanloo has, indeed, developed a powerful set of therapeutic techniques capable of facilitating deep and lasting change in a broad range of patients, many of whom had been resistant to any other form of treatment.

At this time, ISTDP is the only empirically validated treatment for many personality disorders (Abbass, 2003b; Abbass et al., 2000; Magnavita, 1997). Davanloo's ability to break down the resistances that, left unattended, sabotage treatment efforts seems to be responsible for his success with this population. The effectiveness of these techniques in breaking down defence and resistance and exposing the core conflicts within these patients has provided all of us with the opportunity to obtain evidence regarding the genesis and development of psychopathology.

Davanloo (1990) has taken an "uncompromising stance on many issues that are still a matter of widespread controversy and confusion. I believe that dynamic psychotherapy can be not merely effective but uniquely effective, that therapeutic effects are produced by specific rather than non-specific factors, and that the essential factor is the patient's experience of his true feelings about the present and the past" (p. 2). Conversely, he has hypothesized that the patient's defences against these painful, anxiety-laden feelings is the primary factor responsible for the creation and maintenance of neurotic suffering. He goes further and adds that, in many cases, the patient's suffering is a disguised form of self-punishment, driven by the guilt he unconsciously feels about his angry, sadistic impulses towards loved ones. According to Davanloo (1990), "These feelings are complex and they have their genetic roots in all the unresolved feelings and impulses in relation to the past. The patient's major unconscious anxiety has its links with repressed sadistic impulses as well as guilt-laden, grief-laden unconscious feelings in relation to the people in her past life orbit" (p. 242).

These defensive patterns, when established early in life, tend to be perpetuated in the patient's current life, with the result that no one can get close to him. Patients who are driven by a need to punish themselves often destroy one relationship and one opportunity after the other, with no awareness of their unconscious need to do so. This need to suffer and to punish the self is often so all-pervasive that it will lead the patient to defeat the therapist. Even in cases where the patient is consciously committed to treatment and cooperation, these unconscious resistances can sabotage genuine progress if they are not identified and removed as soon as possible. Freud (1937c) became very pessimistic about fighting these self-punitive forces and suggested that "we must bow to the superiority of the forces against which we see our efforts come to nothing". Davanloo did not bow to these forces, but learned to take them head-on in such a way as to defeat them and, in so doing, give patients a chance at life. He has found that "it is possible to acquaint the patient with the unquestionably sadistic, self-punitive mechanisms that have permeated his or her life, and to bring to the surface the impulses—the sadistic, murderous impulses—the major grief and guilt-laden unconscious feelings for which the self-punishment was designed" (Davanloo, 1990, p. 336). By facilitating "the systematic de-repression of repressed sadistic impulses and guilt and grief-laden unconscious feelings in relation to the past, the therapist can bring about a major restructuring of the superego, finally causing it to cease its destructive activity altogether" (p. 336).

The empirical evidence presented in chapter 3, along with the data presented on the seven cases described in the present volume, offer strong support for the contention that breaking through defences and liberating buried feelings is a reliable route to emotional freedom. Furthermore, the cases presented here provide compelling evidence that this treatment model facilitates more than a mere cessation of suffering; it helps patients to embrace whole-heartedly the very feelings and impulses that had previously caused cause such anxiety, guilt, and self-punishment. As a result, these patients have come alive. They are able to revel in their feelings, open up to creativity, love and be loved, and live life to the fullest.

THE ROLE OF GUILT AND SELF-PUNISHMENT IN PSYCHOPATHOLOGY

Put very simply, Davanloo contends that patients suffer from anxiety and guilt about the angry, sadistic feelings and impulses they harbour towards loved ones. While it is almost inevitable that we will all have mixed feelings towards those closest to us, when one's basic needs are frustrated and thwarted—or, worse, neglected and abused—a violent rage is often experienced. The competing impulses to kill and preserve the loved one can create an unbearable conflict for the child. Due to anxiety and guilt over the sadistic, murderous impulses towards loved ones, the other is often preserved at the cost of the self. The aggression is turned inward towards the self and constitutes both a punishment for sadistic wishes and a disguised expression of these same wishes. In other cases, both self and loved one are protected and these unacceptable feelings are displaced onto others and often acted upon. In either case, it is the defences against these impulses that cause the problems, not the feelings and impulses themselves.

In some cases, like The Good Girl with Ulcerative Colitis, The Woman with Dissociation, The Self-Loathing Headmistress, and the Reluctant Fiancée, the internalization of the sadistic impulses towards others took both physical and emotional forms. These women suffered from lifelong anxiety and depression, but they also attacked themselves physically in very specific ways that support Davanloo's notion that there is a direct, one-to-one correspondence between the suppressed sadistic impulse towards the other and the symptomatic suffering of the patient. In the case of The Good Girl with Ulcerative Colitis, she internalized the impulse to attack the other (mother, brother, and lover) in the gut and created pain in her own abdomen. The Reluctant Fiancée, who suffered from headaches nearly all her life, had the impulse to smash the heads of her father and brother. In each of these cases, this one-to-one correspondence between the repressed sadistic impulse and the patient's presenting symptoms became self-evident once the previously repressed sadistic impulses towards the other were exposed.

In other cases—most notably the Masochistic Artist, The Man Divided, and The Cold-Blooded Businessman—internalization of rage resulting in depression existed alongside the tendency to act out warded-off aggression by having sexual affairs outside their marriages. Other forms of self-destructiveness—such as drinking and driving, or under-functioning at work—were also noted in the two men in this treatment sample. There seems to be a greater tendency on the part of men to act out their pain and rage than of women, though there are exceptions.

In any case, in order to relieve patients of the need to suffer, they need to accept, and even learn to enjoy, the very feelings and impulses they have previously associated with anxiety, guilt, and shame. How is this kind of emotional freedom achieved? In the case of The Good Girl with Ulcerative Colitis we can observe this process in a very clear way. She began by barely being able to verbally acknowledge some anger towards her mother without feeling pain in her abdomen. Once she became aware that she was doing to herself what she wanted to do to others, she came upon "the most painful discovery of all"—that there was sadistic pleasure in experiencing her rage and imagining getting her revenge on the other. She had been punishing herself for these impulses for years. By going immediately to self-punishment, the patient had remained completely unaware of feelings of guilt. When guilt was experienced directly, the love lying beneath was also experienced.

How is it that the experience of all these feelings promotes healing? Leigh McCullough Vaillant (1997) has suggested that patients become phobic of their own feelings and, when they are exposed to their feared emotions without the negative consequences they anticipate, they learn that their fears have been groundless. Neuroscientists in Canada have documented changes in the brain following psychotherapy (Begley, 2004) that may explain why psychotherapy is superior to medication in preventing the relapse of depression. These changes take place in the cortex, or the "rational brain". The fact that brain activity shifts from the limbic system (the "emotional brain") to the cortex provides concrete evidence that emotional reactivity, much of which was unconscious, becomes conscious (neocortical activity) as the result of insight-oriented psychotherapy. The ability to recognize, acknowledge, and consciously modulate feelings is consistently associated with measures of emotional and physical health.

LENGTH OF TREATMENT

The goal of ISTDP is to free patients of their emotional (and often physical) suffering in as rapid a fashion as possible. Abbass (2003b) has demonstrated remarkable and lasting changes in a highly dysfunctional sample in an average of only 15 sessions. In the current volume, four patients, all of whom were in a state of current crisis in their lives, achieved both symptom removal and character change in only 14–32 sessions. This end was achieved in cases of severe abuse (The Woman with Dissociation and The Reluctant Fiancée, for example) and long-standing, debilitating symptoms. While their symptoms and character pathology were chronic, when in a current crisis they were highly motivated and proved capable of rapid and sustained change. As Lindemann (1944, 1945, 1979) discovered decades ago, an external crisis seems to create an openness in the unconscious, as characteristic defences have been overwhelmed and rendered inoperable by the trauma. Given this, the appropriate intervention can have rapid, dramatic, and long-lasting effects, as seen in the cases detailed in this volume.

Other patients, not in crisis but mired in their character defences, like The Cold-Blooded Businessman, The Self-Loathing Headmistress, and The Good Girl with Ulcerative Colitis, took a good deal longer to treat. The entire process of weakening the defences, which had been brought about by external factors for those in current crisis, needed to be painstakingly undertaken in each case, doubling or tripling the time required to eliminate symptoms and change character.

CHAPTER 14

Coda

In this final chapter, we return to one of the themes of chapter 1: the theoretical and practical consequences of possessing a therapeutic method of such power.

VALIDATION WITHOUT CONTROLS

Because there is so much scepticism among many professionals, it is important to spell out the ways in which the work presented here validates both the theory and the practice of dynamic psychotherapy. The most important of these are as follows:

1. Convincing evidence is provided by the fact that therapeutic effects in *long-standing* disturbances appeared in therapy consisting of a *relatively small number of sessions*. Taken to the limit, in one patient a lifelong disturbance was permanently cured in one session. This virtually proves that the changes *were due to therapy*, but by itself it says nothing about the factors that were responsible.

2. However, in all seven patients, therapeutic effects appeared immediately after identifiable *specific* events in therapy. These events mostly consisted of the emergence into consciousness ("de-repression") of many kinds of buried feeling, predominantly anger and grief.

3. The de-repression of *anger* is followed by a distinct sequence, essentially repeated over all seven patients: grief, power, love, therapeutic effects, reconciliation. This sequence has also been observed in another series of patients treated by the same method.
4. Several patients reached *spontaneous* insight about links in the Triangle of Person—that is, similarities among neurotic patterns in the *transference*, in *current* relationships, and in *distant-past* relationships. These links are generally regarded as important factors in all forms of dynamic psychotherapy. In some patients, this insight was followed immediately by therapeutic effects.

A scientific experiment based on prediction

Some—not all—scientific advances are made through the generally recognized sequence of hypothesis→prediction →experiment→experimental result. We also have been able to employ this procedure, which may be introduced as follows: Let us suppose that the therapist had asked two independent judges (1) to view the videotape (or read the transcript) of the initial interview, *before each patient was taken into treatment*, and (2) to form hypotheses and make predictions of the important issues that (a) needed to be dealt with in therapy and (b) would be most likely to lead to therapeutic effects; then there is no doubt that the comparison between these predictions and actual events would possess all the essential characteristics of a scientific experiment. Yet as long as the judges were kept in ignorance of all events subsequent to the initial interview, *there is clearly no reason why the predictions should not be made at any time*. The fact that the experiment had already been carried out—even years before—is neither here nor there. This was the situation in the present work.

Both judges independently formulated, among their many dynamic hypotheses, that buried *anger with one or both parents* was an important factor in all seven patients, and both made the corresponding prediction that therapeutic effects would follow if the anger could be brought to the surface. These predictions were confirmed (for exact details, see chapters 8 and 10).

Therefore, we have (1) made a series of hypotheses, (2) formulated predictions, (3) performed experiments, and (4) found the hypotheses confirmed by subsequent events. This leads to a number of important theoretical and practical consequences.

First, it is quite clear from the accounts of therapy that the anger—or at least the sadistic quality and the true extent of it—was *largely uncon-*

scious when the patient came to treatment. It is necessary to point this out because the idea of "the unconscious" is not accepted by everyone. It is also clear, from the resistance that each patient put up and the guilt and anxiety expressed, that these feelings had been kept out of consciousness because they were painful and unacceptable. When the feelings eventually began to be allowed into consciousness, they were found not to be as intolerable as originally feared; anxiety, guilt, and self-punishment evaporated; and the patient experienced great relief and a sense of power. There followed other immediate therapeutic effects, sometimes—as described above—in disturbances that had lasted for many years.

All this validates the theory and practice of dynamic psychotherapy: the origin of neurosis in the repression of intolerable feelings—that is, the existence of the "repressed unconscious"—and the therapeutic effects of bringing these feelings into consciousness.

VALIDATION WITHOUT PREDICTION

It has to be remembered that this sequence of hypothesis→prediction →experiment→experimental result is not always possible, and hypotheses may have to be tested simply by collecting and examining evidence, as in a court of law. Therefore, it is perfectly acceptable to search for this evidence by examining our data retrospectively.

When this is done, we can see that the material is shot through with evidence confirming the validity of what we may call the *science of psychodynamics*. The following phenomena have been observed repeatedly and indisputably (one or more of them occurs on almost every page): defence, resistance, transference, the origin of neurosis in conflict in early life, links in the Triangle of Person, the "compulsion to repeat", self-punishment, unconscious feelings and impulses, de-repression, therapeutic effects. These phenomena go back to Freud, who observed them all. No one who reads this material can possibly deny their relevance.

THE CENTRAL ASPECTS OF TECHNIQUE

Here we need to pick out the central—and, indeed, unique—aspects of the technique of ISTDP. It has become clear that the essential interventions are to *ask* patients what they feel and then to block the *tactical defences*, including those in the transference, persistently and systematically, until the buried feelings can be truly experienced. Often this is accomplished through the state of "dreaming while awake", in which patients re-live in fantasy their deepest and most heavily defended feelings and impulses, *which were intolerable originally, but—with greater maturity—can now be faced*. This bringing-into-consciousness of feelings of which patients were formerly unaware is the basic principle of all dynamic psychotherapy, and here it is entirely validated by the therapeutic effects that follow from it.

PROCESS AND OUTCOME

It is worth reiterating that in this form of therapy, properly conducted, the transference neurosis does not develop, termination presents no problem, at follow-up there is no evidence of unresolved transference, and the results typically amount to *total resolution* of even severe neuroses.

THE CONSEQUENCES FOR THERAPEUTIC PRACTICE

In chapter 1 we wrote of the practical consequences of the more general adoption of this form of therapy, in terms of the efficiency of therapeutic clinics and the allocation of funds. However, it remains to be seen how far such hopes will be fulfilled, since their fulfilment represents a very considerable challenge.

First of all, this work requires therapists who possess special characteristics. They must be capable of deep empathic understanding; they must be comfortable with bearing not only their patients' pain but, when necessary, their sadism; and they must be capable of leading patients relentlessly towards these feelings and to carry them through the process without becoming in any way sadistic themselves.

Moreover, those trained in psychoanalysis and traditional dynamic psychotherapy need to undergo a huge reorientation in thinking and in "therapeutic reflexes". For instance, in the early stages of therapy they need to curb entirely one of the fundamental aspects of their training— namely, their tendency to give *interpretations*.

Another difficulty is equally serious: among some therapists trained in traditional methods, there is considerable resistance against even hearing about this technique. Perhaps they can be forgiven, because these results taken out of context do seem to be almost unbelievable. Yet surely it is not unfair to use the following analogy: Suppose a team of reputable physicians were to report that they had discovered a uniquely effective, widely applicable, and permanent cure for cancer:

would traditional oncologists simply decide that they "didn't want to know"?

THE TWO MOST IMPORTANT DISCOVERIES

The first of the two most important discoveries is that of the hitherto unrecognized state of "dreaming while awake", which—as described above—enables patients to experience and express safely in fantasy their most heavily defended feelings and impulses.

For the second we can continue another of the themes of chapter 1, the *quality of therapeutic results*, which may be introduced by two observations. The first of these is that, in the later stages of therapy, two of these patients (The Good Girl with Ulcerative Colitis, The Masochistic Artist) described how a sensation of *inner emptiness* was no longer present because the emptiness had now been *filled by their true feelings*. They only discovered the emptiness when it was filled, so that it could never have been part of their original complaints, nor could we have referred to it in our Criteria for a successful outcome. Yet it clearly had been crucial, for it indicated the former absence—and now the rediscovery—of important parts of their personality.

The second observation is as follows. In James Robertson's 1952 film, *A Two Year Old Goes to Hospital*, we saw the little girl pass through Bowlby's stage of *protest*, to a state of quiet acceptance, in which she played by herself and caused no further trouble and gave hardly any discernible evidence of inner pain. Yet when she was visited by her family, what we saw—after initial difficulty—was an entirely different child, bouncing about on the bed and laughing and participating in everything around her. It became obvious that previously she had been in Bowlby's third state, of *denial*, and that although nobody noticed that there was anything wrong, large parts of her personality had been lost.

The parallel is exact. Let us suppose that the symptoms shown by our seven patients had been removed—as might happen with any therapeutic method that bypasses the unconscious and deals directly with the patient's most prominent disturbances. We now know the burden of hidden anger, grief, pain, and guilt that these patients would still be carrying around with them and having to keep permanently at bay. What would be the price in terms of the loss of essential aspects of their personality, a loss that would be immensely real but might well not be noticed by anyone, least of all by the patients themselves?

Follow-up on these seven patients reveals the answer in terms of parts of their personality that had been lost but were now resurrected.

These consist of emotional freedom, spontaneity, joy, compassion, the capacity for closeness, and, above all, real happiness—qualities that far exceed our necessarily rather pedestrian Criteria and result from *true harmony* between these former patients and their unconscious. We may recall with sympathy, but now with scepticism, Freud's pessimistic statement that the best we can hope for is to convert "neurotic unhappiness" into "normal unhappiness".

This leads naturally to Schnarch's (1991) classification of human beings described in chapter 11 , the first two categories of which were the "pathological" and the "normal". If there is one aspect of this work that stays in the memory more than any other, it is the ability to convert the *appallingly traumatized* not into the *normal*, but into the third category, the *blessed few*—something that no one would ever have dreamed possible. Yet this supposedly unattainable dream has become reality.

REFERENCES

Abbass, A. (2002a). Intensive short-term dynamic psychotherapy in a private psychiatric office: Clinical and cost effectiveness. *American Journal of Psychotherapy, 56*: 225–232.

Abbass, A. (2002b). Short-term dynamic therapies in the treatment of major depression. *Canadian Journal of Psychiatry, 47*: 193.

Abbass, A. (2003a). "Davanloo's Intensive Short-term Dynamic Psychotherapy: Recent Clarifications of His Technique for Direct Access to and Experience of Unconscious Feelings." Paper presented at conference on Reaching the Affect: The Healing Force in Psychodynamic Therapy, Washington, DC, October.

Abbass, A. (2003b). The cost-effectiveness of short-term dynamic psychotherapy. *Journal of Pharmacoeconomics and Outcomes Research, 3*: 535–539.

Abbass, A., Gyra, J., Kalpin, A., Hamovitch, G., & Sheldon, A. (2000). "A Multicentre Controlled Evaluation of Short-Term Dynamic Psychotherapy of Patients with Personality Disorders." Proceedings of the Canadian Psychiatric Association, Victoria, British Columbia, October.

Ablon, J. S., & Jones, E. E. (1999). Psychotherapy process in the National Institute of Mental Health Treatment of Depression Collaborative Research Program. *Journal of Consulting and Clinical Psychology, 67*: 64–75.

Alexander, F. (1957). *Psychoanalysis and Psychotherapy.* London: George Allen & Unwin.

Alexander, F., & French, T. M. (1946). *Psychoanalytic Therapy: Principles and Application.* New York: Ronald Press. [Reprinted New York: Wiley, 1974.]

Anderson, E., & Lambert, M. (1995). Short term dynamically oriented psychotherapy: A review and metaphysical analysis. *Clinical Psychology Review*, 15: 503–514.

Balint, M., Ornstein, P. H., & Balint, E. (1972). *Focal Psychotherapy: An Example of Applied Psychoanalysis*. London: Tavistock.

Barber, J. P., Connolly, M. B., Crits-Christoph, P., Gladis, L., & Sinqueland, L. (2000). Alliance predicts patients' outcome beyond in-treatment change in symptoms. *Journal of Consulting and Clinical Psychology*, 68: 1027–1032.

Barlow, D. H. (1994). Psychological interventions in the era of managed competition. *Clinical Psychology: Science and Practice*, 1: 109–122.

Baumeister, R. F., Dale, K., & Sommer, K. L. (1998). Freudian defense mechanisms and empirical findings in modern social psychology: Reaction formation, projection, displacement, undoing, isolation, sublimation, and denial. *Journal of Personality*, 66: 1081–1124.

Beck, A. T., & Steer, R. A. (1987). *BDI, Beck Depression Inventory: Manual*. San Antonia, TX: The Psychological Corporation.

Beck, A. T., & Steer, R. A. (1990). *BAI, Beck Anxiety Inventory: Manual*. San Antonia, TX: The Psychological Corporation.

Beeber, A. R. (1999a). The perpetrator of the unconscious in Davanloo's new metapsychology. Part I: Review of classic psychoanalytic concepts. *International Journal of Intensive Short-Term Psychotherapy*, 13 (3): 151–157.

Beeber, A. R. (1999b). The perpetrator of the unconscious in Davanloo's new metapsychology. Part II: Comparison of the perpetrator to classic psychoanalytic concepts. *International Journal of Intensive Short-Term Psychotherapy*, 13 (3): 159–176.

Beeber, A. R. (1999c). The perpetrator of the unconscious in Davanloo's new metapsychology. Part III: Specifics of Davanloo's technique. *International Journal of Intensive Short-Term Psychotherapy*, 13 (3): 177–189.

Begley, S. (2004). New hope for battling depression relapses. *The Wall Street Journal*, 6 January.

Bergin, A. E., & Strupp, H. H. (1972). *Changing Frontiers in the Science of Psychotherapy*. Chicago, IL: Aldine Press.

Beutler, L. E., Clarkin, J. F., & Bongar, B. (2000). *Guidelines for the Systematic Treatment of the Depressed Patient*. Oxford: Oxford University Press.

Bohart, A. C. (1977). Role playing and interpersonal conflict reduction. *Journal of Counseling Psychology*, 24: 15–24.

Bowlby, J. (1969). *Attachment and Loss, Vol. 1: Attachment*. London: Hogarth Press; New York: Basic Books.

Bowlby, J. (1973). *Attachment and Loss, Vol. 2: Separation, Anxiety and Anger*. London: Hogarth Press; New York: Basic Books.

Bowlby, J. (1980). *Attachment and Loss, Vol. 3: Loss, Sadness and Depression*. London: Hogarth Press; New York: Basic Books.

Carveth, D. L. (2001). The unconscious need for punishment: Expression or evasion of the sense of guilt? *Psychoanalytic Studies*, 3: 9–21.

Clark, D. (1995). Perceived limitations of standard cognitive therapy: A consideration of efforts to revise Beck's theory and therapy. *Journal of Cognitive Psychotherapy, 9*: 153–172.

Cloitre, M., Koenen, K. C., Cohen, L. R., & Han, H. (2002). Skills training in affect and interpersonal regulation followed by exposure: A phase based treatment for PTSD related to childhood abuse. *Journal of Consulting and Clinical Psychology, 70*: 1067–1074.

Coughlin Della Selva, P. (1992). Achieving character change in IS-TDP: How the experience of affect leads to the consolidation of the self. *International Journal of Short-Term Psychotherapy, 7*: 73–87.

Coughlin Della Selva, P. (1996). *Intensive Short-Term Dynamic Psychotherapy: Theory and Technique*. New York: Wiley.

Coughlin Della Selva, P. (2001a). Dynamic assessment of ego functioning in Davanloo's ISTDP. In: J. ten Have-de Labije (Ed.), *The Working Alliance in ISTDP: Whose Intrapsychic Crisis?* (pp. 1–39). Amsterdam, the Netherlands: VKDP (havelaby@euronet.nl).

Coughlin Della Selva, P. (2001b). Working to identify and remove tactical defenses. *Quaderni di Psichiatria Pratica, 17/18*: 37–47.

Cramer, P. (2000). Defense mechanisms in psychology today: Further processes for adaptation. *American Psychologist, 55*: 637–646.

Cramer, P., & Blatt, S. J. (1993). Change in defense mechanisms following intensive treatment, as related to personality organization and gender. In: W. Ehlers., U. Hentschel., G. Smith., & J. G. Draguns (Eds.), *The Concept of Defense Mechanisms in Contemporary Psychology* (pp. 310–320). New York: Springer-Verlag.

Crits-Christoph, P. (1992). The efficacy of brief dynamic therapy: A meta-analysis. *American Journal of Psychiatry, 149*: 151–158.

Damasio, A. (1994). *Descartes' Error: Emotion, Reason, and the Human Brain*. New York: Putnam. [Reprinted London: Macmillan, 1996.]

Damasio, A. (1999). *The Feeling of What Happens: Body and Emotions in the Making of Consciousness*. New York: Harcourt [reprinted 2000] .

Damasio, A. (2003). *Looking for Spinoza: Joy, Sorrow and the Feeling Brain*. New York: Harcourt.

Danner, D. D., Snowdon, D. A., & Freisen, W. V. (2002). Positive emotions in early life and longevity: Findings from the Nun study. *Journal of Personality and Social Psychology, 83*: 804–813.

Davanloo, H. (1978). *Basic Principles and Techniques in Short-Term Dynamic Psychotherapy*. New York: Spectrum.

Davanloo, H. (1980). *Short-Term Dynamic Psychotherapy*. New York: Aronson.

Davanloo, H. (1986). Intensive short-term dynamic psychotherapy with highly resistant patients. I. Handling resistance. *International Journal of Short-Term Psychotherapy, 1*: 107–133.

Davanloo, H. (1988). The technique of unlocking the unconscious: Part 1. *International Journal of Short-Term Psychotherapy, 3*: 99–159.

Davanloo, H. (1990). *Unlocking the Unconscious.* New York: Wiley.

Davanloo, H. (1996a). Management of tactical defenses in intensive short-term dynamic psychotherapy, Part 1: Overview, tactical defenses of cover words and indirect speech. *International Journal of Short-Term Psychotherapy, 11*: 129–152.

Davanloo, H. (1996b). Management of tactical defenses in intensive short-term dynamic psychotherapy, Part 2: Spectrum of tactical defenses. *International Journal of Short-Term Psychotherapy, 11*: 153–199.

Davanloo, H. (2000). *Intensive Short-Term Dynamic Psychotherapy: Selected Papers of Habib Davanloo.* Chichester: Wiley.

De Angelis, T. (2003). When anger's a plus. *Monitor on Psychology, 34*: 44–45.

Derogatis, L. R., Abeloff, M. D., & Melisarato, S. N. (1979). Psychological coping mechanisms and survival time in metastatic breast cancer. *Journal of the American Medical Association, 242*: 1504–1508.

Dodge, K. A. (1991). Emotion and social information processing. In: J. Garber & K. Dodge (Eds.), *The Development of Emotion Regulation and Dysregulation.* Cambridge: Cambridge University Press.

Epstein, S. (1994). Integration of the cognitive and psychodynamic unconscious. *American Psychologist, 49*: 709–724.

Fenichel, O. (1945). *The Psychoanalytic Theory of Neurosis.* New York: Norton.

Ferenczi, S., & Rank, O. (1925). *The Development of Psychoanalysis. Classics in Psychoanalysis Monograph Series, Monograph 4*, ed. G. H. Pollack, trans. C. Newton. Madison, CT: International Universities Press, 1986.

Foote, J. (1992). Explicit empathy and the stance of therapeutic neutrality. *International Journal of Short-Term Psychotherapy, 7*: 193–198.

Fosha, D. (2000*). The Transforming Power of Affect*: *A Model for Accelerated Change.* New York: Basic Books.

Foxhall, K. (2000). Research for the real world. *APA Monitor, 31*: 28–36.

Frank, J. D., & Frank, J. B. (1991). *Persuasion and Healing: A Comparative Study of Psychotherapy* (3rd edition). Baltimore, MD: Johns Hopkins University Press.

Frankl, V. E. (1959). *Man's Search for Meaning.* New York: Washington Square Books.

Freud, A. (1966). *The Ego and the Mechanisms of Defense.* Madison, CT: International Universities Press; London: Hogarth Press, 1986.

Freud, S. (1917e [1915]). Mourning and melancholia. *Standard Edition, 14*, pp. 243–258.

Freud, S. (1923b). *The Ego and the Id. Standard Edition, 19*, pp. 13–59.

Freud, S. (1926d [1925]). *Inhibitions, Symptoms and Anxiety. Standard Edition, 20*, pp. 87–156.

Freud, S. (1937c). Analysis terminable and interminable. *Standard Edition, 19*, pp. 209–254.

Fromm-Reichmann, F. (1950). *Principles of Intensive Psychotherapy.* Chicago, IL: University of Chicago Press.

Garfield, S. L. (1990). Issues and methods in psychotherapy process research. *Journal of Consulting and Clinical Psychology, 58*: 273–280.

Glover, E. (1955). *The Technique of Psycho-Analysis*. London: Baillière, Tindall, & Cox.

Goldfried, M. R., & Wolfe, B. E. (1996). Psychotherapy, practice and research: Repairing a strained alliance. *AmericanPsychologist, 51:* 1007–1016.

Goleman, D. (1995). *Emotional Intelligence*. New York: Bantam Books.

Gottman, J. (1994). *Why Marriages Succeed or Fail: And How You Can Make Yours Last*. New York: Simon & Schuster.

Gottman, J., & Silver, N. (1999). *The Seven Principles for Making Marriage Work: A Practical Guide from the Country's Foremost Relationship Expert*. New York: Random House.

Greenberg, L. S. (2001). *Emotion-Focused Therapy: Coaching Clients to Work Through Their Feelings*. Washington, DC: American Psychological Association.

Greenberg, L. S., Elliott, R. K., & Lietaer, G. (1994). Research on experiential psychotherapies. In: A. E. Bergin & S. L. Garfield (Eds.), *Handbook of Psychotherapy and Behavior Change* (4th edition, pp. 509–531). New York: Wiley.

Greenberg, L. S., & Paivio, S. (1997). *Working with Emotions in Psychotherapy*. New York: Guilford Press.

Greenberg, L. S., & Pinsoff, W. (Eds.) (1986). *The Psychotherapeutic Process: A Research Handbook*. New York: Guilford Press.

Greenberg, L. S., & Safran, J. D. (1987). *Emotion in Psychotherapy: Affect, Cognition, and the Process of Change*. New York: Guilford Press.

Gross, J. J., & John, O. P. (1997). Revealing feelings: Facets of emotional expressivity in self-reports, peer ratings, and behavior. *Journal of Personality and Social Psychology, 72*: 435–448.

Gutrel, F. (2002). What Freud got right. *Newsweek,* 11 November, pp. 50–51.

Hamer, E. (1990). *Reaching the Affect: Style in Psychodynamic Therapies*. Northvale, NJ: Aronson.

Havens, L. (1994). Some suggestions for making research more applicable to clinical practice. In: P. F. Talley, H. H. Strupp, & S. F. Butler (Eds.), *Psychotherapy Research and Practice: Bridging the Gap* (pp. 88–98). New York: Basic Books.

Hendricks, G. (1999). *The Ten Second Miracle: Creating Relationship Breakthroughs*. San Francisco, CA: Harper.

Hendricks, M. N. (2002). Focusing-oriented/experiential psychotherapy. In: D. Cain & J. Seeman (Eds.), *Humanistic Psychotherapy: Handbook of Research and Practice* (pp. 221–256). Washington, DC: American Psychological Association.

Hill, C. E., Corbett, M. M., Kanitz, B., Rios, P., Lightsey, R., & Gomez, M. (1992). Client behavior in counseling and therapy sessions: Development of a pan-theoretical measure. *Journal of Counseling Psychology, 39*: 539–549.

Hillard, R. (1993). Single-case methodology in psychotherapy process and outcome research. *Journal of Consulting and Clinical Psychology, 61*: 373–380.

Høglend, P., & Perry, J. C. (1998). Defensive functioning predicts improvement in major depressive episodes. *Journal of Nervous and Mental Disease, 186*: 238–243.

Horvath, A. O., & Luborsky, L. (1993). The role of the therapeutic alliance in psychotherapy. *Journal of Consulting and Clinical Psychology, 61*: 561–573.

Howard, R. C. (1999). Treatment of anxiety disorders: Does specialty training help? *Professional Psychology: Research and Practice, 30*: 470–473.

Ilardi, S. S., & Craighead, W. E. (1994). The role of nonspecific factors in cognitive-behavioral therapy for depression. *Clinical Psychology: Science and Practice, 1*: 138–156.

Ingram, B. L., & Mulick, J. A. (2005). Letter to Editor. *APA Monitor on Psychology, 36:* 4.

Iwakabe, S., Rogan, K., & Stalikas, A (2000). The relationship between client emotional expressions, therapist interventions, and the working alliance: An exploration of eight emotional expression events. *Journal of Psychotherapy Integration, 10*: 375–401.

James, W. (1902). *The Varieties of Religious Experience: A Study in Human Nature.* New York: Penguin Books, 1985, 2003; New York: Simon & Schuster, 1997; New York: Random House, 1994.

Janoff-Bulman, R. (1992). *Shattered Assumptions.* New York: Free Press.

Jones, E. E. (1993). Introduction to special section: Single case research in psychotherapy. *Journal of Consulting and Clinical Psychology, 61*: 371–372.

Jones, E. E., Ghannam, J., Nigg, J. T., & Dyer, J. F. P. (1993). A paradigm for single-case research: The time series study of a long-term psychotherapy for depression. *Journal of Consulting and Clinical Psychology, 61*: 381–394.

Kassinove, H., Sukhadolsky, D. G., Eckhardt, C. I., & Tsytsarev, S. V. (1997). Development of a Russian state-trait anger expression inventory. *Journal of Clinical Psychology, 53*: 543–557.

Kennedy-Moore, E., & Watson, J. C. (1999). *Expressing Emotion: Myths, Realities, and Therapeutic Strategies.* New York: Guilford Press.

Kiesler, D. J. (1971). Patient experiencing and successful outcome in individual psychotherapy of schizophrenics and psychoneurotics. *Journal of Consulting and Clinical Psychology, 37*: 370–385.

Klein, D. N., Schwartz, J. E., Santiago, N. J., Vivian, D., Vocisano, C., Castonguay, L. G., Arnow, B., Blalock, J. A., Manber, R., Markowitz, J. C., Riso, L. P., Rothbaum, B., McCullough, J. P., Thase, M. E., Borian, F. E., Miller, I. W., & Keller, M. B. (2003). Therapeutic alliance in depression treatment: Controlling for prior change and patient characteristics. *Journal of Consulting and Clinical Psychology, 71*: 997–1006.

Knight, D. C., Nguyen, H. T., & Bandettini, P. A. (2003). Expression of conditional fear with and without awareness. *Proceedings of the National Academy of Sciences of the United States of America, 100* (25): 15280–15283.

LeDoux, J. E. (1986). Sensory systems and emotion: A model of affective processing. *Integrative Psychiatry, 4*: 237–243.

LeDoux, J. E. (1992). Brain mechanisms of emotion and emotional learning. *Current Opinion in Neurobiology, 2*: 267–289.

LeDoux, J. E. (1996). *The Emotional Brain: The Mysterious Underpinning of Emotional Life*. New York: Simon & Schuster.

Lerner, J., Gonzalez, R., Small, D., & Fischoff, B. (2003). Effects of fear and anger on perceived risks of terrorism: A national field experiment. *Psychological Science, 14*: 144–150.

Levine, P. A. (1997) (with Frederick, A.). *Waking the Tiger, Healing Trauma: The Innate Capacity to Transform Overwhelming Experiences*. Berkeley, CA: North Atlantic Books.

Ligiéro, D. P., & Gelso, C. J. (2002). Countertransference, attachment and the working alliance: The therapist's contribution. *Psychotherapy: Theory/ Research/Practice/Training, 39*: 3–11.

Lindemann, E. (1944). Symptomatology and management of acute grief. *American Journal of Psychiatry, 101*: 141–148.

Lindemann, E. (1945). Psychiatric aspects of the conservative treatment of ulcerative colitis. *Archives of General Neurology and Psychiatry, 53*: 322–325.

Lindemann, E. (1979). *Beyond Grief: Studies in Crisis Intervention*. Northvale, NJ: Aronson.

Luborsky, L., Singer, B., & Luborsky, L. (1975). Comparative studies of psychotherapies: Is it true that "Everyone has won and all must have prizes"? *Archives of General Psychiatry, 32*: 995–1008.

Luhrmann, T. M. (2000). *Of Two Minds: The Growing Disorder in American Psychiatry*. New York: Knopf.

Magnavita, J. J. (1997). *Restructuring Personality Disorders: A Short-Term Dynamic Approach*. New York: Guilford Press.

Mahoney, M. J. (1991). *Human Change Processes: The Scientific Foundations of Psychotherapy*. New York: Basic Books.

Mahrer, A. R. (1989). *The Integration of Psychotherapies: A Guide for Practicing Therapists*. New York: Human Sciences.

Main, M. (1991). Metacognitive knowledge, metacognitive monitoring, and singular (coherent) versus multiple (incoherent) models of attachment: Findings and directions for future research. In: C. M. Parkes., J. Stenson-Hinde., & P. Marris (Eds.), *Attachment Across the Life Cycle* (pp. 127–150). London: Routledge.

Main, M. (1995a). Discourse, prediction, and recent studies in attachment: Implications for psychoanalysis. In: T. Shapiro & R. N. Emde (Eds.), *Research in Psychoanalysis: Process, Development, Outcome* (pp. 209–244). Madison, CT: International Universities Press.

Main, M. (1995b). Recent studies in attachment: Overview, with selected implications for clinical work. In: S. Goldberg, R. Muir, & J. Kerr (Eds.), *Attachment Theory: Social, Developmental and Clinical Perspectives* (pp. 407–474). Hillsdale, NJ: Analytic Press.

Main, M. (1996). Introduction to the special section on attachment and psychopathology: 2. Overview of the field of attachment. *Journal of Consulting and Clinical Psychology, 64*: 237–243.

Main, M., & Goldwyn, R. (1984). Predicting rejection of her infant from mother's representation of her own experience: Implications for the abused–abusing intergenerational cycle. *Child Abuse and Neglect, 8*: 203–217.

Main, M., & Hesse, E. (1990). Parents' unresolved traumatic experiences are related to infant disorganized attachment status: Is frightened and/or frightening parental behavior the linking mechanism? In: M. T. Greenberg, D. Cicchetti., & E. M. Cummings (Eds.), *Attachment in the Preschool Years: Theory, Research, and Intervention* (pp. 161–182). Chicago, IL: University of Chicago Press.

Main, M., & Morgan, H. (1996). Disorganization and disorientation in infant strange situation behavior: Phenotypic resemblance to dissociative states? In: L. K. Michelson & W. J. Ray (Eds.), *Handbook of Dissociation: Theoretical, Empirical and Clinical Perspectives* (pp. 107–138). New York: Plenum.

Main, M., & Solomon, J. (1990). Procedures for identifying infants as disorganized/disoriented during the Ainsworth Strange Situation. In: M. T. Greenberg., D. Cicchetti., & E. M. Cummings (Eds.), *Attachment During the Preschool Years: Theory, Research and Intervention* (pp.121–160). Chicago, IL: University of Chicago Press.

Malan, D. H. (1963). *A Study of Brief Psychotherapy*. London: Tavistock. [Reprinted New York: Plenum, 1975; London: Routledge, 2001.]

Malan, D. H. (1973). The outcome problem in psychotherapy research: A historical review. *Archives of General Psychiatry, 29*: 719–729.

Malan, D. H. (1976a). *The Frontier of Brief Psychotherapy*. New York: Plenum.

Malan, D. H. (1976b). *Toward the Validation of Dynamic Psychotherapy: An Example of the Convergence of Research and Clinical Practice*. New York: Plenum.

Malan, D. H. (1979). *Individual Psychotherapy and the Science of Psychodynamics*. London: Butterworth (2nd edition). London: Arnold, 2001.

Malan, D. H. (1980). The most important development in psychotherapy since the discovery of the unconscious. In: H. Davanloo (Ed.), *Short-Term Dynamic Psychotherapy* (pp. 13–23). New York: Aronson.

Malan, D. H. (1996). Foreword. In: P. Coughlin Della Selva, *Intensive Short-Term Dynamic Psychotherapy: Theory and Technique*. New York: Wiley.

Malan, D. H., & Osimo, F. (1992). *Psychodynamics, Training, and Outcome in Brief Psychotherapy*. Oxford: Butterworth-Heinemann.

Martin, D. J., Garske, J. P., & Davis, M. K. (2000). Relation of the therapeutic alliance with outcome and other variables: A meta-analytic review. *Journal of Consulting and Clinical Psychology, 68*: 438–450.

McCullough, L. (2003). "The Experience of Touch and the Deepening of Affect." Paper presented at conference on Reaching the Affect: The Healing Force in Psychodynamic Therapy, Washington School of Psychiatry, Washington, DC, October 10–12.

McCullough, L., Winston, A., Farber, B., Porter, F., Pollack, J., Laikin, M., Vingiano, W., & Trujillo, M. (1991). The relationship of patient–therapist interaction to outcome in brief psychotherapy. *Psychotherapy, 28*: 525–533.

McCullough Vaillant, L. (1997). *Changing Character: Short-Term Anxiety-Regulating Psychotherapy for Restructuring Defenses, Affect, and Attachment.* New York: Basic Books.

Menninger, K. (1958). *Theory of Psychoanalytic Technique.* New York: Basic Books.

Miller, A. (1996). *The Drama of the Gifted Child: The Search for the True Self* (revised edition). New York: Basic Books.

Mineka, S., & Thomas, C. (1999). Mechanisms of change in exposure therapy for anxiety disorders. In: T. Dalgleish & M. Power (Eds.), *Handbook of Cognition and Emotion* (pp. 747–764). New York: Wiley.

Mohr, D. C. (1995). Negative outcome in psychotherapy: A clinical review. *Clinical Psychology: Science and Practice, 2*: 1–27.

Neborsky, R. J. (2001). Davanloo's method of intensive short-term dynamic psychotherapy. In: M. F. Solomon, R. J. Neborsky, L. McCullough, M. Alpert., F. Shapiro, & D. H. Malan (Eds.), *Short-Term Therapy for Long-Term Change* (pp. 16–53). New York: Norton.

Osimo, F. (2003). *Experiential Short-Term Dynamic Psychotherapy: A Manual.* Bloomington, IN: First Books.

Pennebaker, J. W. (1991). *Opening Up: The Healing Power of Confiding in Others.* New York: Morrow.

Pennebaker, J. W. (1997). *Opening Up: The Healing Power of Expressing Emotions.* New York: Morrow.

Piliero, S. A. (2003). "Patients' Experience of Experiential STDP: What Patients Really Think." Paper presented at conference on Reaching the Affect: The Healing Force in Psychodynamic Therapy, Washington, DC.

Pos, A. E., Greenberg, L. S., Goldman, R. N., & Korman, L. M. (2003). Emotional processing during experiential treatment of depression. *Journal of Consulting and Clinical Psychology, 71*: 1007–1016.

Reich, W. (1933). *Character Analysis.* New York: Touchstone.

Roth, A., & Fonagy, P. (1996). *What Works for Whom? A Critical Review of Psychotherapy Research.* New York: Guilford Press.

Safran, J. D., & Muran, J. C. (1994). Toward a working alliance between research and practice. In: P. F. Talley, H. H. Strupp, & S. F. Beutler (Eds.),

Psychotherapy Research and Practice: Bridging the Gap (pp. 206–226). New York: Basic Books.

Salerno, M., Farber, B. A., McCullough, L., Winston, A., & Trujillo, M. (1992). The effects of confrontation and clarification on patient affective and defensive responding. *Psychotherapy Research, 2*: 181–192.

Schnarch, D. (1991). *Constructing the Sexual Crucible: An Integration of Sexual and Marital Therapy*. New York: Norton.

Schnarch, D. (1997). *Passionate Marriage: Keeping Love and Intimacy Alive in Emotionally Committed Relationships*. New York: Owl Books.

Schnarch, D. (2003). "Resurrecting Sex: Solving Sexual Problems and Revolutionizing Your Relationship." Cape Cod Summer Institute, Eastham, MA, August.

Seligman, M. E. P. (1995). The effectiveness of psychotherapy: The consumer reports study. *American Psychologist, 50*: 965–974.

Seligman, M. E. P. (1996). Science as an ally of practice. *American Psychologist, 51*: 1072–1079.

Seligman, M. E. P. (1998). *Learned Optimism: How to Change Your Mind and Your Life*. New York: Pocket Books.

Shaw, B. F. (1989). Cognitive-behavioral therapies for major depression. *Psychiatric Journal of the University of Ottawa, 14*: 403–408.

Siegel, D. J. (1995). Memory, trauma and psychotherapy: A cognitive science view. *Journal of Psychotherapy Practice and Research, 4*: 93–122.

Siegel, D. J. (1999). *The Developing Mind: Toward a Neurobiology of Interpersonal Experience*. New York: Guilford Press.

Silberschatz, G., Fretter, P., & Curtis, J. (1986). The role of therapeutic alliance in psychotherapy. *Journal of Consulting and Clinical Psychology, 54*: 646–652.

Silver, J. (2003). What you don't know can hurt you. *Journal Watch Psychiatry* (newsletter, December).

Sjödin, I., Svedlund, J., Ottosson, J.-O., & Dotevall, G. (1986). Controlled study of psychotherapy in chronic peptic ulcer disease. *Psychosomatics, 27*: 187–196.

Smith, M. L., Glass, G. V., & Miller, T. I. (1980). *The Benefits of Psychotherapy*. Baltimore, MD: Johns Hopkins University Press.

Stanton, A. L., Danoff-Burg. S., Cameron, C. L., Bishop, M., Collins, C. A., Kirk, S. B., & Sworowski, L. A. (2000). Emotionally expressive coping predicts psychological and physical adjustment to breast cancer. *Journal of Consulting and Clinical Psychology, 68*: 875–882.

Strachey, J. (1969). The nature of the therapeutic action of psycho-analysis. *International Journal of Psychoanalysis, 50*: 275–290.

Strupp, H. H. (1993). The Vanderbilt psychotherapy studies: Synopsis. *Journal of Consulting and Clinical Psychology, 61*: 431–440.

Strupp, H. H., & Binder, J. L. (1984). *Psychotherapy in a New Key: A Guide to Time Limited Psychotherapy*. New York: Basic Books.

Svedlund, J. (1993). Psychotherapy in irritable bowel syndrome: A controlled outcome study. *Acta Psychiatrica Scandinavica, Supplement 67* (306): 1–68.

Tafrate, R. C., Kassinove, H., & Dundin, R. (2002). Anger episodes in high- and low-trait anger community adults. *Journal of Clinical Psychology, 58*: 1573–1590.

Tang, T. Z., & DeRubeis, R. J. (1999). Sudden gains and critical sessions in cognitive-behavioral therapy for depression. *Journal of Consulting and Clinical Psychology, 67*: 894–904.

Tavris, C. (1989). *Anger: The Misunderstood Emotion.* New York: Fawcett.

Vaillant, G. E. (1993). *The Wisdom of the Ego.* Cambridge, MA: Harvard University Press.

Vuilleumier, P., & Schwartz, S. (2001), Modulation of visual perception by eye gaze direction in patients with spatial neglect and extinction. *NeuroReport, 12* (10): 2101–2104.

Warwar, N., & Greenberg, L. (2000). "Emotional Processing and Therapeutic Change." Paper presented at the annual meeting of the International Society for Psychotherapy Research, Indian Hills, IL.

Weinberger, D. A. (1990). The construct validity of the repressive coping style. In J. L. Singer (Ed.), *Repression and Dissociation: Implications for Personality Theory, Psychopathology, and Health* (pp. 337–386). Chicago, IL: University of Chicago Press.

Weinberger, D. A., Schwartz, G. E., & Davidson, R. J. (1979). Low anxious, high anxious, and repressive coping styles: Psychometric patterns and behavioral and physiological responses to stress. *Journal of Abnormal Psychology, 88*: 369–380.

Weinberger, J. (1995). Common factors aren't so common: The common factors dilemma. *Clinical Psychology: Science and Practice, 2*: 45–69.

Weiss, J. (1990). Unconscious mental functioning. *Scientific American,* March, pp. 103–109.

Weiss, J. (1993). *How Psychotherapy Works: Process and Technique.* New York: Guilford Press.

Weiss, J., Sampson, H., & the Mount Zion Psychotherapy Research Group (1986). *The Psychoanalytic Process: Theory, Clinical Observations and Empirical Research.* New York: Guilford Press.

Whalen, P. J., Rauch, S. L., Etcoff, N. L., McInerney, S. C., Lee, M. B., & Jenike, M. A. (1998). Masked presentations of emotional facial expressions modulate amygdala activity without explicit knowledge. *Journal of Neuroscience, 18*: 411–418.

Winnicott, D. W. (1960). Ego distortion in terms of true and false self. In: *The Maturational Processes and the Facilitating Environment* (pp. 140–152). London: Hogarth Press & The Institute of Psychoanalysis, 1965.

Winston, A., McCullough, L., Trujillo, M., Pollack, J., Laikin, M., Flegenheimer, W., & Kestenbaum, R. (1991). Brief psychotherapy of personality disorders. *Journal of Nervous and Mental Disease, 179*: 188–193.

Wiser, S., & Goldfried, M. R. (1993). Comparative study of emotional experiencing in psychodynamic-interpersonal and cognitive-behavioral therapies. *Journal of Consulting and Clinical Psychology, 61*: 892–895.

Wiser, S., & Goldfried, M. R. (1998). Therapist interventions and client emotional experiencing in expert psychodynamic-interpersonal and cognitive-behavioral therapies. *Journal of Consulting and Clinical Psychology, 66*: 634–640.

INDEX